LAWFARE

Judicial Warfare in Spain

The LSE Spanish History Series

General Editor: Professor Paul Preston, London School of Economics

From 2021, under the auspices of the Department of International History of the London School of Economics, the Cañada Blanch / Sussex Academic Studies on Contemporary Spain continues publication as the LSE Spanish History Series. A list of all published titles in the series is available on the Press website. More recently published works are presented below.

Peter Anderson, *Friend or Foe?: Occupation, Collaboration and Selective Violence in the Spanish Civil War.*

Germà Bel, *Disdain, Distrust, and Dissolution: The Surge of Support for Independence in Catalonia.*

Carl-Henrik Bjerström, *Josep Renau and the Politics of Culture in Republican Spain, 1931–1939: Re-imagining the Nation.*

Darryl Burrowes, *Historians at War: Cold War Influences on Anglo-American Representations of the Spanish Civil War.*

Steven Byrne, *Independence, Language and Identity in Modern Catalonia: A Study in Socio-Cultural and Socio-Political Allegiance*

Andrew Canessa (ed.), *Barrier and Bridge: Spanish and Gibraltarian Perspectives on Their Border.*

Damià del Clot, *Lawfare – Judicial Warfare in Spain: The Strategy of Repression Against the Catalan Independence Movement.*

Kathryn Crameri, *'Goodbye, Spain?': The Question of Independence for Catalonia.*

Pol Dalmau, *Press, Politics and National Identities in Catalonia: The Transformation of La Vanguardia, 1881–1931.*

Francisco Espinosa-Maestre, *Shoot the Messenger?: Spanish Democracy and the Crimes of Francoism – From the Pact of Silence to the Trial of Baltasar Garzón.*

María Jesús González, *Raymond Carr: The Curiosity of the Fox.*

Helen Graham, *The War and its Shadow: Spain's Civil War in Europe's Long Twentieth Century.*

Mandie Iveson, *Language Attitudes, National Identity and Migration in Catalonia: 'What the Women Have to Say'.*

Gabriel Jackson, *Juan Negrín: Physiologist, Socialist, and Spanish Republican War Leader.*

Xavier Moreno Juliá, *The Blue Division: Spanish Blood in Russia, 1941–1945.*

Francisco J. Leira-Castiñeira, *Franco's Soldiers: Transnational and Sociological Analysis of Recruitment and Combat in the Spanish Civil War (1936–1939).*

David Lethbridge, *Norman Bethune in Spain: Commitment, Crisis, and Conspiracy.*

Guiomar Acevedo López, *Refugee Displacement during the Spanish Civil War, 1936–1939: The Republican Experience before Exile.*

Antonio Miguez Macho, *The Genocidal Genealogy of Francoism: Violence, Memory and Impunity.*

Carles Manera, *The Great Recession: A Subversive View.*

Jorge Marco, *Guerrilleros and Neighbours in Arms: Identities and Cultures of Antifascist Resistance in Spain.*

Jorge Marco and Gutmaro Gómez Bravo, *The Fabric of Fear: Building Franco's New Society in Spain, 1936–1950.*

Emily Mason, *Democracy, Deeds and Dilemmas: Support for the Spanish Republic within British Civil Society, 1936–1939.*

Soledad Fox Maura, *Jorge Semprún: The Spaniard who Survived the Nazis and Conquered Paris.*

Martin Minchom, *Spain's Martyred Cities: From the Battle of Madrid to Picasso's* Guernica.

Raphael Minder, *Feeling the Heat: A Decade as a Foreign Correspondent in Spain – From the Financial Crisis to the Pandemic.*

Linda Palfreeman, *Tartan Angels: The Scottish Ambulance Unit in Madrid during the Spanish Civil War (1936–1939).*

Fernando Puell de la Villa and David García Hernán (eds.), *War and Population Displacement: Lessons of History.*

Rúben Serém, *Conspiracy, Coup d'état and Civil War in Seville, 1936–1939: History and Myth in Francoist Spain.*

Gareth Stockey, *Gibraltar: "A Dagger in the Spine of Spain?"*

Maggie Torres, *Anarchism and Political Change in Spain: Schism, Polarisation and Reconstruction of the* Confederación Nacional del Trabajo, *1939–1979.*

Antoni Vives, *SMART City Barcelona: The Catalan Quest to Improve Future Urban Living.*

To the memory of
Miquel Strubell i Trueta

LAWFARE
Judicial Warfare in Spain

The Strategy of Repression Against the Catalan Independence Movement

DAMIÀ DEL CLOT

LSE Department of International History

LIVERPOOL UNIVERSITY PRESS

The Author acknowledges the editorial assistance of Liz Castro in the preparation of this work.

First published 2023 by
Liverpool University Press
4 Cambridge Street
Liverpool L69 7ZU

Published in collaboration with the Department of International History of the London School of Economics.

British Library Cataloguing-in-Publication data
A British Library CIP record is available

Paperback ISBN 978-1-78976-190-0

Typeset & designed by Sussex Academic Press, Brighton & Eastbourne.
Printed and bound by CPI Group (UK) Ltd, Croydon CR0 4YY.

Contents

The LSE Spanish History Series

Formerly The Cañada Blanch Centre for Contemporary Spanish Studies

In the 1960s, the most important initiative in the cultural and academic relations between Spain and the United Kingdom was launched by a Valencian fruit importer in London. The creation by Vicente Cañada Blanch of the Anglo-Spanish Cultural Foundation has subsequently benefited large numbers of Spanish and British scholars at various levels. Thanks to the generosity of Vicente Cañada Blanch, thousands of Spanish schoolchildren have been educated at the secondary school in West London that bears his name. At the same time, many British and Spanish university students have benefited from the exchange scholarships which fostered cultural and scientific exchanges between the two countries. Some of the most important historical, artistic and literary work on Spanish topics to be produced in Great Britain was initially made possible by Cañada Blanch scholarships.

Vicente Cañada Blanch was, by inclination, a conservative. When his Foundation was created, the Franco regime was still in the plenitude of its power. Nevertheless, the keynote of the Foundation's activities was always a complete open-mindedness on political issues. This was reflected in the diversity of research projects supported by the Foundation, many of which, in Francoist Spain, would have been regarded as subversive. When the Dictator died, Don Vicente was in his seventy-fifth year. In the two decades following the death of the Dictator, although apparently indestructible, Don Vicente was obliged to husband his energies. Increasingly, the work of the Foundation was carried forward by Miguel Dols whose tireless and imaginative work in London was matched in Spain by that of José María Coll Comín. They were united in the Foundation's spirit of open-minded commitment to fostering research of high quality in pursuit of better Anglo-Spanish cultural relations. Throughout the 1990s, thanks to them, the role of the Foundation grew considerably.

In 1994, in collaboration with the London School of Economics, the Foundation established the Príncipe de Asturias Chair of Contemporary Spanish History and the Cañada Blanch Centre for Contemporary Spanish

Studies. It is the particular task of the Cañada Blanch Centre for Contemporary Spanish Studies to promote the understanding of twentieth-century Spain through research and teaching of contemporary Spanish history, politics, economy, sociology and culture. The Centre possesses a valuable library and archival centre for specialists in contemporary Spain. This work is carried on through the publications of the doctoral and post-doctoral researchers at the Centre itself and through the many seminars and lectures held at the London School of Economics. While the seminars are the province of the researchers, the lecture cycles have been the forum in which Spanish politicians have been able to address audiences in the United Kingdom.

From 1998 to 2021, the Cañada Blanch Centre has published a substantial number of books in collaboration with several different publishers on the subject of contemporary Spanish history and politics. An extremely fruitful partnership with Sussex Academic Press began in 2004 and continued until 2021. Full details and descriptions of the published works can be found on the Press website. From 2021, under the auspices of the Department of International History of the London School of Economics, the collection continues life as the LSE Spanish History Series.

An area in which this series has made a significant contribution to scholarship is the analysis of the tension between Catalonia and the central government in Madrid over the last one hundred and fifty years. The conflict between the two in the late nineteenth and early twentieth century was examined in Pol Dalmau's *Press, Politics and National Identities in Catalonia*. The period during which Catalonia enjoyed its highest level of autonomy, the Civil War years from 1938 to 1939, was the subject of the Arnau González's edited collection, *The Illusion of Statehood: Perceptions of Catalan Independence up to the End of the Spanish Civil War*. Post-war reconstruction, as dominated by the Francoist dictatorship, was the subject of Olivia Muñoz-Rojas's path-breaking study, *Ashes and Granite: Destruction and Reconstruction in the Spanish Civil War and its Aftermath*.

The resurgence of Catalan independence sentiment in post-Franco Spain has been the subject of several volumes. These have included Germà Bel's analysis of the damage done to the Catalan economy by Spain's dysfunctional transport and communications model, in *Infrastructure and the Political Economy of Nation Building in Spain, 1720–2010* and Ramon Tremosa's *Catalonia, An Emerging Economy*. The scale of inter-regional distrust since the emasculation of the revised autonomy statute in 2010 has been examined by Germà Bel's *Disdain, Distrust and Dissolution: The Surge of Support for Independence in Catalonia*, Andrew Dowling's *Catalonia since the Spanish Civil War: Reconstructing the Nation* and Kathryn Crameri's

GOODBYE, SPAIN? The question of independence for Catalonia. Mandie Iveson's *Language Attitudes, National Identity and Migration in Catalonia* offered an original insight into the role of women in keeping alive Catalan language and culture from the 1960s to the present crisis.

The present volume by Damià del Clot i Trias examines the impact of the Spanish legal system in effectively criminalising the Catalan independence movement. It traces the historical continuity of the essentially anti-Catalan prejudice of the juridical establishment from the Franco regime to the constitutional mechanisms of the post-transition state. In doing so, it explains much of the ongoing bitterness in the aftermath of the independence referendum of October 2017.

Preface by Carles Mundó

For centuries the Spanish State has proved to be an expert system for repressing political dissent and any threat that could jeopardize the maintenance of the status quo. It has done so by using all the institutions and all the arenas of power that were necessary, for the end has always justified the means.

In this book, Damià del Clot takes an accurate panoramic photograph of the mechanisms of repression that the Spanish State has been building up and perfecting over the past century, but which rest upon a long tradition that has been amply tried out in multiple episodes of colonization and assimilation. Specifically in the case of Catalonia, there have been countless attempts by those in power in Spain to wipe off the map all the features that shape Catalan national identity, from its language and its culture to its institutions and civil law, and to repress, at any cost, the political movements that have raised the banner of freedom.

The invention of an external enemy against which one needs to protect and defend oneself has served to forge its own identity and to oil a machinery which throughout history has taken various forms, but always with the same logic. In the Spanish repressive tradition, the attempt to legitimize, with apparent legality, ways of behaving designed to persecute the enemies of the Fatherland, has been unending.

Victor Hugo, in *Le droit et la loi*, published in 1875, raised the debate between what is legitimate and what is legal. Laws are an imperfection of justice, he said. He therefore argued that those who write the laws should be guided by the Republican values of liberty, equality and fraternity. Just laws can only be passed by righteous men and women, and when that isn't the case, we have unjust laws, which institutionalize abuse and imposition.

As Damià del Clot explains very well in this book, the obsession of state apparatuses, both throughout the Franco period and since, has been to transform into a legal corpus what is nothing more than an ideological project, finding in legality a way of imposing it. What is legal and what is democratic have been uncritically confused by those who had the coercive power to impose laws. In practice, it has been the way to say that anything that deviates from the law can be prosecuted, if necessary, by means of criminal proceedings.

The entire institutional fabric of the State is at the service of a legality that is tailor-made to prosecute and repress dissent. During the Franco regime, an institutional architecture was created and consolidated that today, conveniently legitimized under the umbrella of the post-Franco Constitution, continues to function on the basis of the same patterns. This book makes a complete inventory of the institutions and bodies that serve to go after everything that does not fit into the notion of a uniform Spain.

The portrait offered here of the judicial system and how it has developed is especially enlightening. What is argued and documented is that the end of the Franco dictatorship and the beginning of the democratic period occurred without a break. The same people who handed down sentences the day before on behalf of Caudillo Franco continued to do so the following day in the name of His Majesty the King. The Spanish judiciary has uncritically submitted itself to the *rule of law* in order to perpetuate a specific model of state and society, leaving in the background the ideal of justice to be expected of a law court.

This book also presents an x-ray of the confusion of powers that exists in Spain today. As the 19th-century Italian jurist Francesco Carrara stated, when politics enters a law court, justice jumps out of the window. On paper, in Spain there is a separation between the legislature, the executive and the judiciary, which is the defining element of a democratic state and the rule of law. But reality falls well short of this aim. The politicization or, to use the author's words, the partisanship of the judiciary in Spain has meant that judges have been gaining more and more prominence in political activity, and we have seen the full splendour of this phenomenon very recently, with the persecution and repression of the Catalan independence movement.

Explaining a dynamic that comes from way back, Damià del Clot helps us to understand that nothing we have experienced during the past decade in Catalonia, coinciding with the historic surge of the independence movement, which reached its peak with the holding of the referendum of October 1, 2017, is the result of chance or improvisation. On the contrary, it is the result of the inertia and expertise of a system that activates the mechanisms of repression in all areas and modalities. The judiciary, the prosecution, the police forces, the state administration and the propaganda apparatuses, which are sometimes confused with the media, have functioned in a synchronized manner and with a shared goal.

Recently, the political offensive on the part of the judiciary to go after an ideology or a political movement with the tools of the rule of law has come to be known as *lawfare*, a concept that is spelled out throughout the book. In fact, the 'general case' against independence is becoming a paradigmatic example of lawfare. Instead of resolving a question of a political nature through the mechanisms of politics, following the well-known model of Scotland and Great Britain or Quebec and Canada, Spain chose to take the matter to court, considering that legitimate aspirations as to the political future of Catalonia were purely a matter of legality.

The scheme applied follows a well established model: to formulate exaggerated and unjustified accusations that reflect an obvious political intentionality and to let the judges apply laws designed to combat those accusations. The efforts of the State apparatus have not focused on adjusting the accusations to specific facts, but quite the opposite: twisting reality as much as necessary to square the facts with the desired criminal category. In short, all mechanisms have been activated in order to transform the presumption of innocence into a presumption of guilt, with an aberrant war of propaganda and disinformation to degrade the image of the persecuted and thus to be able to legitimize the lawfare and give satisfaction to all those who have understood that the enemies of the Fatherland have to be punished.

A good example of this was the unfounded and fanciful accusation of rebellion, to which I myself have also been subjected. The fact that it was written by the Civil Guard in collaboration with the Public Prosecutor's Office was no unintended mistake. It was a perfectly deliberate strategy that allowed the criminal case against the Government of Catalonia, against the Speaker of the Catalan Parliament and against the leaders of Catalan social organizations to be dragged to the Supreme Court in Madrid so that it was nice and close to political power. The suspension of the politicians' ministerial posts was achieved by applying a provision of the Penal Code which had been included with regard to terrorism. That, in turn, was made to justify arbitrary pre-trial imprisonment, to be maintained on the grounds of the gravity of the accusation. In the end, the Supreme Court ruling did not accept this thesis, but the political goal, clad in legality, had already been achieved. Obviously, however, none of these abuses or arbitrary decisions will be grounds for punishing those who have kept innocent people in prison, because one of the virtues of the repressive system is the impunity of those who serve the purpose of repression.

Lawfare. The Strategy of Repression Against Catalan Independence is a rigorous and readable book which makes it possible to understand how the mechanisms of repression of modern States work. It is a panoramic black and white photograph that, portraying the past, also portrays the present, and that is very helpful in understanding the complexities of a defensive political system and State model that are incapable of seducing or convincing those citizens who do not share a single view of reality.

But, more powerful than repression and unjust laws is the strength of the people, who – with their votes and their democratic, civic and peaceful commitment – can make what today seems impossible become inevitable tomorrow.

CARLES MUNDÓ
Catalan Minister of Justice, 2015–2017

Prologue by Jaume Alonso-Cuevillas i Sayrol

In September 2017, I accepted the legal defence of the President of Catalonia, Carles Puigdemont, and other members of his Government. The following October 1, a Referendum on the independence of Catalonia was to be held, an initiative considered illegal by Spanish justice. The Catalan Parliament had just passed the legal framework that was to facilitate the Referendum. On the merits of this recently introduced legislation (which would rapidly be invalidated by the Spanish Constitutional Court), on the night of September 6, ½ the Catalan Government issued the Decree calling for the Referendum and another supplementary decree, with the corresponding organizational regulations. The response was immediate: the following day, the Superior Prosecutor's Office of Catalonia (ascribed to the General Prosecutor's Office of the Spanish State) announced the filing of a lawsuit against all members of the Catalan Government for the offences of disobedience (for disobeying the – generic – prohibition by the Spanish Constitutional Court) and embezzlement of public funds (for allocating public resources to activities considered illegal). The complaint was immediately filed, admitted for judicial inquiry and leaked to the press, even before being notified to the defendants (on the second business day after its filing). In this tense environment, I received a phone call that would end up changing my professional life.

Until then I had been a lawyer with no political affiliation, with the sole merit of being relatively well known in Barcelona. I was the senior Professor of Procedural Law at the University of Barcelona. as well as former Dean of the Barcelona Bar Association, President of the Council of Lawyers of Catalonia, and President of the European Bars Federation. I had also made relatively frequent appearances on the Catalan media (television, radio and press) as an analyst of legal issues. But I had no political links and, apart from the Catalan Minister of Justice, I simply knew some Ministers in the Government in a formal context. So I assumed the defence, not out of political allegiance but guided by the professional rigor demanded for such an honorable assignment.

With the urgency that the issue required (the procedural admission was notified on Tuesday, September 12, granting us just five days to appeal against the resolution), I organized a legal team with various assistants from both the professional and the academic fields. Apart from the professional excellence of the team, what is relevant here is their political plurality: they were voters of various different parties, and many of them identified with parties contrary to the independence of Catalonia. However, the technical diagnosis was unanimous. Both the complaint from the Public Prosecutor's Office and the Admission Order for processing by the Superior Court of Justice of Catalonia had more political than legal content. I would even go further. Pro-independence and anti-independence supporters agreed that the arguments not only lacked legal logic, but that in many points they ostensibly deviated from long consolidated legal interpretations. The Law that I had become acquainted with, studied, applied and taught for thirty-three years, had been severely twisted, with the obvious purpose of criminalizing and persecuting political dissidents. After more than three decades of professional practice as a lawyer, I found myself faced by an indisputable case of lawfare, a phenomenon I knew about on a theoretical level but had never expected to be faced with in the courts of a State that was supposed to have left behind it the grim period of the Franco dictatorship and become homologated to the club of solid democracies.

My twofold disappointment, as a lawyer and as a citizen, was as profound as it was ever-increasing. Indeed, far from being an isolated episode, the phenomenon was to reach heights unimaginable at the time. After the peaceful celebration of the illegal Referendum (the only violence exerted there was that of the Spanish police), President Puigdemont's government was accused of rebellion, the most serious offence in the Spanish Penal Code, punishable with up to 30 years in prison, but which implies an armed uprising. Likewise, provisional prison was also decreed for members of the Government, the Speaker of the Parliament and the leaders of two civicpro-independence associations (Òmnium Cultural and the Catalan National Assembly), various elected officials were suspended, and a fully-fledged general case against the Catalan independence movement was launched. A recent book by journalist Jordi Panyella (its translation into other languages is essential) lists almost 4,000 cases of reprisal against pro-independence activists at the hands of the Spanish justice system.

During the following months I combined my work as defence lawyer – now focused on the President and the Ministers who followed him into exile – with the task of giving publicity to events through the media and in numerous lectures throughout Catalonia. What was happening was so incomprehensible to any lay observer that we lawyers became media stars in the attempt to explain it. Despite the fact that Spain was theoretically a full State of Law, in the Catalan case the Law was being applied in a fashion construed to criminalize political dissidence with the purpose of deterring and demobilizing supporters of Catalan independence.

In this new role as legal commentator, I met a key character in this story and the undisputed architect of the English edition of this book that I have the honor to preface, the recently deceased Anglo-Catalan sociolinguist Miquel Strubell, to whom I take the opportunity to pay the highest honors here.

Strubell has been an important man in the recent history of Catalonia. A fully committed cultural activist (especially in the field of sociolinguistics and language), he was involved in the first municipal referendums on independence in 2014 and was a founder member of the Catalan National Assembly, a plural, civic association created with the explicit objective of promoting the independence of Catalonia. It has tens of thousands of members and has for a decade organized the massive demonstrations on Catalonia's National Day, with over a million participants. From a sociological perspective, Strubell was especially concerned about the war of fake news and disinformation being waged by the major Spanish media, in clear collusion with senior Spanish State authorities and official bodies. The book *Lying for Unity. How Spain Uses Fake News and Disinformation to Block Catalonia's Independence,* written in English by Miquel Strubell, is a key to understanding the strategic use of fake news in the fight against Catalan independence. Fake news not only sets out to impose a certain false account of reality, but also, as Damià del Clot explains – and I have had the opportunity to verify personally – it is also used as incriminating material in lawsuits against independence activists. Strubell masterfully explains, with abundant and rigorously documented references, the numerous falsehoods invented by the Spanish media and by authorities of all ranks (including politicians, officials and judges) to try to convert the wholly peaceful civic independence movement into an allegedly violent one. In so doing, it uses the same template that the Spanish State had applied to fight against Basque terrorism in the past. The Spanish authorities had always affirmed that "Without violence you can talk about everything." Yet, faced with an essentially civic pro-independence phenomenon like that of the Catalans, they chose to distort reality, trying to portray as violent a peaceful movement that has always condemned every type of violence. Strubell explains this and demonstrates it in a most convincing way. But he also understood that, for a better international understanding of the real situation, it would be important to write another book explaining how the Spanish judicial system was misrepresenting facts and rights, in order to criminalize and repress Catalan political dissidence. Strubell was an irresistible seducer and quickly convinced me to start writing a book with him in order to explain, in English, the way in which lawfare was being used against the Catalan independence movement. We met on several occasions, we designed the outline of the work and, just when we were about to start writing, we discovered the great book that I have now been asked to preface.

A good friend, who is a judge and a client of mine (Josep Maria Noales, one of the few magistrates to have been especially belligerent with the lawfare practiced in Spain) showed me the book *Lawfare* by his friend Damià del Clot. I read – or rather, devoured – the book with genuine surprise and fascination. Damià del Clot had been a student of mine at the Faculty of Law some decades ago. But the work that emerged from his doctoral thesis on Constitutional Law and Political Science was, without a doubt, much better than what Strubell and I had in mind to write. As I told Del Clot at the first public presentation of his book, it was the book that I would have liked to have written, because, over and above his solid legal knowledge, its author also has a very firm footing in Political Science – a subject of which he was Associate Professor at the Autonomous University of Barcelona, having moved on to become Associate Professor of Constitutional Law there today – as well as commanding an elegant, clear and entertaining prose style.

I told Strubell about Del Clot's book, and this led us to give up our original plan. We immediately agreed that we should convince Del Clot to get his book translated into English. With the author's approval, Miquel and his brother Toni – another important character in the recent history of Catalonia – began to translate it and contacted the prestigious hispanist Paul Preston, who facilitated the appearance of this edition, which is sponsored by the London School of Economics. Henry Ettinghausen kindly revised the translation and helped undertake the proof-reading.

As the patient reader will be able to verify, my role in this story is that of a secondary actor. Damià del Clot's book is bound to be a key work in identifying the lawfare that the Spanish courts are applying to the Catalan independence movement. I do not think I exaggerate if I say that it will be a legal, political and historical reference book for decades. It is therefore a great honor to be asked to preface the English version. During his last days, Miquel Strubell had the satisfaction of knowing that the English edition of Del Clot's *Lawfare* would be published. This prologue must also serve as a posthumous tribute to Miquel Strubell, to whom we owe so much.

JAUME ALONSO-CUEVILLAS I SAYROL
Professor of Procedural Law, University of Barcelona, March 2022

Glossary of Terms and Abbreviations

ANC, 'Assemblea Nacional Catalana': 'Catalan National Assembly', an organization that seeks the political independence of Catalonia from Spain.

Cs, 'Ciudadanos': 'Citizens', a Spanish centre-right liberal party that rejects autonomous communities' right to self-determination.

CUP, 'Candidatura d'Unitat Popular': 'Popular Unity Candidacy', a left-wing to far-left pro-Catalan independence political party which has traditionally focused on municipal politics. In 2012, the CUP decided for the first time to run for Catalan parliamentary elections, gaining three MPs out of 135. In the 2015 elections they obtained ten MPs.

ERC, 'Esquerra Republicana de Catalunya': 'Republican Left of Catalonia', a Catalan social-democratic political, focusing in recent years on the creation of an independent Catalan Republic. ERC played an important role during the Second Republic, the Civil War, the anti-Francoist resistance and the transition to democracy.

Generalitat, 'Generalitat de Catalunya': Government of Catalonia, the institutional system whereby Catalonia organizes its self-government, formed by the Parliament of Catalonia, the Presidency of the Generalitat, and the Executive Council of Catalonia. Its origins lie in the 13th century. The modern Generalitat was established in 1931 as the institution of self-government of Catalonia within the Spanish Republic. Exiled after the Civil War in 1939, it was re-established in 1977.

JxCat, 'Junts per Catalunya': 'Together for Catalonia', a Catalan electoral and parliamentary alliance, registered as a political party in 2018, originally envisaged as a platform comprising the Catalan European Democratic Party (PDeCAT), successor of the late Democratic Convergence of Catalonia party (CDC) and independents and centered upon the candidacy of former Catalan president Carles Puigdemont ahead of the 2017 Catalan regional elections.

Òmnium Cultural: An association based in Barcelona, created in the 1960s to promote the Catalan language and spread Catalan culture. Over the years it has increased its involvement in broader political issues. In 2012 it committed itself to Catalan independence, specifically demanding the right of self-determination for Catalonia.

PP, 'Partido Popular': 'People's Party', the Spanish conservative and Christian-democratic political party, founded as 'Alianza Popular' (AP) in 1976, and renamed PP in 1989, by authorities and supporters of the Franco dictatorship. It has alternated in governing Spain with the PSOE.
Procés: The ongoing attempt to achieve the independence of Catalonia from Spain, begun specifically in 2010, after the watering down by the Spanish State of a revised Statute of Autonomy for Catalonia and culminating in the Referendum on Independence held on October 1, 2017. The Referendum had been preceded by an unofficial ballot held on November 9, 2014.

PSOE, 'Partido Socialista Obrero Español': 'Spanish Workers' Socialist Party', a mainstream social-democratic political party founded in 1879. The PSOE has been in government longer than any other party in modern Spain, namely from 1982 to 1996, from 2004 to 2011 and currently since 2018. Historically a Marxist party, it abandoned Marxism in 1979.

Transition: The 'Transición', i.e. the political post-dictatorship developments in Spain that occurred after the death of Franco in 1975.

UP, 'Unidas Podemos': 'United We Can', a democratic socialist electoral alliance of left-wing to far-left parties to contest the 2016 Spanish general elections. Part of the anti-austerity movement, it advocates direct democracy, federalism, and republicanism in Spain. After the November 2019 Spanish general elections, it formed a coalition government with the PSOE.

VOX: An extreme right-wing or far-right-wing Spanish political party, founded in 2013. It entered the Spanish parliament for the first time in the April 2019 general elections, and became the country's third political force after the November 2019 elections, securing 3.6 million votes and 52 seats. Its public support is on the rise, according to results of subsequent regional elections and opinion polls.

"All suppressed truths become poisonous"

NIETZSCHE, *Thus Spake Zarathustra*

Introduction

Repressing the Enemy

The political history of Spain is a history of violence. Dozens of military coups d'état – both failed and successful – the assassination of four prime ministers between 1870 and 1973, the civil wars – from the Carlist wars to the Civil War of 1936–1939 – and two authoritarian dictatorships in the 20th century, are ample proof. But, if the political history of the Spanish State is a history of violence, that of the relations between the Spanish State and Catalonia is a history of repression, persecution, intolerance, revenge, humiliation, and also of violence. This violence has reappeared when Catalonia has aspired to achieve more political power, either through a statutory reform that would improve its self-government or its national recognition, or because it has sought to hold a consultation or a self-determination referendum, exercising the right to decide its future. This alone explains why eight of the last ten Presidents of the Generalitat – the Catalan government – have suffered repression. Some were imprisoned, others were (and are) exiled, others barred from public office and subjected to seven-figure fines, and one – President Lluís Companys – assassinated in what is the only execution of a democratically elected president that Europe experienced in the whole of the twentieth century.

These violent impulses are a consequence of the climate of confrontation and intolerance with which the Spanish State has a habit of coping with political problems. The lack of a democratic culture has fuelled a dichotomous view of policies more appropriate in a war setting. We or Them. Friend or Foe. This binary vision of the struggle, which would set its roots in the conquest of America, resurfaced crudely during the Civil War and was established, in its theoretical and legal dimension, during the Franco regime. It is then that the regime looked to Fascist Italy and to Nazi Germany in search of intellectual references to help build a *New State* with an authoritarian structure. Carl Schmitt was one of them, the most important one. But he was not the only one. The definition of the enemy was to be accompanied by the creation of a new political regime that was to seek, via the violence of weapons and the force of law, the control of all political, social and economic space. And, in this totalitarian ambition, the judiciary was to become a fundamental cornerstone.

Little has been written about the judiciary, both recently and in the past. During the Franco regime, judges were turned into the body on which the regime sought legitimacy. It was then that a fundamental variable of repression was successfully tested: the judicialization of all social spheres, with special emphasis on politics. For Francoism, politics and all values – such as parliamentarianism, political pluralism and territorial decentralization, associated with the Second Republic – had to disappear from public debate. That is, they had to be eliminated. This is one of the legacies that forty years of a dictatorial, Fascist, authoritarian and violent regime has left us: almost the same period as we have known democracy. It is a legacy based on uncritical submission to the law, the denial of plurinationality, the aversion to territorial decentralization and the phobia of citizen participation in the most important political issues – all of which the political and social right and far right have found it simple to continue subscribing to. In addition displaying a fierce defence – by whatever means – of the unity of the State. This book speaks about this legacy, which has simultaneously become a way of understanding the exercise of politics.

We propose to explain how, in the face of the demand of a majority, expressed at the polls and in the street, based on parliamentary resolutions and governmental actions, which claims to exercise the right to decide first and the right to self-determination later, the Spanish State responds with repression. But not just with repression. It responds just as dictatorships always do in the face of a threat. First, invoking the law to deny politics. Then deploying a communication strategy aimed at targeting the enemies in order finally to dehumanize them. And lastly, to call in the judiciary (it was the military that used to be called in) with the political goal of eliminating them. This is the basis of a lawfare strategy: to seek an alliance of the actors of the judicial system with the hegemonic media, promoting the dissemination of ideas and the co-opting of public opinion in order to anticipate the pernicious effects of a criminal trial procedure. This is a far cry from Canada or the United Kingdom's responses to a similar problem of a deficit in territorial fit on the part of a minority like Quebec or Scotland.

This work aims to explain how Spanish democracy has been transformed into a *legalistic democracy*. And, as in any *legalistic democracy*, the political system lives installed in a permanent delirium of complaints. Legal complaints – or the vice of resolving any issue, however trivial, in the hands of the courts – have been the strategy chosen to respond to legitimate demands of a clearly political nature. The aim of this work is to provide a theoretical and practical view of the construction of this political strategy.

It is a tactic on the basis of which there is a poorly disguised desire to twist the law, a clear intention to manipulate a servile toga-wearing power and the need to take advantage of media willing to deploy a narrative from a pre-war language, perfectly chosen to stigmatize political dissent: stigmatizing first to eliminate later.

To explain this, the book starts with a first chapter in which the concepts are examined which, when duly deviated or duly reinterpreted, make up the vocabulary of lawfare. After this first chapter, the book is divided into two parts. The first part – entitled *The Repression of the Enemy in Spanish Judicial Culture* – has a clearly theoretical intention. In this sense, the second chapter delves into the elements that characterized the repression of the enemy during the Franco period, especially in the role played by doctrine (theorizing repression), legislation (legalization of repression) and justice (legitimation of repression). The third chapter narrates the Francoist culture that the Transition is unwilling to leave behind. More than that: it inherits it, launders it and offers the continuation of one of the estates most identified with repression: the judiciary. In addition, this chapter offers a theoretical view of what is at the root of repression or what repression seeks to defend: the *raison d'état*.

The fourth chapter dissects the design of judicial institutions in the Constitution. This is what we call the double soul of the Constitution. One thing is the written letter and another its effective deployment. It is what Juan Ramon Capella calls the *Tacit* Constitution and what Alejandro Nieto calls an "*anti*-regulation framework". That is, the mechanisms by which there is a transfer of power from the executive and the legislature to the judiciary. This phenomenon has been referred to in various terms – *juristocracy* (Hirschl), *judicial democracy* (Kaluszynski) or *judicial shift* (Martin). We shall call it the *judicialization* of politics. We shall see how those debates not started or directly banned during the Transition (basically monarchy and territorial unity, which are at the basis of the *raison d'état)* are protected, thanks to mechanisms surreptitiously concealed in the Constitution itself. We shall look at those that have to do with the body in charge of protecting them: the high courts set up in a kind of *Deep State*. In the fifth chapter we shall analyse the way in which judicial elites are recruited and the system of servitudes that has been installed in the Spanish judicial leadership.

The second part of the book has a clear practical dimension, but without shying away from formulating a theoretical view of the concepts that will be used. With this aim, the sixth chapter is dedicated to framing the elements that characterize a legal battle in its triple dimension: strategic, judicial and communicational. Chapter Seven is based on a duality that is activated the moment the Deep State decides that reasons of State need to be protected through the effective deployment of lawfare. It is a typology of duality that Ernst Fraenkel had theorized about in connection to the Nazi State and that, once adapted to the reality of the Catalan sovereignty process, helps to decipher the real goal of the exceptional, arbitrary and disproportionate measures that are at the heart of the repression of the Catalan independence movement. The application of the criminal and procedural law of the enemy is explained by a distinction between good and evil: the good Spaniards and the anti-Spaniards. This is the starting point of the conception of the secessionist challenge, not as a political problem, but as a war in which the enemy has to be eliminated.

From Chapter Eight onwards, the book examines the culmination of the lawfare strategy deployed against the dissident independence movement. It is based on the transformation of the Spanish State into a *judicial State*, dominated by the opinion of the judges and conditioned by the content of their resolutions. Starting with the analysis of the macro-cause against the Catalan independence movement in the various Spanish judicial bodies, in this chapter we anatomize, with the aid of statistical data, the sociological profile of the judges of the Constitutional Court and the Supreme Court, the Spanish courts within which lawfare has been undertaken. In the ninth chapter we narrow the focus and concentrate on the construction of the political trial – special case 20907/2017 – the never-hidden goal of which has been to eliminate the most outstanding leaders in the Catalan independence movement. Or, in the words of Soraya Sáenz de Santamaría, to decapitate it.

The analysis of special case 20907/2017 will help us to cross-reference theory and practice once again. Using Otto Kirchheimer's theoretical considerations, in this ninth chapter we will delve into the punitive elements that are at the root of the criminal case against the leaders of the *Procés*, going so far as to transform it into a political trial. We shall see how the successful end of the criminal process – or the exercise of the *ius puniendi* of the State – is placed above the protection of fundamental rights. We shall analyse how the law is twisted in order to criminalize the whole of a peaceful, good-natured, transversal, intergenerational, grassroot social movement, which has been expressed in very large numbers in the streets and squares of the country. Even Brussels and Madrid have witnessed it! We shall study how, with the deployment of lawfare, the independence movement has been depicted as a subversive, violent movement supposedly aimed at bringing about a *coup d'état*.

Finally, the tenth chapter addresses the weakness of Spanish lawfare: the international dimension of the legal battle. We shall examine how the European arrest warrants and the Junqueras doctrine have been the Achilles heel of Spain's jurisdictional strategy and may in the future become the basis of, or prelude to, a judicial *fracas* of considerable proportions. The work ends with an epilogue – an attempt at a brief conclusion intended to define where we were a few years ago and where we are today, if only to see that in many matters inherent in the fundamental pillars of what should be a law-abiding State – protection of fundamental rights, defence of liberties, application of the law in accordance with democratic principles – we have not moved on from a scenario that we thought had been put behind us but that turns out to inspire the logic of Spain's politics and high courts.

This book was not born with the aim of being an academic text. It neither seeks to achieve that purpose nor responds to the literary style that works of that nature ought to present. It's an essay. As such, it raises a number of issues that have to do with politics, though it is not a document that belongs to political science. It also talks about law, though it is not conceived as a legal text, either. It speaks of history, philosophy and sociology, although it cannot be considered a historiographical, philosophical or sociological document. Consequently, it is a book that combines all these disciplines of the social sciences, but without any ambition to become a scientific document. Footnotes are used for identifying the bibliographical sources that have helped me the most in writing the work.

The ideas presented come from my experience of more than twenty years as a lawyer, from my status as an active politician, from my academic side as a researcher-doctoral student at the Autonomous University of Barcelona and, this academic year 2020–2021, from my new post as Associate Professor of Political Science at the University of Barcelona. The coming pages are thus a sum of hours of libraries, court writs – complaints, lawsuits, appeals, reversals, reforms, cassation – allegations in courtrooms and lectures in political and academic tribunes of a varied nature. They are also hours of reflection and conversation, of debate and reformulation of positions in relation to concepts that until now had not emerged in all their clarity.

Damià del Clot

Written at

VILASSAR DE MAR – BIGUES I RIELLS – MONASTERY OF MONTSERRAT.

Chapter 1

Conceptual Framework

The Importance of Language in the Lawfare Strategy

It was in the early years of the 21st century that a linguist warned that American Conservatives had been investing millions of dollars in think tanks since the 1970s. The aim was to fund research, publications and conventions devoted to perfecting a better way of structuring and communicating their ideas. Deep down, what the Republicans wanted was to destroy, by using language – though not only from the point of view of language – the prestige and the political credibility of their opponents. And they succeeded. The Conservatives defined the big political issues and labelled their enemies using their own language, using their own political interests, and using their own deeply or markedly conservative values. From there, they deployed a political communication strategy aimed at defining goals, using the appropriate tools, an articulated discourse, and an effective staging. A complete success.

The creation of a conceptual framework in clear connivance with associated media allowed the American Right to coin concepts such as the "war on terror", which defined world politics in the first decade of the 21st century. In actual fact, they characterized it so much that the concept of "war on terror" became a mantra capable of activating feelings associated with everything to do with fear – above all, fear of the unknown, which had of necessity to be violent, destructive and deadly. And, in order to fight terror, the President of the United States was no longer just the President; he became the Commander-in-Chief of the US Armed Forces, for only the Commander-in-Chief could deal with Saddam, Al Qaeda or Iraq, for Saddam, Al Qaeda or Iraq (that is, the "Axis of Evil") were the enemies. And the enemies had to be eliminated. John Yoo, a lawyer and professor at the University of Berkeley and author of *War by Other Means*, was in charge of the entire judicial architecture of lawfare, following the logic of Carl von Clausewitz: using the law to achieve a military goal. Guantánamo is a consequence and example of this lawfare, as is the Patriot Act.

The linguist who warned of all this was George Lakoff. And Lakoff reflected on this issue – and other issues related to language and the ability of language as a tool or weapon capable of mobilizing feelings, values and goals in a context of high media coverage of politics – in the now classic *Don't Think of an Elephant!*.[1] The fact is that the reflection that Lakoff made in the early years of the 21st century has not lost its validity: on the contrary. It has been shown to be a strategy that, properly perfected, has aroused phenomena initially linked to the use of language. Lawfare is one of them, for in its initial conception, lawfare becomes a battlefield in which words replace swords.[2]

The phenomenon we propose to analyse – the lawfare strategy applied to the Catalan case – also has its own conceptual framework. It is a language duly adapted to the needs of the protection of legal assets to be defended by means of legal instruments of coercion that are at the heart of the judicial war. Next we shall analyse these concepts, the meanings of which, incidentally, have had to be reformulated or rewritten so as to adapt them to the new playing field in which it is claimed they are to be applied: that of the battle of the togas.

1.1 Lawfare as a Strategy of Repression

Lawrence Freedman, a professor of military history at King's College, referred to a well-known contemporary definition of strategy to describe it as being about "maintaining a balance between ends, ways, and means; about identifying objectives; and about the resources and methods available for meeting such objectives."[3] Strategy comes into play when a real or potential conflict arises or persists, in which there are colliding interests and decisions are needed in the search for solutions (Freedman. 2013: xi). But strategy – we continue with Freedman – is also presented in scenarios in which there are two opposing positions, and this reflects the military origins of the concept. The link between military strategy and the objectives of politics was offered by Carl von Clausewitz in his well-known work *On War*, when he stated that war was the continuation of politics but using other means.[4] Using this abstraction, war did not necessarily require the use of weapons. It could refer to a confrontation between two parties with conflicting interests, such as a criminal trial.

But it is clear that a judicial process is not conceived of as a battle for confronting political positions. Nor can the judicial process be used as a tool to destroy a minority by a majority. Or to liquidate the enemy. A lawsuit has other purposes, but not these. When the analyst or scholar takes on the goal of defining a phenomenon as complex and, at the same time, as fashionable as lawfare, the judicial process appears as one of the strategic elements that characterize it. But it is not the only one. We know, then, that when defining the term lawfare we are confronted with a polysemous concept or, at the very least, with a concept on which there is no consensus. It is often used pejoratively. It is no coincidence that it has elements – such as the misuse of justice or the distortion of law for political purposes – that make it controversial in popular and political discourse. Its influence on the recurring harangue of American conservatism during the years of the "War on Terror" after the 9/11 attacks has made lawfare an unpleasant concept.

In the 1990s, lawfare was conceived of as the misuse of legal instruments for the purposes of political persecution, destruction of the public image (whether of a politician, a political party or a social movement) in the endeavour to disqualify the adversary or enemy. Consequently, a definition of lawfare, according to the premises of the nineties, would be a strategy that combines actions of legal appearance with other political actions, with ample media coverage, with the aim of bringing pressure to bear on the enemy or adversary and its immediate social environment. The adversary or enemy is thus more vulnerable to the instruments of judicial coercion. Lawfare therefore appears in contexts of political crisis, where the government – or as we shall see, the State apparatus – chooses to push aside politics as a means of resolving the conflict and to transfer this responsibility to the courts. This is called imposing the law from above.

The use of the term lawfare – the combination of law and warfare – responds to a desire to define the concept especially in terms of military strategy. For Silvina Romano, lawfare is a military strategy of a jurisdictional nature that comes to be transformed into an unconventional method of warfare.[5] In this strategic aspect, the law is used as a means to achieve a military goal. It is no coincidence that the concept in question came to be used in political and military language after the publication, in 2001, of an article written by U.S. Air Force General Charles J. Dunlap, of Duke Law School.[6] Two years earlier, in 1999, two Chinese People's Liberation Army colonels, Qiao Liang and Wang Xiangsui, had written *Unrestricted Warfare*, in which they offered arguments for China to defeat a technologically superior opponent, such as the United States,. through a war that did not necessarily have to be military.

Let us return to Silvina Romano to point out that the concept of lawfare is asymmetrical and extorting, one typical of colonial contexts. In 2001, John L. Comaroff, in his paper *Colonialism, Culture and the Law*, conceived of lawfare as the coercive use of the law to achieve the subordination, conquest and control of subordinate populations and, in general, of minorities.[7] Lawfare, now and before, has always been a tool within the reach of privileged elites who reorganize the political and social scene in favour of the interests of the transnational power network (Romano: 2019: 22). But of late, as Carol Proner tells us, lawfare has become a tool of power at the service of neo-Fascism.[8] According to Proner, this hybrid war strategy penetrates spaces where there are social elements of popular crisis to nurture the narrative of systemic corruption, rejection of politics and politicians, and the weakness of parliament as opposed to a supposedly incorruptible judiciary.[9] And it works on an element that is a very cornerstone of Fascism: co-opting popular bases and achieving the politicization of society in an authoritarian direction (Proner 2019: 36).

The Spanish State is no stranger to the phenomenon of lawfare. Far from it. Spain has a long history of designing strategies for the use of the judiciary and the law to persecute political dissent. In the following sections we shall argue how concepts are distorted by the Spanish State to the point of twisting their meaning around to serve the ends of the judicial war strategy.

1.2 The Language of Lawfare

When Curzio Malaparte, in *Technique du coup d'état* – a book that was banned during the Franco regime – explores the mechanisms of seizing power (the case of the Bolshevik coup and Trotsky's tactics in October 1917) or defending the State (the case of Joseph Stalin and the defence of the Soviets' power against Trotsky in 1927), he insinuates that violence is not necessary. All that is needed, according to this controversial writer – who was both a Fascist and an anti-Fascist at the same time and who was, above all, an excellent narrator and polemicist – is a well-organized group. The same can be said of the promoters of lawfare against Catalan independence. In parallel with the start of the deployment of lawfare, a campaign was launched to criminalize the Catalan sovereignty movement, calling it *putschist*. This expression was used precisely because in the Spanish collective imagination the coup came to be a mechanism for taking control of power which was clearly associated with violence. In the desire to present the independence movement as a violent movement there was a more sophisticated intention. So why, then, was a social movement with a clearly peaceful dimension treated as putschist?

To answer we need to return to George Lakoff and his classic *Don't Think of an Elephant,* or go back as far as George Orwell and his no less classic political essays on power and language. To put it another way: the desire to portray the peaceful and civic independence movement as a subversive force with a putschist vocation hid the intention of framing particular actions within a specific narrative, a fictitious narrative in which the concepts are not what they are or are what those who use them want them to be – in a twisted way, to be sure. Language and narrative are two variables that are part of lawfare. And in what we have called the Catalan case, before analysing the unfolding of the legal war, we need to dissect a series of concepts that will form part of the narrative that the strategists will use.

These are not unknown concepts. On the contrary, they will appear distorted. Or at the very least, the concepts in question will not fit into the function they are traditionally given. That is why it is appropriate to fit each concept into the coordinates in which it will be used. Unless we do this, unless we specify each concept in the political and judicial framework in which it will be used, the reader may end up in some confusion. Words, as George Lakoff reminds us, are relevant for framing specific situations associated with political issues, especially when we try to analyze a legal war strategy where the media dimension of the conflict is essential – or very nearly essential – in winning the support of public opinion as regards the future court ruling.

1.2.1 The Law and Laws

Although in the Spanish political rhetoric of recent years they may seem synonymous, law and the Law form two different realities that should be defined at the outset. The law, in itself, is just one more expression of power. Law, on the other hand, aspires to achieve expectations and values. The relationship that connects law with the Law is justice. Justice is invoked when a law is overbearing, arbitrary or excessively violent, so that values such as conscientious objection or civil disobedience are brought up. A law can therefore be unjust. And when it is said that a law is unjust, what is being said is that it will not achieve the ideal of justice, so law does not fulfil the function it has been given: to serve values and principles such as freedom, democracy, political pluralism, social equality and the defence of human rights. A political system legitimized by unjust laws responds to what Michel de Montaigne called *legalistic legal absolutism,*[10] in other words, laws at the service of an absolutist State.

There is no need to go very far to identify States that have sought their legitimacy by constantly invoking submission to the law. This logic, although not expressly stated, implies the expression "force of the law." Nazism, Fascism and Francoism were States that called themselves lawful States. This did not prevent them from engaging in legalized violence, issuing sentences enforcing laws that provided for the death penalty, or criminalizing conduct that was an expression of the exercise of social and political rights. The Nuremberg Laws were the introduction, in German legislation, of the racist ideology of Hitler and the National Socialist Party, in the same way that the Law of Repression of Freemasonry and Communism or the Law of Political Responsibilities were the expression of the will to eliminate the enemy during the Franco regime. But, as the aphorism points out: *dura lex, sed lex*.

It is pertinent to make this distinction insofar as a desire has emerged, in the Spanish political culture of recent years, to merge the Law and laws and then deploy a legalistic rhetorical discourse that has gone further, in an attempt to confuse both concepts with politics. The aim is to reduce politics to defending the laws. The laws – not Law – are an essential tool for the success of a lawfare strategy. Their interpretation by like-minded gown-bearers for the benefit of the promoters of the hybrid warfare strategy can mark the difference between the success and the failure of a judicial battle.

1.2.2 The Rhetoric of the Rule of Law

As society has challenged and conquered social and economic spaces to exercise fundamental rights and freedoms, both individual and collective, government elites have been strengthening the legalist discourse. The arrival of the constitutional State, with a democratic embedding, has consolidated variables hitherto unknown to the Spanish State: alternating governments, the exercise of fundamental rights and increasingly expansive freedoms, protection of consumers and users against abusive practices of the large financial corporations, and territorial decentralization of political power. But the fact that multilevel governance spaces have been conquered or regulations for the protection of the weakest have been articulated does not mean that democracy has taken root as a form of social organization. The jurisprudence of the international courts of justice has revealed and confirmed the weaknesses of Spanish democracy, especially as regards the level of tolerance with social conquests that the Spanish elites were willing to accept.

The need to strengthen the narrative of the rule of law has been accentuated since the emergence of the 15-M social movement and the emergence of the Catalan independence movement. The first – also known as the *movimiento de los indignados* (the movement of the outraged) – sought to promote a more participatory democracy than the alternating Popular Party-Socialist Party bipartisanship and the domination of the large banks, and to achieve a real division of powers. The Catalan independence movement sought – and still seeks today – the possibility of holding a referendum or poll on the independence of Catalonia, invoking the right to decide first (2010–2015) and the right to self-determination later (2016 until now). The social and political rights that the conquests of these movements amount to become a clear distribution of power, resources and values. And not only that: at the heart of these groups' demands there is a clear will to break with the constitutional political regime inherited from the Franco dictatorship. To combat these social movements in the field of politics, the Spanish State has strengthened the rhetoric of the rule of law and, in the process, the legalist narrative. As a result of this strategy, it has expanded the scope of action and influence of the Spanish judicial elites.

Thanks to this empowerment, the State has deployed a strategy, by means of which the courts have become the only space for resolving the conflict. Before that, though, it changed the rules of the game. It is in this context that two of the most restrictive norms in terms of fundamental rights known to Spanish democracy exist: Organic Law 4/2015, on the protection of public safety – better known as the *Gag Law* – and Organic Law 15/2015, reforming the Organic Law of the Constitutional Court so that it can execute its own judgments. The title of the last law refers precisely to the rhetoric of strengthening the rule of law. What both norms implement, however, is a considerable expansion of the political power of judges. To put it another way, the two norms respond to the desire to build a strategy – rhetorical first and normative later – to raise the judiciary above the legislative and the executive. And raising the judiciary above the legislative and the executive ensures the desired outcome – that is, in the form of measures or convictions – of a judicial battle strategy.

1.2.3 Judicial Elites

Spanish judges, according to the Constitution, are subject to the rule of law. This sentence condenses, in all its force, the principle of legality. And this principle of legality takes shape, when we talk about judges in their interpretation of the law. In the hands of deviant judges, the most exquisite law can become a tool far removed from its function. That is why it says little or nothing about law or the ideal of justice. The certainty of the law overshadows any other characteristic of the judges, just as important, or even more so, than the principle of legality. We refer to judicial independence. In more democratically mature or more confident societies, recourse to the courts has a reparative function for harm done. But in societies riddled with mistrust or lacking in democratic culture, such as the Spanish one, in which political elites have entered into an obsessive litigating delirium to solve social and political discrepancies, independence attains at least as much importance – if not more so – than the judge's subjection to the law.[11] But as judges get closer to power they tend to lose the virtue of independence, and submission to the law gives way to the instructions of political parties.

And it is in this sense that a warning has to be given. When in the coming pages readers see the expressions *toga government* or *judicial elite* or *high judiciary*, or any formulation of a similar nature and content, they should know that we are referring to judges linked to political power, or close to political power. Hence, when readers come across an expression such as *political judge*, it is not our intention to criticize judges for having an ideology or a capacity to govern; we refer to that sector of the judiciary that has decided to act, based on tactics and techniques more typical of an *omertà*, as a conveyor belt of the ideological and political preferences of the parties that have placed them in strategic places at the top of the Spanish judiciary. They wear togas but, strictly speaking, do not fulfil a jurisdictional function – to judge and to execute what has been judged. On the contrary, they take part in the political game in accordance with instructions that come from the leaders of the parties that appointed them.

We are not referring, therefore, to the vast majority of judges who practise the profession in Spain and who do so in very difficult and complex conditions, with scant human, technical and legal resources. Front-line justice is the example of judges who are committed to applying the law and who dignify justice. They are the ones who, far from practising a mechanical application of the legal norm, impregnate their decisions with common sense and hand down their judgments within the parameters of equity. Lawfare does not want these judges. It wants the political judge, or worse: the partisan judge.

1.3 The Aims of Lawfare

Every lawfare strategy pursues a political goal. In Spain, this political goal is not – or cannot be – explained without a brief review of recent history. Let's take a leap into the past, to July 18, 1936. This date helps to explain what was in the past – but also what is in the present – the goal of a lawfare strategy: to destroy the enemy. But not just *any* enemy: we are talking about an enemy that becomes necessary. Umberto Eco wrote that having an enemy is not only important in defining our identity; it is also important "to provide us with an obstacle against which to measure our system of values."[12] Following the illustrious Italian, the Franco regime that arose out of the 1936 *coup d'etat* acted within the logic of knowing that when the enemy does not exist it has to be created. And it created many, one of which was Catalan nationalism in its various expressions.

Catalan nationalism was repressed and vexed, and attempts were made to eliminate it, in the past and also in the present. Indeed, one of the features that marked the degree of repression and brutality that the *coup d'état* of July 18, 1936, entailed was that there was never a single symbolic gesture, or a single political decision, to put a definitive end to the Civil War. Quite the contrary: in the practice of the regime there was a desire to continue the conflict as a way to consolidate peace, while maintaining the divide between the winners and the losers. Proof of what we are saying is that no political amnesties were granted, nor was the existence of political prisoners acknowledged.

The regime acted on the logic of liquidating the adversary, identified with the imagery of the Second Republic. Politics was a harmful activity inasmuch as it emerged as an element of contamination of *good* Spaniards, dividing society and fuelling conflict. Opponents or dissidents were persecuted. This persecution and repression had the function of a warning or social message seeking, ultimately, to achieve a passive society in regard to public issues or affairs. Pluralism was pernicious, so only unity could exist: a single Nation, a single party, a single trades union and a single side from which to separate good and evil.

It is from this logic that the concept of the enemy takes shape. Although the term enemy – and its neutralization[13] – had always been present in Spanish politics, it was during the Franco regime that its doctrinal construction was sought in order to combat it through the use of force: especially the enemy who questioned the main ideological postulates on which the *New State* was to be built. One of these postulates was the principle of unity of the homeland and, consequently, the defence of the Spanish nation. Catalan autonomism – then called *separatism* – was one of the enemies to be eliminated: probably the most hated enemy of all.

1.3.1 Carl Schmitt and Friend-Enemy Rhetoric

When the President of the General Council of the Judiciary and the Supreme Court quoted Carl Schmitt during his inaugural address for the 2020 judicial year, he did not do so in a superfluous or idle way. He did so intentionally. Schmitt's dictum – "Sovereign is he who decides on the exception" – is the confirmation of a totalitarian view of the law.[14] Carl Schmitt's is the most thorough and complete intellectual and doctrinal contribution on the corrosion of the rule of law and legal totalitarianism.

He enjoyed great prestige during the Franco regime and has continued to have followers to this day, as is shown by the highest Spanish judicial authority.[15]

There are two reasons for the special relationship of Schmitt with Spanish totalitarianism: one, the excellent knowledge of Carl Schmitt's work in Spain during the 1930s; two, Schmitt's interest in traditional Spanish legal thinking that was revived during the Franco regime.[16] The visits to German institutions in the 1930s by lawyers linked to the Franco regime, such as Francisco Javier Conde and Luís Legaz Lacambra, also contributed to the knowledge of Schmitt's work. The definitive fit of the work of the German jurist in the field of legal theory allied to the Franco dictatorship comes from the theorization of concepts that suit, and fit in with, a Francoist State with violent and repressive roots.

The Schmittian definition of politics, seen as a distinction between friend and foe, may be the best known of all, but it is not the only one.[17] Here we will focus on the political enemy, who according to Schmitt, "need not be morally evil or aesthetically ugly; he need not appear as an economic competitor, and it may even be advantageous to engage with him in business transactions. But he is, nevertheless, the other, the stranger, and it is sufficient for his nature that he is, in a specially intense way, existentially something different and alien" (Schmitt 2007: 27). The enemy is, then, he who is different, alien, unequal, though he need not be unpleasant. The enemy, says Schmitt, is *hostis*.

As we shall see, the intellectual contribution of the philosopher from Plettenberg transcends the chronological framework in which it was formulated, to such an extent that today it is considered to be one of the greatest contributions to the construction of a totalitarian policy. The Schmittian ideology began to take shape during World War I and gained fame and prestige during the Weimar Republic. But his joining the NSDAP[18] in 1933 meant that Schmitt's ideas came to be adopted in the service of the doctrinal justification of National Socialism. Although this fact was much more pronounced in his followers, such as Ernst Forsthoff or Theodor Maunz, today Schmitt is considered to be the quintessential *kornjurist*. Nazi law cannot be explained without the contributions of Carl Schmitt. Proof of this statement are, as the Sorbonne philosopher Yves-Charles Zarka has written, the Nuremberg Laws.[19] This legal framework led to the entry of Schmitt's political thought into German law by normatizing the racist and discriminatory ideology that Hitler had already left in writing in *Mein Kampf*.

For Zarka, Carl Schmitt's adherence to Nazism was a conscious and deep connection, so it is not possible to study his extensive legal-political work by putting into brackets his commitment to Nazi principles and the credit that his intellectual reflections enjoyed (Zarka 2007: 18). In fact, Schmitt was already a well-known and feared jurist when he joined the Nazi Party in 1933. From then on, he offered coverage for the darkest episodes of Nazism. In 1934 he was entrusted with the direction of the party's main legal propaganda body, the Deutsche Deutscheg, from which he published articles justifying the worst Nazi laws. Suffice it to point out that in that same year he published "The Führer Protects the Law," in which he endorsed the political figure of Hitler after the bloody "Night of the Long Knives" (June 30, 1934).

The Francoist State, then, took on board the radicalism of Schmittian thought, adopting the distinction between friend and foe as a political category. Franco's jurists saw Schmittian political realism as an instrument of recognition and legitimacy of the Spanish reality to replace the one that the Second Republic had developed under the State system of parties based on the recognition of political pluralism. "The nation had ceased to be a state and was actually torn apart in two different states", wrote Luis Legaz Lacambra in 1940.[20] Political pluralism and the decentralization of the State were two of the great enemies which the New State had to cope with, and this circumstance could be seen as the trigger for a civil war. The will was that the internal animosity within the Spanish State should never take place again, and this is why Legaz Lacambra himself proposed the elimination of the enemy, i.e. that of the most representative political leaders, their ideologies and their symbols.

This aspect of Schmitt's political conception is worth underlining insofar as it feeds the logic from which, when this division occurred within the State, political unity was fractured and the Civil War broke out. And the Civil War could only have one of two consequences: the annihilation of the enemy or the secession of a part of the territory. Heinrich Meier has highlighted this Schmittian theory, which did not appear in the edition of *The Concept of the Political* published in 1927, yet did in the version published in 1932.[21] For Schmitt in 1927 there could only be one policy, which was foreign or international. From 1932 onwards, this concept changed, and the existence of domestic politics burst into his theses as did, in consequence, the existence of an enemy within the territory, or in a part of the territory. As we shall see, this is the conception of the foe that, in the opinion of important theorists of current criminal doctrine, was to inspire Günther Jakobs to formulate the theory of the criminal law of the enemy.

The derivation in terms of criminal legislation from the political conception of the enemy was, as the jurist Marino Barbero observed, a transposition of German National Socialist legal and judicial policy.[22] Action-based criminal law was replaced by on-demand criminal law. Classic criminal dogmatics, based on the formalism of the analysis of criminal actions, gave way to criminal law that focused its *raison d'être* on the criminalization of the elements that define the offender: his personality, behaviour, race or ideas. This new Criminal Law only made sense if the goal was to fight a political enemy; it would never apply to ordinary delinquents.

1.3.2 The Internal Enemy. The problem of "España"

Let us take a further step back in time: to 1898. The loss of Cuba and Puerto Rico or, to put it another way, the defeat in the war that meant doing without the overseas colonies by the use of weapons, entailed the dismemberment of more than half of the Spanish colonial empire. According to the historian Xosé M. Nuñez Seixas, the defeat had three immediate consequences.[23] Firstly, posing the "Problem of Spain" in essentialist and metaphysical terms, which led to a recovery of *casticism* by the 1898 intellectual (literary) Generation. Secondly, an obsession with designating a new internal enemy which was to be the peripheral nationalisms: political Catalanism, then Basque nationalism and, later and to a lesser extent, political Galicianism. And thirdly, a return to the exaltation of the value of the people understood as the healthy part of a Nation – the Spanish one – that was calling for regeneration. This movement would be known as Regenerationism.

This regenerationism – a basically intellectual movement – that sought to overcome the decline of Spain as a Nation, contrasts with, and at the same time gets feedback from, a movement that emerged in Catalonia, the Renaixença.[24] This contrast between a dismembered and decadent, demoralized Spanish Nation, lacking an attractive political project, and a Catalonia that enhances its language and culture, its architecture and its commerce, makes Catalanism stand out as the main internal adversary. Basque Nationalism and political Galicianism are also adversaries, but neither of them manages to generate as many antibodies as Catalanism does. Anti-Catalanism which, as we shall see, dates back to the 17th century, has lasted over time, as has Catalanism in many of its expressions: federalist, republican, traditionalist and separatist. No distinctions would be made from Madrid.

Nuñez Seixas singles out a fourth variable, which we connect in the way this Spanish nationalism reacts as regards the internal enemy. This fourth variable is the trend of authoritarian inspiration, which oscillates between the radical right and Fascism, which first looks at Mussolini's Italian model and then – especially from Ramiro Ledesma Ramos, Onésimo Redondo and

José Antonio Primo de Rivera onwards – puts the spotlight on Nazi Germany (Nuñez Seixas. 2017: 57). Its most perfected organic embodiment as genuinely fascist organizations were to be the 'Juntas de Ofensiva Nacional-Sindicalista' (JONS), founded in 1931, and the Falange Española, founded in 1933 and led by Primo de Rivera. The joining of the two organizations was to take place in 1934. And they were to achieve concepts that mixed traditional Catholicism, authoritarianism and populism and an essentialist idea of the Spanish nation, identified with "The Community of Destiny," according to a thesis developed by Ortega y Gasset.

All this conglomerate of traditions linked to an idea of Spanish nationalism was to be put into practice, not by associations or small parties, but by the Army. In its capacity as a leading actor in Spanish political history, the Army considered itself to be the depositary and guarantor of the essences, symbols and, most importantly, unity of the Fatherland. A first practical expression was seen in Barcelona, because of the signing, on September 11, 1923 – by the most radical sectors of Catalan, Basque and Galician nationalisms – of the pacts called 'Galeusca', or Triple Alliance. The aim of the pact was to work together to make possible the exercise of the right to self-determination – echoing the fourteen points of the Wilson doctrine – by the three nations. The answer was not long in coming. Two days later, the Captain General of Catalonia, Miguel Primo de Rivera, led the *coup d'état* that was to establish a dictatorship with the approval of King Alfonso XIII.

Violence and repression became the medicine to be administered to the Catalan internal enemy. Primo de Rivera yielded to the wishes of the deeply anti-Catalan sentiments of the military leadership and rejected – as Franco would later – Catalan culture and language.[25] Moreover, he banned the display of symbols, such as the Catalan flag, and prevented the teaching of Catalan in schools.

1.3.3 The Catalan Independence Movement. "A por ellos" (Go get 'em!)

Let us now take a leap forward, to the 21st century. Carl Schmitt's friend–enemy dichotomy is still alive. The verbalization of expressions such as blackmail, annihilation or betrayal, and the warlike rhetoric so typical of the Franco regime – and yet so present – addresses a new concept: tension. Joaquín Estefanía has best defined tension as: "a permanent and systematic disagreement with certain initiatives of the political antagonist, presented from the other side as a sign of spurious changes of the rules of the game, as a threat to coexistence or to democratic consensus".[26] Antagonism and hostility as a form of political exercise are nothing more than the survival of Schmittian doctrines. Politics, understood as a war or as a space where two antagonistic positions fight each other, in which there can only be winners and losers, allows one to offer a view of the position of the governments of the Popular Party – the only interlocutor during the years of greatest intensity of the Catalan independence *Process* – against any initiative that arose from Catalonia with the intention of increasing its political power. The sovereignty Process is the latest example, but it is not the only one.

The history of the first twenty years of the 21st century shows us that two initiatives were sought in Catalonia: first, obtaining a new constitutional framework, an increase in self-government within Spain; and, second, when this attempt failed, asking the citizenship what political framework they wanted to enjoy and whether that framework should be within or outside Spain. Both have been the subject of court judgments. The reform of the Statute of Autonomy, which ended with a severe cut in Catalan aspirations through judgment 31/2010, handed down by the Constitutional Court, showed the end of the autonomous State. As for the sovereignty Process, it was prosecuted and submitted to the verdict of the courts. The best known of all was the judgment handed down by the Supreme Court in special case 20917/2017, which sent the nine defendants to gaol for a total of 99 years. Though not the only judgments, these are the most important ones.

Since the *Procés* began, the "secessionist challenge" – an expression often used in Madrid's media and political forums – has intensified the anti-Catalan impulse, which is neither new nor born with democracy or, looking back, even with Francoism. As Francesc Ferrer i Gironès tells us, the first outbreaks were manifested in the *Gran Memorial* written in 1624 by the Count-Duke of Olivares who proposed to the King the repeal of Catalonia's constitutions.[27] With the Count-Duke, an anti-Catalan sentiment arose that, over the years and events – the War of the Reapers (1640–1652) and the loss of Catalan institutions in 1714 were to be the most important – transmuted into Catalanophobia. Catalanophobia was born as a reaction to Catalanism's desire to claim greater political power and greater national recognition.

Anti-Catalanism, then, has revived the authoritarian impulses of Spain. As Juan Carlos Moreno Cabrera has written, the (independence) Process has woken up a Spanish nationalism that has featured a strong aggressive, negationist (to defend the Catalan nation is to deny the Spanish Nation, which is the only one that exists) and ethnocidal nature. This Spanish nationalism – I continue with Moreno Cabrera – is incompatible with the freedom of other nations because of its exclusionary, supremacist and imperialist character.[28] All these adjectives reawaken when, from Catalonia, a bottom-up, transversal, intergenerational social movement is born, with democratic values, that expresses itself in the streets and in the institutions, claiming the exercise of the right to decide, first, and the right to self-determination, later. It is in this political context, from 2010 to the present day, that anti-Catalanism has acquired its worst face: the face that Carl Schmitt theorized and which took shape long before October 1, 2017, but which became present on that date. That face acquired a voice. It was the cry *"A por ellos!"* (Go get 'em!).

Enric Company, an *El País* journalist, expressed this phenomenon in the following words: "Son gritos de hostilidad."[29] They have been followed by equally sectarian, equally uncivil, slogans, the resurgence of an anti-Catalanism that had been dormant for quite some time, since the years of the Transition, but was still there. If you stir it up, it works, as is well known. Anti-Catalanism was described a long time ago as a mass ideology of Spanish nationalism. The Popular Party pulled it out from the depths of its closet in 2006 when it launched the campaign against the draft Catalan Statute throughout Spain. Anti-Catalanism, which emerged as a result of a collection, made by the Popular Party, of signatures against Catalonia and passing them off as signatures against the Statute of Autonomy, returned to the political scene. But what did the cry *A por ellos!* mean, from a political and social point of view?

The cry *A por ellos!* was not just any old expression.[30] In many statements by leaders of the Spanish Government, of the Popular Party or of Ciudadanos, as well as journalists and commentators on Spanish radio stations and television channels, uttered in the heat of *A por ellos*, there was a clear determination to unfold a narrative of conflict. It was a warlike language, with a rhetoric and a tone that demonstrated, once again, the persistence of the political vision of Francoism linked to the dialectical confrontation between Them and Us. It sounded like the prelude to an outbreak of violence.[31] *They* were the enemies, the foe, the different ones; *We* were the defenders of the unity of the Fatherland. It was the demonstration of the ineffectiveness of politics in resolving a conflict that was neither new nor unheard-of. It was a conflict tolerated and managed – granting breadcrumbs was a form of tolerance and management – during forty years of theoretical democracy, but a conflict that resurfaced, amplified and supported by a majority social movement in Catalonia, calling for the deployment of the finest virtues of politics.

But it was not to be. As early as 1929, Francesc Cambó had warned, when he wrote *Per la concòrdia (For Concord):* "I hope that there is no separatist who is candid enough to believe in the possibility of obtaining the separation of Catalonia by persuasion, something like what happened with the separation of Norway and Sweden. [...] Spain would never adopt Sweden's attitude: the whole of history attests to this."

PART ONE

The Repression of the Enemy in Spanish Judicial Culture

Chapter 2

Francoism

Repression in its Historical Dimension

Extreme violence – especially that exerted against civilians – the punishment of the non-combatant population, the culture of war, the expulsion of the enemy – potential or imaginary – and the militarization of civilian spaces that characterized the Spanish Civil War all came in response to a determination to build a fascist state. We have already noted that the Franco regime was an ally of Nazi Germany and fascist Italy, from which it received logistical support to to implement in the coup of July 18, 1936. But what we are interested in highlighting about Nazism and fascism is that these two political regimes were the main ideological reference point for what was to be called the New State. This New State, as Javier Rodrigo writes, was fascist both in substance and in form: warlike origin, single party, charismatic leadership, display of impunity, contempt for death and regulation of social spaces and the nuclear elements of political, economic and social life.[1]

In Spain – we continue following Javier Rodrigo – there was a coagulating substance that united different elements to build a political identity capable of homogenizing Spanish fascism, which was ultra-Catholic and militaristic: violence (Rodrigo. 2011: 81–82). But not any old violence. We are talking about extreme violence. Violence used in a massive, disproportionate, structural and, also, preventive fashion. A violence that was used to create loyalties, to arouse fear in dissidents, to paralyse and destroy, to stigmatize. But also as a necessary condition for building the nation. And the nation required violence while lacking reference points.

Victorious Francoism had, in the earlier dictatorship of General Primo de Rivera, an important reference point from which to pursue the destruction of parliamentary democracy which was to be replaced by a model of corporate representation, a task in which the Francoists received the support of the Traditionalist monarchists, the Falangists and the Catholics. Together they formed the grand coalition that led to the *coup d'état* of July 18, 1936. The subsequent victory in the Civil War in 1939, gave the winner

– Francisco Franco – the largest share of power that any ruler in the history of Spain has ever known. This fact, as we shall see, was no minor trifle.

Needless to say, the exercise of this power also required a doctrinal corpus, a political culture aimed at defining and excluding the enemy. The goal was to wipe out all opposition. The use and abuse of violence had to be accepted – even normalized. Trials, physical elimination and assassinations were not conducted solely for individual reasons related to a particular action of the victim: the reasons for putting an end to the opponent's life were "supra-individual". In other words, the real crime committed was to belong to the enemy side or to represent the values of what was to be eliminated: to be a communist, a separatist, a republican or simply a democrat. A criminal law had to be created to combat dissidence, a criminal law capable of building spaces of exceptionality within an apparent rule of law. These were the characteristic features of the construction of the New Fascist State. What the ideologue Dionisio Ridruejo called a "true national community."

In this sense, the Franco dictatorship was inspired by the reactionary and traditionalist thinking of authors such as Ramiro de Maeztu, José Maria Pemán and José Calvo Sotelo. The theoretical foundations of Francoism arose mainly from Falangism and reactionary Catholicism. They rejected everything that the Second Republic had stood for, that would come to be seen as alien. In addition – and this is one of the most interesting aspects of this work – Francoism became an effective apparatus for the repression of dissidence that remained operational throughout the dictatorship, based on a legal structure that from the outset guaranteed impunity. It started to do so as from two special courts: the Court of Political Responsibilities and the Special Court for the Repression of Freemasonry and Communism. Thereafter aided by the military courts. The army also played a key role in the repression of the more or less organized forms of political dissidence, insofar as it reached the command of the forces of law enforcement, the Armed Police corps, created in 1941, and the Civil Guard, both bodies being of a clearly military nature.

However, the Political Responsibility Law of February 1939 – which remained in force until 1966 – became the tool that put in place a special jurisdiction for the purging of political dissidence. It would become one of the starting points for a cleansing policy bathed in legality which would work towards a new legal structure that would bring about a massive process to replace people. This replacement operation affected society as a whole, from top government officials to factory workers. But one of the groups of greatest interest was school and university teachers and, in general, intellectuals. Its replacement meant the emergence of a current of thought of right-wing ideological and National Catholic allegiance, which embraced various areas of knowledge, amongst which the legal field stands out. The search for legitimacy offered by arguments founded in law was one of the objectives of the dictatorship in order to justify the *coup d'etat* of July 18, 1936.

2.1 The Doctrinal Construction of Repression

The destruction of the social sciences – particularly law – following the uprising of July 18, had a very important political consequence: the colonization of the scientific field by Franco's power. The Civil War had eliminated or, at best, sent into exile the leading intellectuals in the juridical field. The need to build a new law, far removed from republican values, implied the need to look for new intellectual references which would produce legal work. This involved, above all, the two legal disciplines that the regime considered strategic for the design and the doctrinal, institutional and legal deployment of the New State: political law and criminal law.

2.1.1 Political Law. The Construction of the New State

A good example of the "purification" of the scientific field was given in the area of Political Law, a name then given to Constitutional Law. As Sebastián Martín points out, it was considered urgent to renew Political Law, which during the Second Republic had highlighted the relevance of comparative law and the construction of a doctrinal corpus and techniques in the elaboration of constitutional legal science. Amongst its proponents was Nicolás Pérez Serrano, director of the *Revista de Derecho Público,* founded in 1932, and author of one the most prestigious monographs on the 1931 Constitution – *La Constitución española: 9 diciembre 1931. Antecedentes, texto, comentarios* – published in 1932 in *Revista de Derecho Privado*. Another was Fernando Giner de los Ríos, a well-known intellectual who had been a PSOE MP since 1918, Minister of State and Public Education during the Second Republic and, during the Civil War, ambassador to the United States. But the exercise to transform the legal set-up, as pointed out by Martin, only lasted as long as the Second Republic itself.[2]

Pérez Serrano and Giner de los Ríos were two intellectuals that the Francoists sought to do away with, but they were not the only ones. The Civil War sent into exile Political Law professors, such as Francisco Ayala, a disciple of Hermann Heller, or Manuel Pedroso, who went on to teach law in Mexico, where he is still remembered as the teacher of important writers, such as Carlos Fuentes and Sergio Pitol. With the disappearance and exile of these and other Political Law professors and intellectuals, a way of perceiving law from a sociological and constitutional viewpoint was lost. Nevertheless, for the Francoists, the subject of Political Law took on special importance, alongside Philosophical Law, insofar as both disciplines had the mission to contribute to the juridical constitution of the *New State* and its political, social and cultural legitimization. Hence, it is not surprising that the new professors should stand out as pioneering ideologues of the new legitimacy that was sought after. Such was the case of Luis Sánchez Agesta or Torcuato Fernández Miranda. Or, in the Falangist field, the case of Carlos Ollero and the afore-mentioned Francisco Javier Conde.

Francoist mistrust towards the universities, especially in the field of social sciences, led to the creation of a network of extra-university interests, at the heart of which lay the key element in the ideological make-up that was to set up or reinforce the doctrine of dissidence: the *Instituto de Estudios Políticos*. Nicolás Sesma defined this institution as one of the foremost factors in the "construction and evolution *Procés* of the Franco regime, and not only in an ideological and institutional sense, but also from the point of view of its political and intellectual staff."[3] Indeed the *Instituto de Estudios Políticos* became a basic strategic pillar in the formation of academic, political, and judicial elites. The teaching of the discipline of law on the basis of the postulates of the regime was transcendental not only as a form of social control, but also inasmuch as it constructed the arguments and the legalistic rhetoric that were then deployed, adapted to each register, in the realms of politics (speeches), the university (published work), and the courts (sentences).

In addition, this institution was to order ideological training to exercise the doctrinal monopoly of the new political cadres of the Falangist 'Movimiento'. In fact, the submission of the Instituto de Estudios Políticos to the Francoist governmental framework finds its maximum expression in the names of those who were its main directors and most prominent ideologues. When Alfonso García Valdecasas was its director, foreign authors who had contributed to the construction of the doctrines of totalitarian dictatorships cooperated with the Institute – and more specifically with its *Revista de Estudios Políticos* – the most prominent being Carl Schmitt. In 1943, coinciding with the period when the Axis powers started losing the war, Fernando Maria Castiella Maiz took over from Valdecasas and opened the Institution to other Catholics and propagandists like himself. In 1948 Castiella Maiz left the Instituto de Estudios Políticos and began a prominent political career, as did other directors of the Institution, such as the aforementioned Francisco Javier Conde and Manuel Fraga Iribarne.

Another important part of the extra-university structure of the Franco regime was the aforementioned Instituto de Estudios Jurídicos which was attached to the Ministry of Justice. Its first director was the notary and future mayor of Barcelona, Josep Maria de Porcioles. But, beyond the institutions and journals of a deliberately specialized nature, the idea that we are most interested in highlighting in this sense was the scientific interventionism and the submission of the work of social researchers to the interests of the regime. Specialists in Political Law, Administrative Law, Philosophy of Law, along with new disciplines in Political Science, bowed to the demand to legitimize the dictatorship. They were branches of law necessarily aimed at creating an official ideological corpus from which to legitimize the persecution, culling or elimination of political dissidence – the right to reward loyalties and purge betrayals. At the same time, political cadres assumed the ideological and doctrinal postulates of the regime and put them into practice. In a nutshell, it was a question of constructing a *New State* based on the repression of dissidence and the elimination of opponents.

2.1.2 Penal Law. The Dogmatics of Totalitarianism

The influence of the totalitarian regimes that were on the upsurge in Europe, especially in Nazi Germany and fascist Italy, became evident in the principles of criminal policy and criminology that were to become benchmarks for the Francoist *New State*. The leading penal criminologists were Edmund Mezger and Franz Exner and the academics linked to the so-called Kiel School, such as Georg Dahm – a supporter of an inquisitorial procedural system, instead of a liberal prosecution – or Friedrich Schaffestein – a staunch defender of the death penalty and criminal law as a tool for the protection of the people. All of them were prestigious intellectuals who invested their academic capital in order to deform dogmatic categories with the aim of legitimizing the application of inhuman juridical-penal dispositions.[4]

From these and other influences, the New State was transformed into an all-powerful repressive machine, while the individual shrank to the point that he was left with none of the guarantees brought in by the French Revolution. This influence was shown by magazines of the time that sought to define the image of *tabula rasa* from which to forge a criminal law – in this case, a true criminal law of the enemy – which was erected in a chain of legitimacy that began in the governmental narrative and the speeches of the leaders of the dictatorship and ended in the design of concrete techniques that at the same time identified a style of government. An example of this desire to forge a new perspective on criminal policy was the preponderance of Philosophy of Law and political narrative in postwar legal journals to justify new ways of acting legally.[5]

The beginning of large-scale repression was forged through punitive techniques that distorted the facts. For example, Marino Barbero has called the convictions for rebellion justice in reverse: "those who precisely did not take up arms against the Republic, remaining faithful to it, were convicted of joining the rebellion" (Barber. 1977: 68). That is, those who defended the legality of the Constitution were considered rebels. Another example was reverse amnesty. Or, what amounts to the same, an amnesty agreed on, but not in favour of the vanquished, as would be considered normal, but in favour of the victors, creating the necessary legal framework to exercise impunity. Justice on demand, or the right to encourage impunity, a legal technique that once again was to emerge at the time of the Transition after Franco's death.

The most intriguing figure associated with Franco's criminal law was Isaías Sánchez Tejerina, who won the chair at the Central University of Madrid and was active – in a low key – teaching his anti-democratic and totalitarian ideology to generations of students. In his textbook on the subject of Criminal Law, he based this discipline on a moral order imposed by God. Under this premise he defended the death penalty that had been repealed by the Second Republic. To legitimize the death penalty, he invoked the concept of self-defence, not of a person, but of the State, in a so-called "War of Liberation." Years later, the Civil War would be portrayed as an operation of collective defence (Ferré. 2009: 16). Tejerina received a gift that he himself never expected: the Chair of Law at the Central University of Madrid. From that position he continued to teach, ever deepening his anti-democratic ideology.

Another defender of the death penalty was Eugenio Cuello Calón. He had been a professor at the University of Barcelona, but when investigated by Franco's university purge commission, he swore full adherence to the National Movement and claimed, in his defence, always to have taught all his classes at the University of Barcelona in Spanish, having rejected the use of Catalan. Cuello Calón had actively collaborated with the dictatorship of General Primo de Rivera. He even took an active part in the 1928 Penal Code Drafting Commission. It was a Penal Code characterized by its exacerbated rigour and the provision of the death penalty for many crimes.

Another fervent promoter of Franco's criminal law was Juan del Rosal. He argued for a totalitarian criminal policy in an article published in 1942, causing a great impact – "Los Estados totalitarios y el Estado español" (The totalitarian States and the Spanish State) – in which he defended alleged spiritual rights arising from a millennial culture, the role of Christianity above the Bill of Rights of the French Revolution which, according to Del Rosal, did not exist. For Juan del Rosal, the authentic Spanish Criminal Law that forged the New State was a totalitarian instrument at the service of the integrity of the Fatherland.[6] Other criminal specialists at the service of the regime were José Maria Rodríguez de la Devesa, who had also had a military career, and Miguel Fenech Navarro, who wrote an influential work entitled *La posición del juez en el Nuevo Estado* (The Role of the Judge in the New State) in which he pointed to the need to transfer to Spain the principles of the Nazi regime's criminal procedure.

These authors – alongside others, such as Antonio Vallejo Nágera – were to be the intellectuals who, from the pages of books and university classes, inspired the new generations of politicians, magistrates and civil servants of the Francoist State administration.

2.2 The Juridical Architecture of Repression

The declaration of a *state of war* and the adoption, by military command, of power after the removal of the civilian authorities. This was the starting point that justified the explicit prohibition of the exercise of the rights of assembly, demonstration, strikes, expression and free movement of people, according to agents that had to protect the first acts of violence associated with the coup. It sought to replace the lack of legitimacy of all sorts of actions with a justification for legalized violence. Or, as Julio Aróstegui writes, Francoism was transformed into an apparatus of oppressive and repressive power, and not of legitimate power, an apparatus that sought legitimacy from legality.[7] The action – if it was punitive, so much the better – acted as a source of legitimacy. A precedent was beginning to emerge from which only what was legal was legitimate. Or the other way around: things are legitimate only if they are legal.

On the basis of these premises, a new legal architecture was forged to combat the enemy, at the head of which, on July 24, 1936, the National Defence Board was formed, which assumed all the powers of the State. Due to the design of this whole regulatory framework, two concepts that we have already quoted, but have only mentioned in passing, were particularly relevant: on the one hand, the criminal law of the author; and, on the other, the crime of rebellion, on the basis of which the will to create special jurisdictions to judge, imprison and liquidate dissent was founded.

2.2.1 Legal Repression. The Criminal Law of the Author

From a chronological point of view, one of the first initiatives of the new regime would be to build a regulatory framework to combat, judge and physically and civilly eliminate the enemy, even though doing this would violate basic elementary principles, such as that of the non-retroactivity of criminal law or the principle of *non bis in idem*. The construction of this legality would begin with the Law of Political Responsibilities. This regulation is defined by historian Manuel Álvaro Dueñas as a "repressive instrument effectively conceived to eliminate at the root any political or ideological referent discordant with the postulates of the victors." It sought to eliminate civilly (with disproportionate prison sentences and disqualification) and to strangle economically (with disproportionate civil responsibilities that often involved the seizure of all assets).

This norm closely linked the purge of political responsibilities with the military jurisdiction. But the worst thing about the law was its appalling nature in legal terms. This generated all sorts of criticism from qualified lawyers.[8] Retroactivity (which allowed judging deeds that had formerly been legal), the waiver of the presumption of innocence and the annulment of the most basic rights for the defendant (such as the use of all means of proof in the exercise of their right to defence) were the pillars of a so-called exceptional law that transformed war enmity into an effective criminal law of combat (Tébar 2017: pp. 97–128).

The Law for the Repression of Freemasonry and Communism stood out as one of the greatest examples of the criminal law determined by who the accused was in the Franco era. It was yet another example of the application of criminal law that divided between citizens and enemies. Criminal conditions were established, such as being a Freemason, a Communist or a member of other clandestine societies that were never defined, leaving the object of criminalization absolutely open. By not defining exactly which ideological organizations or postulates were outlawed, the Franco government could, at any time, add to the Freemason or Communist organizations any others it might deem necessary (art. 1 of the Law). The assets of these organizations were considered illegal and were assigned to the jurisdiction of Political Responsibilities (art. 2). The confiscation of assets and prison sentences of more than 20 years for the guilty – and more than 12 years for those cooperating – assimilated this conception of the the law determined by who the accused was to the conception made by the most important legal operators – the Constitutional and Supreme Courts – in more recent stages of our history.[9]

The Law of July 12, 1940, on the basis of which the Code of Military

Justice was re-established, meant the legalization in peacetime of the "hyperextension" of military jurisdiction, based on the implementation of prosecution formulae provided by war contexts (Tébar 2017: 55). The reduction of procedural guarantees and deadlines for the prosecution allowed judges and prosecutors to have a greater inquisitorial capacity and to apply a greater severity in terms of prison sentences and financial responsibilities. After the State Security Act, it would end up fixing a wide range of criminal categories that would fall under this military jurisdiction and regulate the death penalty as the only possible punishment to be imposed. This rule came to legalize an obsession of the Franco regime: to lay down a set of criminal typologies to severely sanction conduct that violated the prestige and security of the State. It sought to condemn all forms of rebellion against the established political power.

When looking for examples, Catalonia becomes an unbeatable source, insofar as Catalanism was one of the staunchest enemies for the Franco regime. Paul Preston explains that hatred of everything Catalan became an openly racist affair: "The deep anti-Catalan sentiment that had been generated on the rebel side was inevitably reflected in the subsequent repression. The entry of the Francoist victors into any conquered city or town must be followed immediately by the prohibition of the native language, although many of the inhabitants could not speak any other. [...] The scope of a hatred with almost racist overtones is illustrated in the case of Manuel Carrasco i Formiguera" (Preston 2017: 600). Indeed, Hilari Raguer was of the opinion that the Civil War was, above all, a war against Catalonia.[10] Pierre Vilar wrote that, among the reasons for the uprising of July 18, 1936, was a deep feeling against Catalan autonomism, which the military coup referred to as separatism.[11]

There are two cases that deserve looking into insofar as they are convincing proof of this hatred of Catalanism and of the application of the criminal law as determined by who the accused were. As Preston himself explains, in an atmosphere of revenge and prejudice against the Catalan people, on April 9, 1939, Manuel Carrasco i Formiguera, a veteran founder of the Christian Democratic party (Unió Democràtica de Catalunya), was executed, accused of being a Republican and a Catalanist. It was the prelude to the execution of the President of the Catalan Government, Lluís Companys, who was arrested on August 13, 1940, in the town of La Baule-les-Pins, in Brittany, and taken to Paris. There he was handed over to Pedro Urraca Rendueles who transferred him to Madrid. Imprisoned in the basement of the Directorate General of Security for five weeks, the President of the Generalitat was subjected to harassment, torture and beatings. On October 3, he was transferred to Barcelona, his clothes stained with blood.

He was sentenced to death in a summary trial in which he was charged with the crime of military rebellion, with no possible defence and in an oral hearing that lasted just an hour. On the morning of October 15, 1940, at Montjuic Castle, he was executed by a firing squad of Civil Guards, the alleged cause of death being "traumatic internal haemorrhage."

Lluís Companys became the first President in Europe to be executed, a classic case of the criminal law determined by who the accused was. But it also became a clear example of the will to exterminate a political leader, a dissident, the death sentence – and its subsequent execution – being presented as yet another victory by the victor and a form of humiliation for the vanquished. Execution is the most unspeakable expression of the culmination of revenge.

2.2.2 Judicial Repression. Special Jurisdiction

Rebellion was made into the crime on which to build an inquisitorial network at the service of the Franco regime. The regime was able to weave a network of permanent exchange of information. Those taking part were entities as wide-ranging as the State Delegation for the Recovery of Documents, the Courts Martial, the Purge Commissions, those holding the post of mayor, the Falangist party, the Civil Guard, the Church, private informants, etc.[12] This conglomerate of an inquisitorial nature was also backed up by the two main special courts that the regime created: the Court of Political Responsibilities and the Special Court for the Repression of Freemasonry and Communism.

These two courts consolidated the doctrine of the internal enemy, a military feature that was present in much of the jurisdiction of the Franco regime. Insofar as they were exceptional courts, they achieved mixed representation. The presidency was always in the hands of the Army. The other institutions involved were the Falangist Party and the judiciary. In relation to the judiciary, both the Court of Political Responsibilities and the Special Court for the Repression of Freemasonry and Communism meant the involvement of the judiciary in the most brutal form of political repression and in the application of the criminal law as determined by who was to be accused. In addition, the presence of judges and magistrates contributed to giving the idea that there really were judicial guarantees for the defendants. Consequently, the judiciary operated as a body that helped whitewash the regime before the general public.[13]

To understand the regime's repressive machinery in depth, it is necessary to look, albeit very succinctly, at their Presidents, at the faces of those leading the regime's ideological persecution. Manuel Álvaro Dueñas draws a parallel between the presidencies of the two courts. This symmetry perfectly defines the common features of the personality sought by the regime by crossing them with the goals it pursued.

Álvaro Dueñas writes that there are a number of coincidences between Enrique Suñer and Wenceslao González Oliveros that are in no way accidental: their link to the Primo de Rivera regime, their having been "persecuted" when the Republic was proclaimed, their limited significance in the political life of the Republican period, their contribution to the ideological justification of the Civil War as a crusade against anti-Spain, and their unconditional public support for the new Regime and Franco" (Álvaro Dueñas. 1999: 148). In addition, González Oliveros, in Paul Preston's opinion, had another attribute that made him especially apt for the Court of Political Responsibility: he was "a pro-Nazi who had distinguished himself in the fierce persecution of the Catalan language and culture" (Preston 2011: 656).

A similar ideological line was held by the President of the Court for the Repression of Freemasonry and Communism, Isaías Sánchez Tejerina. This Professor of Criminal Law was a staunch supporter of the death penalty; moreover, he considered it irreplaceable, intimidating and exemplary, as long as the error of pardon was not incurred and execution was carried out rapidly. The real aim of Sánchez Tejerina was to reintroduce the Inquisition (Ferré 2009: 16). In fact, the Court of Repression was a new version of the Court of the Holy Office, mainly because of its inquisitorial procedures and its ideological nature. The participation of the judiciary in these trials was enthusiastic, servile and uncritical. It seemed that everything was in order for the rule of law to work properly. But in fact they were contributing to the promotion of barbarism. As Fernando Tocora writes regarding Nazi justice – but it could apply just as well to the Spanish judiciary – "the vast majority of German judges renounced their power to think and their power to act in the face of dictatorship and arbitrariness."[14]

The public order jurisdiction also operated as a special jurisdiction with the creation of the Court of Public Order (known as the TOP). This was an anomalous court, which seemed inspired by the Nazi People's Court (*Volksgerichtshof*), presided over by the infamous and much feared Roland Freisler. Freisler was a judge who thought that it was not up to judges to question the laws of a State but to interpret them according to the Führer's superior point of view (Tocora 2019: 100). This magistrate was at the head of a judicial institution which, in reality, was nothing more than a jurisdictional artefact conceived by the elimination of ideological discrepancy. The extent to which the creation of the TOP, like the creation of the *Volksgerichtshof*, implied a blatant will to vindicate and punish, must be borne in mind. One single fact proves it. As Paloma Aguilar explains, in other military dictatorships just as violent or even more so than Spain's – such as Chile's or Argentina's – no civilian court was created for repression.[15] The TOP thus stands as a genuinely Spanish invention aimed at exercising functions of repression of political dissent and social control of the civilian population.

With the creation of the TOP in 1963 – the seed of what would later become the National High Court ('Audiencia Nacional') – the regime was endowed with an instrument of legal exceptionality, given that the repression and persecution of dissent continued to be exercised, but now in a civil context.[16] That is, *civilized* repression took place instead of *militarized* repression. But, when all was said and done, it was repression with a vengeance, since the mere exercise of rights was judged to be a crime. But the TOP, despite the fact that the regime was looking for ways to legitimize the system and improve its international image, was still a jurisdiction of a special and political nature in which political conduct was repressed. The TOP did nothing but confirm the zero separation that existed between the judiciary and the government.

2.2.3 Police Repression. Political Police

Parallel to the creation of new judicial structures, the legal and police-orientated basis was laid for a dictatorship that was to last forty years. The first police measure was the Police Act, which aimed to restructure the state security forces into two: the General Police Corps and the Armed and Traffic Police Corps. The latter pointed the way to the militarization of the police forces. It is interesting to note the reasons given in the preface for the new Law of Surveillance and Security, of March 8, 1941, insofar as it exposed the real motivation for restructuring this police corps. At no time did it hide its true totalitarian conception and the real objectives that it pursued: "The victory of the Spanish arms, in establishing a Regime that seeks to avoid the errors and defects of the old liberal and democratic organization, demands greater efficiency and capacity of the bodies responsible for the State, as well as those modalities that are necessary for the rigorous and intense surveillance of all enemies."

The regime brought in other measures to ensure repression, such as the creation of the Directorate General of Security (DGS), which was organically dependent on the intelligence services of the military police, the SIMP. It had four major general police corps: Borders, Information, Public Order and Identification. The forces directly responsible for repression had a military structure and were fully military bodies: the Civil Guard, the

Armed Police, the Political Police itself and the Social Investigation Brigade, later known as the Social Political Brigade. In this sense, the DGS – which, as directly responsible for the Armed Police and the Social Investigation Brigade – extended its legal-administrative powers to the entire peripheral administration of the State, thus becoming a *de facto* military police force. This set-up lasted throughout all the forty years of the Franco dictatorship. In addition, its collaboration with the Gestapo helped to strengthen its repressive potential. The directors of the DGS were always military, and their basic organizational core were the Brigades, especially the aforementioned Social Political Brigade, which was transformed into a preventive police force, whose power to repress and exert coercion was extremely active at the end of the Franco regime.[17]

In the mid-1960s – and in a more mobilized and active international context, especially with the emergence of the new social movements that were awakening – Francoism was forced to introduce modifications into its repressive model. This does not mean, however, that the major role in repression was removed from the Army, which was, throughout the dictatorship, a fundamental element for the maintenance of the Regime and went on to have a leading and decisive role during the Transition. A key instrument, then, in the coercive machinery of the State over the population was the disproportionate use of special jurisdictions and, very specifically, military jurisdiction to judge purely political activities or the mere exercise of civil rights. Its use, especially in the late sixties, fulfilling the function of repression and consolidation of the regime, is essential to understanding the Franco regime as one of the most harsh, intense and persistently repressive systems of the twentieth century.[18]

2.3 Rebellion in Francoist Culture

The appeal to the unity of the Spanish nation was one of the obsessions of the Franco regime. Not only was its motto "Spain: One, Great and Free!" but, in addition, the indissoluble unity of the Fatherland was to be its glorified *leitmotiv*. This glorification process involved – cause and effect – the repression of national or particular feelings, or, as the regime referred to them, "regional" ones. It was in this sense that the need was seen to condemn any attack on this glorified Spanish unity by classifying it in the Penal Code as a crime of rebellion. In this sense, the Laws of March 2, 1943 were to criminalize cultural and identity expressions of a peripheral national character in order to subject them to the regime's main instrument of repression: the Code of Military Justice. As Paul Preston says, quoting Luis

Jiménez de Asúa, it sought to condemn dissidents on the basis of a rebellion applied in reverse. That is, not having given support to the military uprising of 1936 was considered a crime of rebellion, and therefore, liable to be subjected to a court martial.

In this way, the Franco regime began a new punitive stage in which it was no longer necessary to appeal to the state of war to apply military legislation. In this conception of repression, the approval of two measures aimed precisely at regulating, in the broadest sense, the crime of military rebellion played a very important role. The law that established the new criminal category of rebellion was called "*Rebelión. Definición y Sanción. Modifica los artículos 237 a 242 del Código de Justícia Militar y los 128 a 135 del Código Penal de Marina*" ("*Rebellion. Definition and Sanction. Articles 237 to 242 of the Code of Military Justice and 128 to 135 of the Penal Code of the Navy are modified*") and was subtitled "*Rebelión Militar: hechos que constituyen este delito*" ("*Military Rebellion: facts that constitute this crime*"). Franco's repression, from its very beginnings, needed to be based "on a generalized and analogous application of the crime of military rebellion already foreseen in the July 28 edict which, after the war, was applied to behaviour completely devoid of political relevance."[19]

The new definition of rebellion would therefore become the legal instrument with which to pursue and repress opposition and dissent by extending its application against political conduct – now a crime – prior to the Civil War. This punitive typology was constructed in an extraordinarily broad sense in order to equate it to the other crimes. The fear of the Franco regime was that the result of the Second World War – a result that at the time was already felt to be unhappy for the forces of the Axis powers – would encourage the internal opposition in Spain. It was therefore decided to build a criminal policy that would deter the opposition from questioning one of the legal assets of special protection by the regime: the unity of the Spanish State and Nation – both elements which, by themselves, justified any government action, even if outside the law.

One further fact to finish up with. Military rebellion was what the accusation, trial and conviction of Catalan President Lluís Companys and his entire government boiled down to. As Pere Bosch has pointed out, the proclamation of the Catalan State as part of the Spanish Federal Republic on October 6, 1934, was met with a disproportionate wave of judicial and military repression.[20] To the imprisonment of the Catalan President and the Catalan Government one has to add the suspension of Catalan home rule (the Generalitat government) and all the social advances achieved in Catalonia during the Second Republic.

2.4 The Judiciary as a Tool for the Legitimization of Repression

As very little has been said so far about the judiciary, in this last section we shall address the role it played in repression, in both its clandestine and its official varieties, as practised by the Franco regime.

The judiciary did not limit itself to maintaining a complicit silence in the face of the constant and repeated violation of fundamental rights; it also became a fundamental part of the repressive machinery itself. The judicial elites achieved direct participation in courts martial and in the special jurisdictions that were created for the very purpose of repressing political dissent. Justice was converted into a medieval guild, an estate subject to the exclusive service of the power it served. The constant invocation – both in speeches and in sentences – of the rule of law was erected as a mere propaganda resource that was empty, false and outdated (Del Águila 2001: 39). The aim was to offer an appearance of legality by passing off Franco's legislation as the expression of a popular will that was non-existent. From this discourse of legality, Paloma Aguilar observes – and rightly so – that the more official and "legal" the repression of the opposition has been, the more the judiciary will have been involved in it.[21]

This is no minor question. From the outset, the need to reconstruct the State's most important institutions, once the war was won – or even creating ones *ex novo* – called for the creation of a body of high-ranking civil servants which would be faithful to the new authority led by Franco, in accordance with the rhetoric and dialectics of "Friend-or-Foe." In the case of the judiciary, this will to forge a loyal defensive power as from the highest echelons of the State was carried out by way of the coordinated reconstruction of the administration of justice. Firstly, by proceeding to purge the judiciary; then, by articulating a system of government appointments which, according to Cano Bueso, responded purely and simply to criteria of proven allegiance to the "Caudillo" and to all that the July 18 uprising had stood for (Cano Bueso 1985: 129; Tébar 2017: 34).

Justice, then, became a fundamental pillar of institutional repression. There is a phrase written by the historian Manuel Álvaro Dueñas that, due to its forcefulness, deserves to be transcribed: "To exterminate 'anti-Spain', not only in an ideological but also a physical way, Franco's state used special jurisdictions."[22] This was the true function of the special jurisdictions: the extermination of political dissidence.[23]

The public order jurisdiction also operated as a special jurisdiction, although, to the outside world, it was intended to pass as ordinary justice. In the opinion of Francisco J. Bastida and Manuel Ortiz, the TOP did not mean the end of justice as a key pillar of coercion and the repression of dissent; on the contrary, it confirmed that the role of ordinary Spanish justice was not limited to its jurisdictional function. The world of the judiciary cooperated with the dictatorship, based on the dictation and execution of sentences in which the Francoist ideology was clearly upheld.[24] For example, the identification of the judiciary with the Francoist ideal went so far as to assume that, when taking office as a judge or magistrate, the oath of "unconditional adherence to the Caudillo of Spain" had to be formally declared. As Mónica Lanero points out, this did not leave much room for impartiality.[25]

A very important fact is that the oath began to be taken in 1938 with regard to entering the careers of judge or prosecutor, so that all judges, magistrates and prosecutors who carried on their careers in the Transition to democracy had taken this oath. The creation of the Judicial School as a tool for selection and subsequent political indoctrination helped to forge a conservative judicial class. One example is that in the Judicial School, along with legal subjects, "moral" and "religious" education were also taught; as well as the concept of a hierarchical body spirit based on obedience to superiors. According to Mónica Lanero, the will of the Franco regime had been to create a judicial "militia" willing to follow the instructions of General Franco (Lanero. 2013: 269 and 272).

It was in this sense that the judiciary became an ally and, at the same time, an instrument for defending concepts that were at the core of the Francoist ideology, such as national unity. This concept has not been – either before or during the Transition – a minor matter. It was to be even less so during the sovereignty process, to the extent that it would come under question. The Catalan independence process is a total challenge to the principle of unity. But the principle of unity of the State – with the consequent repression of those who dare to question it – would be defended from the most diverse watchtowers, the judiciary being an indispensable bulwark of doctrinal protection, which would lead judges to achieve powerful political activism. If today the decision of a judge or magistrate is not alien to politics or to a certain ideological conception of life, during the Franco regime judicial activism proved vital in order to defend a central and fundamental idea of the Francoist state.

Moving on to the specifics, what concept of national unity was adopted by the Francoist judiciary? From a jurisprudential point of view, national unity was indestructible (Supreme Court judgment 189/69), intangible (Supreme Court judgment 42/67), indissoluble (Supreme Court judgment 123/69), and one of the inspiring principles of the State. This unity is, moreover, "surpassing past times whose memory cannot be explored by encouraging, with it, the deplorable, lamented and painful action of some tending to its destruction" (Supreme Court judgments 42/67 and 170/69). As Francisco J. Bastida explains, the ambiguity and breadth of Franco's regulations when regulating national unity allowed the Supreme Court to "maintain a notion of national unity identified with centralism and to link decentralizing demands to what are described as separatist leanings" (Bastida. 1986: 71).

The position of the Supreme Court – as the highest judicial instance of the Spanish State and, in consequence, as the main guarantor of the interpretation of the legal concepts that form part of the normative framework of the Franco regime – leads it to a judicial activism of a clearly political nature. And, during the Catalan independence Process, we shall see this judicial activism again. The Supreme Court, during the Franco era, was not limited to protecting Spain's unity from separatist attacks; it assumed this defence clearly when it argued for "an idea of national unity by condemning what is commonly understood as different ways of conceiving the unity of the Fatherland: regional autonomy and federalism" (Bastida. 1986: 71). By not recognizing any kind of political power in the regions or any kind of political category, the judiciary considers that any attempt to alter this dependence of the region on the State, either claiming more political power or intensifying its national character, becomes an attempt to break Spanish unity. The denial of national unity incurred the crime of rebellion.

Chapter 3

The Transition

Repression as an Inheritance

A rigorous analysis of recent Spanish history cannot escape the fact that the transition to democracy operated without making a clean break with the Franco regime. This burden, political and social, conditions Spanish democracy itself, to such an extent that today certain institutions – or the ways in which these institutions act – cannot be understood without taking on board this basic premise. This is the only way to explain the forging of a new, seemingly democratic constitutional regime in which politics is transformed into an exercise in the interpretation of legality; or to understand that, in a system of rights and freedoms, the Constitution ends up becoming the benchmark of legality of what is, or is not, politically correct. The constitutional framework is the red line that separates what can and what cannot be talked about. This is what the post-Franco Transition did: it built this retaining wall under the guise of democratic institutions.

Today there is no shortage of critical voices that compare the Transition with the story of a self-serving myth, the main purpose of which was to legitimize the shortcomings of the current democratic system.[1] The fact that the Franco dictatorship has often been defined as an institutionalized criminal regime that enjoyed an excessively long life thanks to a system of impunity forged from a network of loyalties, complicities and the exchange of political favours, has helped to raise questions about the subsequent transition to democracy. Impunity was a fundamental pillar on which the dictatorship leant, but it was not the only one. The endorsement of this impunity, in the words of Bartolomé Clavero, was "the massively prevaricating ordinary courts."[2] The excesses of the Franco regime cannot be explained without the complicity of the judiciary.

In this chapter, then, we shall analyze the Transition using three elements that, on their own, can explain it and can help to explain other things. We refer to the trusteeships of the Franco regime – we shall call them legacies – the reasons of State that underlay all this poisoned inheritance and, finally, the executor or figure in charge of defending the last wishes of the testator.

3.1 The Legacies of the Franco Regime

The institutional design that emerged from a new constitutional framework, comparable to that of European liberal democracies, has not been sufficient to pinpoint the existence of a "functional and organic continuity between the Francoist state and the state of the new democracy." To ascertain this, we shall focus on three elements present in the Transition, but which have been more or less latent throughout all the years of the consolidation of democracy. These are violence and fear, silence and oblivion, and the abuse of the rule of law. Violence and fear, because these elements have conditioned the whole process of building the new constitutional system. Silence and oblivion, because they have impacted the transition process as a limitation to public debate – a pathology that has survived to this day. (As will be seen later, it is deemed better not to talk about certain issues so as not to create a social divide.) And the abuse of legality, because this need to create a rule of law after forty years of a state of emergency put the law at the epicentre of political debate, so that anything that is not legal would not be politically viable.

These three elements – fear, silence, and the law – ratify the maxim that Giuseppe di Lampedusa embodied in *Il Gatopardo*: If we want things to stay as they are, things will have to change. Things would have to change because, at the heart of the Transition, was the will to build a constitutional framework that would allow the transition from a dictatorship to a democracy. This step was to be taken by creating an apparent space for dialogue and consensus, in which everything could be talked about. Democracy was to be built on the basis of inclusive institutions that would indeed enable the expression of preferences and discrepancies, including those that questioned the nuclear elements of democracy itself. This is what the Constitutional Court has always called "non-militant democracy." But things were to stay as they were, because the real design of certain cornerstones of the constitutional framework had been conceived of by Francoism, precisely in order to ensure its survival.

3.1.1 Culture of Violence and Fear

The French historian Sophie Baby, an expert on political violence, made a notable reflection on the recurring presence of violence in the political sphere of contemporary Spain.[3] Violence in Spain, she tells us, is at the heart of its political and symbolic challenges. During the Transition, this violence appeared, as has already been said, as a reality, present in the memory of many citizens. But, at the same time, violence is also present because it resides at the very core of the process of transforming an authoritarian State – based on the repression of political dissent – into a democratic State that guarantees individual rights and civil liberties (Baby 2018: 32–33). This leads to one of the questions that this section seeks to answer: did the transformation of the Spanish state into a democracy arising out of the Transition that the approval of the 1978 Constitution entails, inactivate, on its own, forty years of *hyper-violent* dictatorship preceded by an outright Civil War?

The answer is no. Violence has never disappeared from the political scene. Spain's sediment of violence has manifested itself when it has been unable to offer a democratic response to a problem of a political nature. This, in our opinion, is one of the keys to understanding how the State has dealt with Catalonia's independence Process. This is the only way to explain the police response – disproportionate, not to say cruel, brutal or savage – to the independence referendum of October 1, 2017, under the slogan of "*A por ellos!*" – (Go get 'em!) and the strategy of judicial battle or lawfare.

The omission and lack of political debate on issues needed to consolidate a democratic system based on the values of pluralism and the right to autonomy – values that had been removed from political debate throughout the Franco regime – consolidated a way of doing politics where keeping quiet was preferable to speaking out. It was safest not to talk about certain issues. This self-censorship, which occurred during the Franco regime and continued during the Transition, especially when building the consensus on which the 1978 Constitution was based, has emerged yet again during the independence *Procés*.[4]

This is one of the legacies that help us to understand certain attitudes that are rooted in the democratic quality that emerged from a transitional process built upon psychological violence and fear. If we add this to the fact that certain people – we could almost say whole institutions – linked to the Francoist repressive apparatus (whether they were in the police forces, the army or the judiciary), continued to offer their services in strategic places of power, many of the reactions of a repressive and judicial nature that the independence Process has been met with can be easily understood. That is why we cannot analyze the Transition whilst leaving out the latent violence, defined in a sufficiently well-known phrase in the Spanish collective imagery: *ruido de sables* (sabre-rattling). Though the data show that it was also a process with plenty of physical violence and deaths in the streets, the

Transition was marketed as a manufactured product based on consensus, debate and giving way.[5]

We also need to highlight the deterrent aspect of violence. The fear of confrontation is, in the opinion of Josep Maria Colomer, one of the most important elements when the political attitude of some of the leading actors in the Transition is analysed and understood;[6] as is also the way those actors designed the chief institutions that resulted in the change of regime (Colomer 1998: 174–175); and how those actors did not do enough, or did not insist enough, on radically modifying institutions in search of a real change of regime. Aversion to fear is a key variable in the transition process that, in itself, explains fundamental aspects of a Transition negotiated from within the regime. In other words, it was the reformists of the Franco regime who, during the negotiations, continued to maintain the main centres of power – political, economic, judicial and military – which compelled the opposition to cede terrain in aspects related to the past that could arouse the annoyance of the armed forces, the institution with the greatest power to subvert the transition process.

The strategy of tension – a strategy that, with various nuances, has survived to this day, and has been very present during the Catalan independence *Procés* – played with the threat, perfectly credible for that matter, of destabilizing the democratization process and leading to situations of institutional violence.

3.1.2 Culture of Silence and Amnesia

The adoption of the 1978 Constitution was preceded by expressions such as consensus, amnesia, reconciliation and the closure of wounds, among others. These are expressions that dominated the political debate that culminated on December 29, 1978, when the constitutional text was published. Efforts were then being made to leave behind the legacy of fear established since the July 18, 1936, uprising and which had featured brutal repression that had sought to glorify the victors and humiliate the defeated. The transition from an authoritarian, repressive and violent dictatorship to a democracy did not entail – as usually happens with all profound political transformations[7] – a call for the need on the part of the main civil, military and judicial institutions inherited from the regime to recognie their responsibilities, nor did it entail the creation of "truth commissions" to investigate human rights violations, nor did it call for trials of those responsible for deaths, torture and illegal detention. That meant that there was no break. The "politics of silence" – the reformist option – prevailed.

This preference cannot be understood unless we analyze various elements of Spanish politics that are well known today and which appear to us as anomalies that hinder political debate. The pact of amnesia was certified through the passage of the Amnesty Law, which sought to regulate the *oblivion* of the regime's atrocities. This law put the torturers and the tortured on an equal footing, the police brutality of the regime with the actions of the opposition. In essence, there was a clear will to conceive of amnesty as a genuine law of impunity, a real law of termination. It is clear, although the Constitutional Court does not want to acknowledge it, that the Amnesty Law is unconstitutional. Its contents violate international human rights law and, in general, the Covenant on Civil and Political Rights in force in Spain since the adoption of the Constitution. The Constitutional Court, through numerous rulings, such as Sentence No. 11/81, of April 8, has endorsed the culture of silence, amnesia and impunity.

In the official discourse of the Spanish political elites, the appeal to national reconciliation as the supreme value has always prevailed. This has led to amnesty for anti-Francoists and amnesia for Francoists (Colomer. 1998: 177). Regulating amnesia and silence by law was tantamount to accepting that the institutional violence perpetrated throughout the Franco dictatorship should go unpunished. Yet again, the absence of a public debate on whether it was necessary to call for justice for the crimes of the dictatorship was taken for granted. This renunciation of debate cannot be understood without the latent and present fear of confrontation and the obsessive desire to avoid another civil war. This is why we speak of a reform and not of a break. The consequence of not breaking away was, as Paloma Aguilar writes, "the subsequent abandonment of certain institutional reforms which, if successful, would probably have led to a better functioning of democracy" (Aguilar. 2013: 12).

The executive branch also helped to consolidate a culture of impunity. Policies were activated to destroy all material that could bring back to the surface a criminal past whose burial was to be implemented. The decision by the then Minister Rodolfo Martín Villa to destroy the police files of the victims of torture in the General Directorate of Security dungeons, was presented as a radical policy of conciliation.[8] It seemed to respond to the logic that what did not exist had never happened. But it did exist. And not talking about what existed and building an institutional design to never discuss what happened – and, preferably, would never happen again – has caused it to finally resurface. It did so by adopting the same totalitarian face and the same thirst for repression.

3.1.3 Culture of Legality

Ignacio Sánchez-Cuenca explains this when he analyses the legal instrument that guaranteed legal continuity between the Franco regime and the new democratic regime[9] – the Law for Political Reform. In this desire for legality, as if legality could erase the dictatorship's forty years of aberrant practices, this Law for Political Reform – the eighth and last Fundamental Law of the political and legal system that emerged from the July 18 uprising – became the tool that allowed the transition from one regime to the other, always – and this fact is also relevant – following the institutional procedures of the legal system of the dictatorship. Franco's legislation conditioned, foreshadowed and is at the root of the political system that was to establish the 1978 Constitution. Significantly, the Law for Political Reform and the Royal Decree Law of April 1977, for the elections of June 15, 1977 – elections that, in spite of everything, were never called as elections to the Constituent Assembly – were pre-constitutional norms, the principles of which remain perfectly valid, especially in electoral matters.[10]

Far from a break, the umbilical cord was maintained between the two realities that now became one. The mantra of the Transition – from law to law – was merely the need of the Francoists to keep the situation under their control; it allowed them to modulate the pace of reforms at their convenience. Not to change anything or keeping everything the same – and this is what is most striking – so that the *de facto* powers, those from whose offices politics and finance continued to be directed, were the Francoist elites who left the interpretation of the new constitutional legal system in the hands of a judiciary that had shortly before contributed to brutal repression. The repression was unprecedented, but of course it was legal. These were judicial elites who overnight became the guarantors of a democratic system based on respect for fundamental rights and public liberties that, hours before, had been decried and, in the worst cases, persecuted by means of their sentences.

3.2 *Raison d'état* and Calculated Deviation

When Machiavelli wrote *The Prince,* he talked, without stating it clearly, about *raison d'état*. In actual fact, *raison d'état* is one of the fundamental topics of Machiavelli's political thought, for only *raison d'état* has the power to legitimize and justify political action. This is the key element: political action. But, whereas Machiavelli did not speak about it clearly, Giovanni Botero – an author relegated to the backstage who challenges Machiavelli's work – did. For Botero, *raison d'état* is a concept to be articulated in a general sense; that is, to be a set of superior and edifying goals that should legitimize the pursuit of politics. Without these goals, politics would be nothing more than a mediocre, superfluous, irrelevant activity. Giovanni Botero set the objectives of the *raison d'état* in his most important and complete work: *Della ragion di Stato*, a ten-volume masterpiece published in 1589.

For Rafael del Àguila, *raison d'état* is a concept linked to evil.[11] We agree, for *raison d'état* is articulated around a general set of higher objectives aimed at guaranteeing the survival and conservation – also the expansion, if such were the case – of the very State. And in this defence of the higher goals of a State, the means are neither here nor there. *The End Justifies the Means.* Machiavelli states that, among the many virtues that the prince must have, there is the will to dig, to stir, to listen . . . in short, to move through the sewers of power.

The literature concerning the Spanish Transition refers to these powers, which exercised influence from the shadows of the State, as *de facto* powers.[12] This is the point: the presence of these mainsprings, which no one sees and no one explains, but which exist. No one has ever denied their existence. Moreover, in the collective imagination it is assumed, uncritically, that they are entrusted with a function of vital importance as executors: guarding and ensuring the maintenance of the essence of the State. When they are called upon to act, these powers awaken with all their legal and political consequences, without assessing the collateral damage that their action may entail. No matter the purpose: only the means matter. They cannot be held to account by anything or anyone. When the resources of the State require the proposed objectives to be reached, as Joan Lluís Pérez-Francesch writes, "the doors to *whatever measures are necessary* are opened, at that very moment, be they state secrets, slush funds or a declaration of state of emergency."[13]

So *raison d'état* justifies everything. But, with the advent – and consequent deployment – of the constitutional and democratic lawful State, *raison d'état* cannot be upheld and defended in a clumsy way. Procedures are needed, and their logic. *Raison d'état* must be adapted to the social and political reality of the moment. And this is not easy. We shall set out below one of these mechanisms that can only be explained from a logic of defending this *raison d'état* over and above other values or principles that are set aside or violated. As we shall see, the mechanism in question will have decisive consequences, albeit very indirectly and almost imperceptibly, on the functioning of the Spanish top judiciary. In short, it is a matter of defending the *raison d'état* while realizing, at the same time, the Lampedusan principle of changing everything to make everything continue as it was. But this mechanism has entailed – and still entails today – a democratic cost that the Spanish political elites are willing to tolerate. This cost is breaking away from the Constitution, with a constitutional principle that ought to inspire the whole legal system: the principle of equality.

This mechanism is known as a *calculated deviation* from the principle of equality. In short, the *calculated deviation* is the introduction of strong correctives to the proportionality of the electoral system, so as to ensure a political regime of dynastic bipartisanship. This anomaly was incorporated, for the first time, in the Law for Political Reform that covered the elections of June 15, 1977. The problem is that the electoral provisions of a law with a transient intention were reproduced in identical form in the electoral constitutional bloc, through the Organic Law of June 19, 1985. And the first consequence, in terms of efficiency of this calculated deviation, is the impossibility of reforming the Constitution: in other words, the impossibility of modifying the renouncements, silences and concessions that are at the basis of the Constitution. It was ensured, by means of reinforced majorities – often three-fifths – that what was 'well tied up' – that is, the *raison d'état* – would remain 'well tied up', one of the many expressions that the Transition bestowed upon us.[14]

It is often said that Spain knows how to write constitutions but does not know how to reform them. This shortcoming, in democratic terms, is a very weighty ballast. The reform of a Constitution becomes a necessity inasmuch as the reform clauses are the mechanism through which to renew the link between the legitimacy of origin and the legitimacy in exercise of the constitutional State.[15] There have been scholars, such as Pedro de Vega, Javier Tajadura and Pérez Royo himself, who have strongly criticized the wording of Part X of the Constitution, which is specifically dedicated to constitutional reform. Part X lays down two procedures: that of Article 167 and that of Article 168. Whereas the first is a mechanism that prevents arbitrary reforms by requiring qualified majorities (three-fifths of both Chambers), the second turns out, in the words of Pedro de Vega, to be not so much a reform procedure as a "procedure to prevent reform."[16] Article 168 of the Spanish Constitution is the mechanism provided for when the reform has to affect particular parts of the constitutional text of different value and varied significance, amongst which what we have called *raison d'état* stands out.

But the calculated deviation from the principle of equality was not only intended to protect the Constitution. The Parliament arising from the direct suffrage of the electorate asserted that it was to feature this *calculated deviation* from the principle of equality with a clear purpose: for the composition of both Houses of Parliament always and at all times, to be in line with a bipartisan-system logic. In other words, a fundamental institution for the proper functioning of democracy was designed with a clear dynastic vocation and a denial of the principle of equality. This is what Pérez Royo calls the "bipartisan Constitution." This flaw was also reflected in the composition of the Upper House, the Senate, so that a province such as Soria, with 100,000 inhabitants, has the same number of Senators as Barcelona, with 5 million inhabitants. This deviation has a clear goal: to protect the Monarchy (which is the most absolute denial of the principle of equality), to prevent federalism and self-determination, and to ensure a bipartisanship that would colonize all spaces of power, including the judiciary.

In essence, what was being done was the construction of legal mechanisms to protect aspects that had been left beyond the walls of the constitutional debate: these aspects, due to their importance or relevance, were considered, in themselves, the *raison d'état*. The imposition of three-fifths of Congress and the Senate for major decisions affecting these key aspects of the new system would be the numerical logic that would finally close the circle. Everything changed so that everything remained under the control of the political elites who had piloted the supposed regime change thanks to a well-known artefact – duly passed through the sieve of prestigious writers and television and radio programmes that extolled the virtues of consensus – known as the Transition.

It is worth noting that this *calculated deviation* from the principle of equality is not just any old phenomenon. For Pérez Royo, during the Transition a real need arose to set up a bipartisan system in the main democratic institutions. This bipartisanship has proved, in practice, to be yet another form of political control clothed in democratic operability, so that nothing and no one can deviate from the script written by the Law for Political Reform. The *controlled* composition of the two Houses of Parliament has led, over eleven legislatures, to a "dynastic bipartisanship" that has divided power by quotas. This is the only way to explain the colonization by the two major parties of the main institutions of political power – it is not a mistake to speak in terms of *political power* – such as the General Council of the Judiciary or the Constitutional Court.

3.3 The Survival of the Francoist Judicial Elite

The configuration of the judiciary that democracy was to inherit from the Transition was another legacy of Francoism. Forty years of authoritarian culture, based on an abusive and disproportionate exercise of violence and protected by *de facto* and legal impunity, made the judicial elites linked to the regime uncritical of abuses of power.[17] They did not condemn the previous regime, and they entered the new democratic system as if nothing had happened, or as if the past were irrelevant. It is noteworthy that, despite the abundant publications that the Transition has generated, the inherited judicial system and its role in the new constitutional system have not generated the literature that a mutation of this nature should have called for.

As Paloma Aguilar rightly says, Francoism became a political regime that, in order to maintain its impunity, built solid networks of complicity through which to retain the privileges it had enjoyed as an elite for forty years (Aguilar. 2013: 304).[18] Only thus can the reluctance of the judiciary to review its past be explained. The mechanisms of intergenerational loyalty, and the fact that the honorability of a body such as the judiciary was taken for granted, have made it difficult to rigorously review the names of judges on each side of the border between the bloody dictatorship and a then incipient democracy. We agree with Jiménez Villarejo and Doñate Martín when they state that the presence of a Francoist ideological bias, with a marked conservative tendency and clear authoritarian content, in the current Spanish judiciary is "a direct consequence of a transition from dictatorship to democracy which affected it little, so it only slowly adopted democratic values" (Villarejo & Doñate. 2012: 17).[19]

This desire to combine amnesia with impunity is exemplified by the State Bulletin of January 5, 1977. The same day that the sinister TOP ('Tribunal de Orden Público', the Court of Public Order) was abolished, a no less sinister National Court was created, which emerged as yet another legacy of the Francoist judiciary. Del Águila explains this mutation, emphasizing the way in which the judges who had taken part in the criminalizing ideology of the regime by holding leading positions in the TOP, found it easy to adapt to the new democratic system. Their destination was the country's highest courts.[20] The absence of a purge and the need to relocate were exacerbated by the judicial system's own inbreeding – the degree of specific self-recruitment – that is to say, judges whose parents were judges, as Juan José Toharia writes, were far more normal in Spain than in nearby systems, such as France or Italy – by the mechanisms of socialization and internal recruitment and by the ingrained *esprit de corps* about which we have already spoken.[21] All this turned the judiciary into an establishment that was hard to adapt to change.

As a result of these historical consequences – framed within an ideological culture featured by strong servitude to governmental power – the way Spain's top judiciary behave reflects the legal culture of the Franco regime. This burden can be observed if, as Judge Ramón Sáez reflects, the analyst looks into the judges' subculture, that is to say, into their professional habitat.[22] In carrying out their jurisdictional work, a double standard directly connected with the practices of the dictatorship can be detected, and this brings justice down to a balance between the protection of caste interests, isolation from society and an *apparent* submission to the law (Sáez 2010: 42). The intellectual training of the Spanish judiciary is an heir of the university elites, and it was forged in the Franco regime as a result of the purges which we referred to at the beginning of this book. This training in values and concepts has been criticized by the judiciary itself.

Another deficit pointed out by the Spanish judiciary is a lower sensitivity, when compared to other European judicial systems, when it comes to the development and implementation of international law, above all as regards institutions such as impunity and the lapsing of certain offences.[23] Their reluctance to apply international law, a closing of ranks as regards Spanish law, flouting the principles of international law – whether it be Criminal or Constitutional – have made the Spanish judiciary an establishment closer to those that lived under Franco than a modern judiciary, comprehensive with the reality of the moment, committed to social changes and respectful of the international principles present in the treaties that the Spanish State is party to.

An uncritical view of the law is another legacy of Francoism. That the Transition was an essentially legalistic product, and that it was carried from *the law to the law*, meant emptying the concept of the lawful State, or making the lawful State comparable to the illegal State or the repressive State. Moreover, it created in the judicial imagination a fallacy consisting of making legality compatible with injustice, as if democratic legality could coexist, as Ramon Sáez says, with the denial of human rights (Sáez: 41–42). The association of judicial independence with the righteous application of the current law is constant in the judicial and academic literature. Ramon Sáez says that this association contains two of the most obvious features of the Francoist judiciary. One, an uncritical submission to the law, as if the law were a merely formal concept that frees the judge from responsibility in the result of its application. And two, the ability of the judiciary to coexist alongside exceptionality, with the impunity of the powerful (Sáez: 42).

Chapter 4

Democracy

The Institutional Design of Repression

We shall now see how the new-born democracy was transferred from the "phobia schema" of Francoism, how it retained the objectives of the *raison d'état,* that is, the defence of the unity of the State, and the Monarchy (now, parliamentarian) as part of the State, the rejection of political pluralism, and allergy to territorial decentralization. This is the only way to explain a Constitution that is refractory to its past. Or a Constitution that enables the omission of all that the Republican Constitution stood for, since both – the one of 1931 and the one of 1978 – are the only democratic constitutions that the Spanish State had in the 20th century. It is difficult to understand the omissions of the text of 1978 in relation to its predecessor. But it is even more difficult to allow connections with Francoist legality, such as the form of a monarchical State, the explicit mention of the Catholic Church, or to put into the hands of the army (one of the fundamental pillars of social control and repression during the Franco regime) the protection of the constitutional order, a step that is completely incomprehensible in democratic terms, having no equivalent in any other European Constitution.

Another of the phobias inherited from the Franco regime was the territorial debate. This was conditioned by the need of the Francoist elites – political, judicial and military – to impose the unity of the state as the supreme value over and above the will to articulate a satisfactory response of a plurinational nature. The state had to be united and impose itself over its territories. It had to leave no room for manoeuvring, so that those territories, especially those with a greater national conscience, could develop their will to self-government. The Army also played a key role in this. It was a key player in the drafting of Article 2 of the Spanish Constitution on the "indissoluble unity of the Spanish Nation, the common and indivisible Homeland of all Spaniards," which was the basis of the principle of unity of the State.[1]

At the same time, Article 2 recognized the principle of autonomy for nationalities and regions. Two principles – unity and autonomy – that had to be treated on an equal footing, or at least in a balanced way. But it has never been like that. The Constitutional Court soon stated that the relationship between unity and autonomy would be a subordinate one. And in this subordination there was, implicitly, a message of assimilation of what differentiated the Constitution: nationalities and regions. This differentiation, plus other indications in the articles of the Spanish Constitution that went in the direction of differentiating territorial realities that were in no case equivalent, has never had a practical application. On the contrary, by putting it in black and white, what was to be called the "coffee for everyone" syndrome was being forged for everybody. Years later, the LOHAPA[2] did the rest, or at least tried to.

As we shall see below, the red lines of Francoism that took on different forms and definitions in the text of the Constitution (but which essentially continued to represent the same thing – an intolerant, repressive, State democracy allergic to decentralization and pluralism), are the lines that were omitted from the political debate. In addition, if any political actor had enough audacity to question them, all the mechanisms that the constitutional state had retained to exercise repression and violence were put into action, be they physical or otherwise, verbal or psychological. We shall see this when we analyse the reaction of the State to the Catalan sovereignty *Procés* and the effective deployment of the lawfare strategy. Let us now see which actors are in charge of governing and activating the mechanisms of repression and, most importantly, what their recruitment system is.

4.1 Governing Democracy

A warning must be made about a reality that has often been omitted in juridical and constitutional literature on the Constitution: a critical reading to see that one thing is the institutional design that was written into the constitutional text and, quite another, the way in which the Constitution has been applied or developed. Experience has shown that there are two Constitutions: a written one and a tacit one, as Juan Ramon Capella says.[3] One may also speak of a constitutional legality and a super-legality that "affected what the visible constituent power could decide" (Capella. 2003: 31). The tacit Constitution is not a sealed norm. It depends on the correlation of political parties, or, to express it in another way, on parliamentary arithmetic. But, above all, it also depends on the interpretation of the Constitution that these operators might make.

As Alejandro Nieto explains, an analysis of the Constitution can imply having to face up to two realities.[4] The first is one situated on the surface.

On this superficial level, scholars are faced with a solemn text regulating a series of institutions and controls that are more than acceptable from the point of view of democratic Constitutional Law. But if this same analyst dips into the deeper situation, he will appreciate that there are also a series of vices, deficits and perversions that lead the official format and the everyday social reality to coincide very little. This is not always the case, but in the case of the high courts, this dichotomy occurs all too often, especially when it is a question of judging matters that are associated with certain political categories that are awkward for those wielding power. The Constitution, as we have said, left many issues unresolved and in the hands of the judicial elites. Politicians failed to rise to the challenge. And it was to be Spain's high judiciary that, when the time came, unflinchingly applied its own criteria to protect the *raison d'état*, amongst other factors.

We now turn to the question of how in other periods of Spain's political history – periods not too distant in the past – power used the judiciary and the law to impose its vision of the State. How courts of justice came to be tools of proven efficiency at the service of the government. How law has always been designed and interpreted to the benefit of the unity of the State. These are the antecedents of what will be our principal subject of analysis: lawfare against the Catalan independence movement. As antecedents, they become highly significant elements in the search to explain why in a judicial State the three powers do not stand apart, but are fused together. They are the same power, to such an extent that the judicial power – as occurs with the executive and legislative powers – lies in the hands of politics. Or rather, in the hands of the two dynastic parties, that is the Partido Popular (PP) and the Partido Socialista Obrero Español (PSOE). It is the party system that places this theoretically independent power at the service of the interests of Power (with a capital P), doing away with its principal function, which is to serve law and justice.

4.2 The Government of Judges

It was in 1921 that Edouard Lambert published a work that was to become a classic. Its title was *Le gouvernement des juges et la lutte contre la législation sociale aux États-Unis.*[5] It was put out by Giard, a distinguished Parisian publisher who coined the famous expression *Government by Judges* (which Lambert, in turn, borrowed from Louis B. Boudin's "Government by Judiciary," an article published in the *Political Science Quarterly* (vol. 26, No. 3, 1911: pp. 238–270). It is an expression which since then has been widely used, both in academic and in political circles. But it has not been the only way to refer to a judicial executive power. Other expressions, such as *judicial oligarchy*, wigged aristocracy or *American judicial supremacy doctrine,* have also helped to identify this social and political phenomenon.

Lambert's objective was to take up positions in the juridical and constitutional debate that were starting up in interwar France showing, on the basis of his American experience, the problems that could arise from a bad design of constitutional justice: the democratic illegitimacy of a constitutional body, bedecked with extraordinary power, with a capacity to make the Constitution say what is denied and to impose limits where the Constitution said nothing. It was a question, therefore, of generating a debate on the need – or not – of granting the political system an organ ready to substitute democratic legitimacy with a legitimacy of a bureaucratic and judicial nature, when called for. If this formula was the one opted for, it would be tantamount to declaring the triumph of the Constitution and awakening constitutionalism. Indeed, and parallel to this, what Lambert was doing was taking up an old debate on the judicial activism of the United States.

But this judicial activism, when bouncing back to Europe, had to be tied to concentrated systems of constitutional jurisdiction in which this activism was expressed, by way of the Constitutional courts, through its own sentences. When this very debate was opened up in Spain's Transition period, a decision was taken to create a Constitutional court (TC) to set it apart from the Francoist judiciary, which was all too present and influential in the judicial power area. No thought was then given to the possibility that the justice system could become, *de facto*, a true government in the shadows from which to impose the vision of the State or from where to defend – ex officio – the *raison d'état*.

4.2.1 The Constitutional Court as the Guardian of the Constitution

The phobias of Francoism, that had reproduced themselves during the Transition period and been included in the Constitution, were woven into the new reality by way of the judicial mantra of the principle of unity. The defence and preservation of this principle had to combine with the need to show Spain as a democracy equivalent to those of other European countries. An institutional body had therefore to be created which, though coming short of being a power of the State, should ensure compliance with the constitutional order and enable the country to function as a plural and decentralized democracy. The decision was taken to follow the European model, and a Constitutional Court was created. Its design was inspired by Germany's Federal Constitutional Court and the Italian Constitutional

Court, without forgetting Spain's own experience with the Court of Constitutional Guarantees, foreseen in the 1931 Republican Constitution. The Constitutional Court was awarded the monopoly of controlling the constitutional orthodoxy of new legal regulations. And although it was carrying out a jurisdictional task – passing sentences and resolving conflicts in legal terms – the institution was left out of the judicial power structure.

As we have noted, placing the Constitutional Court outside the realms of the judicial power had a clear motive. The 1978 Constitution did not cause a rift with the Franco legality, nor with many of the institutions that had served the dictatorship with devotion, loyalty and efficiency. One of those institutions was the judiciary. As Isabel Lifante Vidal quite rightly put it, "The judges of the Francoist dictatorship would continue as judges in the new democratic and constitutional period."[6] That was the problem. So much so that leaving the interpretation of the Constitution in the hands of judges and magistrates, who had served – I insist, with fanaticism, reverence and loyalty – during the Franco regime, was tantamount to leaving it in the hands of those who sought to destroy it. This was confirmed when judges, many of them members of the Supreme Court, showed their hostility to the Constitution, denying it its normative value and merely giving it programmatic value. It was necessary, therefore, to separate the judicial power from the Constitutional Court.

But a mistake was made. A decision was taken to put the appointments to the Constitutional Court in the hands of politicians. And this is what was to be the institution's flaw, and still is. Of the twelve members who make up the Court, four are chosen by the Congress and four by the Senate (among the candidates presented by the autonomous parliaments); always with a three-fifths majority vote. A further two are appointed by the Government, and the last two by the General Council of the Judiciary Power. The key lay in the three-fifths vote, both of the Congress and of the Senate. This reinforced majority (in an organ that sets out to have a counterweight mission) along with the *calculated variance* we have referred to above, ensured that the election of magistrates had to be obtained with the approval of the right. And, logically, with that of the left. So, in practice, this had the participation of the two large political groups – PP and PSOE – which had reached an agreement as regards the omissions and gaps in the Constitution.

This leads us to analyse, briefly, a further variable that must be considered, a variable that will reinforce our argument. In the procedure for appointments, the truth is that neither the Congress, nor the Senate, nor the Government or the General Council of the Judiciary Power take part.

Neither do the two large political groups we referred to above, the left and the right. It is the leaderships of the parties that do so – or, at best, in the case of the Congress and Senate, the two parliamentary groups of the big parties – if it isn't simply their leaders.[7] The parties control the parliamentary groups – and, therefore, exert their capacity for control and influence over the Congress and Senate – and, when all is said and done, they also control the Government if they hold a parliamentary majority. Therefore, the Constitutional Court is today in the hands of the two large parties: the Popular Party (PP) and the Socialist Party (PSOE). –

4.2.2 The General Council of the Judiciary as a Government in the Shadows

Any serious construction of the judicial power must be guided by one basic principle: independence. That is to say, it must guarantee the tools to ensure the independence of judges and magistrates in the exercise of their jurisdictional function. This is the meaning of many of the precepts of the Spanish Constitution. But, as we shall now see, the juridical construction of Spain's judicial power has progressively reduced the sphere of its judicial independence to the benefit of political dependence. Today the General Council of the Judiciary – a body created expressly to guarantee this independence – is a body at the service of the parties and wholly given over to party concerns. It is the opposite of what was sought when the Constitution was drawn up.

Inspired by the then prestigious *Consiglio Superiore della Magistratura* of Italy, the aim was to separate the General Council of the Judiciary from the Ministry of Justice, a step that seemed to mean a split from Francoist logic, being constituted as a unique institution in the Spanish State. Initially, this meant separating the General Council of the Judiciary from the autonomous principle to wholly submit it to the unitary conception of the State, a step which did indeed fully link it to the Francoist judiciary.

We shall now analyse how this will to control the executive – which inspired the first legal steps in the construction of an independent judicial power – was watered down as the two major parties settled into the inertia of the two-party system. To see this clearly, let us select the elements of this juridical construction in chronological order and centre on the legal aspect that has most interested the parties and has raised most controversy in political and media circles: the selection system. The control of the General Council of the Judiciary has turned into a major battlefield between the two major Spanish parties as a question of clear political importance: the General Council of the Judiciary is the body responsible for the appointments made to the most important courts and High Courts (including the

Audiencia Nacional) of the Spanish State. This explains its importance in terms of exerting control over the political agenda.

The first Organic Law, that of 1/1980, January 10, called the Law of the General Council of the Judiciary Power, established that the majority of members of the General Council of the Judiciary – twelve out of twenty – were to be chosen from amongst all the judges and magistrates of all the judicial categories: three magistrates from the Supreme Court, six magistrates and three judges by the judges and magistrates themselves. The other eight members, from amongst lawyers and jurists of renowned competence, chosen as follows: four by the Congress and four by the Senate, by a majority of three-fifths. This was the mandate of Article 122.3 of the Spanish Constitution: that twelve members should be chosen from amongst members of the judicial profession (with the sole participation of judges and magistrates) and the remaining eight among jurists of renowned competence: four proposed by the Congress, and four by the Senate. The quorum laid down by the Constitution was three-fifths. Note that the qualified majority of three-fifths crops up once again.

It could appear logical that the judicial power was chosen, at least as regards the majority of its members, by the judges and magistrates themselves, despite the deficit in terms of representational democracy obtained by this power of the State. However, the right wing heirs of Francoism – basically UCD and AP – were quite happy with this system of designation. Being the majority of the Spanish judiciary of the moment, with a distinctly conservative profile, it ensured itself an interpretation of the norms by way of jurisprudence of a clearly conservative nature. –

As from day one, the General Council of the Judiciary was the object of the ideological projections made by the political parties. The conservative right manoeuvred to establish a voting system that would enable the practical occupation of the new judiciary governing body by the more conservative and hierarchical sector. An agreement between the parliamentary majority and the judicial leadership of the time – most conservative and deeply rooted in the Franco regime – wanted to exclude from access to exercising the right to official judicial membership the groups that failed to have at least fifteen percent of the members of the judiciary. The aim was to prevent associative access to the General Council of the Judiciary to the heirs of "Justícia Democràtica," a very minority association of judges and prosecutors with clear democratic convictions. But the instrumentalization of the judiciary was not only to be the practice of the right. Three years after the Socialist Party came to power in 1982, it put into effect a reform of the Organic Law on Judicial Power to introduce a formula that ensured a hegemonic position for progressive magistrates of Spain's left.

But what really ended up happening is that the reform of the Organic Law left the judges' governing body in the hands of the dual-party system! The amendment that put the election of the board members into the hands of the Parliament – and, thus, into the power of electoral interests and party politics – was made by Euskadiko Ezkerra MP and lawyer, Juan María Bandrés. The new Law 6/1985, of July 1, went on to regulate the election of the General Council of the Judiciary, which was established in articles 111 and 113 in the following manner: of the twelve judges and magistrates, six were to be elected by the Congress and six by the Senate, always with a three-fifths vote. The other eight members (lawyers and jurists) remained the same: that is, the Congress and Senate also decided here, also by a three-fifths vote.

It had been Bandrés' intention to democratize the judiciary's governing body.[8] This option was to subject the election of the General Council of the Judiciary to the designs of politics, bearing in mind that politics was not necessarily bad, nor did it have perverse goals, dangerous purposes, or hidden intentions. Politics was sound, good, and had loyal principles that, according to Bandrés, would not pervert the rule that was intended to be reformed. Bandrés' arguments were refuted by Alianza Popular spokesman José Maria Ruiz Gallardón, who ended up challenging the legislative reform before the Constitutional Court. Ruiz Gallardón was of the opinion that the reform opened the door to the control, by the parties, of the other constitutional bodies whose action was to be guided by the principle of independence.

In what context did this reform take place? In 1985, the profile of judges or magistrates in Spain was conservative, having been groomed intellectually and sociologically during the Franco regime. They were practising Catholics, over the age of fifty and mostly – about 90% – men. At that time, the judges and magistrates totalled some 1,800 members – today there are 5,500 – most of them affiliated to the conservative Professional Association of the Judiciary. Inbreeding in the judicial career then reached the point where one in four judges was the son of judges or magistrates. This deep-seated conservative structure played a key role – although this argument was never publicly acknowledged – in changing the system of electing judges.

The Constitutional Court sentence of July 29, 1986, that came in answer to Ruiz Gallardón's appeal, saw out the constitutionality of the reform. But the Constitutional Court also recommended a return to the election system established in 1980 and alerted to a more than probable interference by the perverse logic of the political parties in the jurisdictional field. The Constitutional Court was not far off in its estimate. This was to be the praxis that would preside over the judge and magistrate election arrangements in what is known as the "quotas" system. Its track record in the four periods of office registered between 1985 and the subsequent reform of the Judicial Power Organic Law certified the enactment of the inter-party struggle within the General Council of the Judiciary. This became a body deprived of autonomy and subjected to the line imposed by the political parties which, by way of the appointments made, exerted control over a body that had become opaque in the eyes of public opinion (Andrés 2003: 159). It was even claimed that the principle of judicial independence had been replaced by the principle of political dependence.

The year 2001, during the second term of office of José María Aznar's PP government, saw the passing of Organic Law 2001, of July 28, on the composition of the General Council of the Judiciary. In general, the regulation respected the appointment system of its predecessor (which now benefited a Popular Party with an absolute majority), but again it involved the judicial associations in the election of judges and magistrates. The reform was interpreted – and in practice it worked out – as an electoral competition between parties, but now via these associations. Alejandro Nieto defined the action of judicial associations as "the operative arm of political parties within the General Council of the Judiciary."[9] Time and practice have endorsed the two-way traffic between the most politicized associations and the two major parties: the associations become a mechanism for interaction and pressure on the parties, and the parties use the associations to penetrate the judiciary.

Perfecto Andrés summed up the consequences of a reform that involved the emergence of associations of judges and magistrates, now unmasked, in the political struggle as "an undesirable partisan depoliticisation of the associative movement. The access of the associate judge – as a judge – to the governing body of the judiciary goes through the party, but informally, surreptitiously."[10] The 2013 reform – Organic Law 4/2013, of June 28 – and that of 2018 – Organic Law 4/2018, of December 28 – did nothing to overcome the will to control the General Council of the Judiciary and submit it to the logic of parliamentary arithmetic – the same three-fifths as ever – as applied in the State's other powers.

4.2.3 The Audiencia Nacional (National High Court) as a Tool of Political Repression

Since its founding, the National High Court has been the subject of repeated criticism by both legal practitioners and experts in specialized doctrine. In the collective imagination, the National High Court is proof of the subsistence and sources of the judicial culture of the Franco regime. It is, in practice, another special court. The first major criticism was spelled out in the context of the proceedings of the First Congress of Democratic Justice, in January 1977. There the complaint was made that, due to the system of appointments and jurisdictional matters, the court was really an update of the Francoist TOP, the Court of Public Order (Gallego 2015: 771). More criticism followed, such as that made by Antonio María Lorca Navarrete, who linked the institution with the pre-constitutional regime that had made it possible, arguing that it was a framework of dubious democratic legitimacy. He was as far to the right as was Andrés de la Oliva, who denounced in the weekly *Actualidad Económica* that the National High Court had been undemocratic from the day it was born.[11]

Certainly, the mere existence of the National High Court violates several fundamental rights enshrined in the Spanish Constitution, which is worrying in terms of constitutional justice. The first and foremost is that, being an *ad hoc* court with statewide jurisdiction, it violates the right to be tried by the ordinary judge predetermined by the law required by Article 24 of the Constitution. This anomaly required ratification, in terms of adaptation to the constitutional framework, on two occasions: firstly, by the European Commission in 1986, and then by the Constitutional Court in 1987. It is the only Spanish court that has been required to justify its existence. This means that its competence must be interpreted, always and at all times, in restrictive terms. This restrictive interpretation is obviously in line with its pre-democratic jurisdictional nature. In democratic terms, it is a jurisdictional anomaly. An expansive interpretation of its competence – as was made, as we shall see, during the political trial of the leaders of the independence Process – transforms the ordinary judge into a special judge. Or, what amounts to the same thing, it places the National High Court in clearly Francoist space/time coordinates.[12]

The legitimacy of this exception cannot be explained in legal terms, only in political ones. By breaking the rule of the judge assigned by law by the creation of a special court, the State could deal with all such cases in which the *raison d'état* was at stake. And it could do so with greater efficiency, whilst concealing the breaking of the rule being applied.

However, this concentration in a jurisdictional body of powers, such as the investigation and prosecution of cases related to terrorist offences, violated yet another principle of criminal procedure: that of mediation. That is to say, the criminal acts must be investigated and judged in the territorial context where the deeds take place. The distance between the deed being prosecuted and the court in charge of instructing and judging brought about a dehumanizing effect on justice, which took the model of the National High Court closer to Francoist justice. In the justice of the regime the place where the deed was committed, or the social or local context, had nothing to do with the space in which these facts were to be tried. We will see the importance of this variable when analysing the construction of the lawfare against the Catalan sovereignty movement.

4.2.4 The Court of Auditors as a Tool of Economic Repression

Media literature has referred to the Court of Auditors as a body affected by the nepotism of the leaders of the two major Spanish political parties: the Popular Party and the Socialist Party. This interpretation is correct insofar as its selection system follows the same variables as the other judicial bodies, the Constitutional Court and the General Council of the Judiciary: of the twelve members of the plenary board of the Court, six are appointed by Congress and six by the Senate, by a quorum of three-fifths. As we have seen with the Constitutional Court and the General Council of the Judiciary, the only two bodies involved in the appointment of members of the plenary are politicians or those subject to the logic of political parties and controlled by what we call the "calculated deviation" from the principle of equality. But what is interesting to note is that, while the politicization of the Constitutional Court and the General Council of the Judiciary has been progressive, coinciding with the alternation in government of the two major dynastic parties, the Court of Auditors has been an institution co-opted by the political sphere from day one.

The reasons for this early colonization of the Court of Auditors must be sought in the roles it plays. The main one is the auditing of the public sector and the prosecution of accounting liability. In other words, it ensures that politicians do not engage in corrupt practices in the management of the institutions they control. Another important function – which makes the taming of the Court of Auditors one of the main objectives of the political elites – is to audit the finances of the political parties. In other words, the parties themselves, on the basis of appointments in Parliament, elect those who will monitor them. Which is to say that those who have to control corruption are chosen by those who will be controlled. It is only on this basis that the Court of Auditors is now a hotbed of former politicians and the family members, friends and acquaintances of active politicians.

Only on rare occasions have complaints about the politicization of a Spanish court come from the judicial sector, from the Supreme Court itself. Deep down, the complaint was that nepotism and cronyism within the Court was so scandalous that, in 2011, hand-picked appointments outnumbered those of professional civil servants. It was in this way that profiles with clear political implications and party servitudes had reached the Court, as may be seen from the following list (which includes the most outstanding cases, but is in no way complete):

- Manuel Aznar, brother of José Maria Aznar, former President of the Popular Party and brother-in-law of Ana Botella, Mayor of Madrid at the time of the appointment.
- Ramón Álvarez de Miranda, President of the Court and ex-UCD MP and son of former Speaker of the Congress, Fernándo Álvarez de Miranda.
- Margarita Mariscal de Gante, former Minister of Justice of the Aznar government and daughter of Jaime Mariscal de Gante, former member of the Francoist Public Order Court.
- Maria José Molinuevo, wife of Federico Trillo, a former leading member of the Popular Party (former Speaker of the Congress and former Minister of Defence) and mastermind behind the Popular Party's appeal against the Catalan Statute, the rejection of which is at the genesis of the Catalan independence Process.
- Juan Velarde, former Court member, had been a leading Falangist. During the Catalan independence Process, he actually said he did not discard bombing Barcelona in retaliation.
- Ubaldo Nieto de Alba, who for ten years presided over the institution, was a former UCD Senator and appeared in the famous "Bárcenas Papers" as one of those making secret donations to the Popular Party.

These names reveal the extent to which the Francoist elites were able to secure positions of control in bodies that were absolutely vital for deactivating the mechanisms necessary for democracy to function properly. So much so that these names are proof of the ineffectiveness of the public auditing body and of the financial accounts of political parties. Given the functions that the body has been entrusted with, it can take on a strong political dimension, as it can become yet another tool of financial repression. It is in this sense that we are interested in contrasting these two variables insofar as they reveal the extent to which the partisan control of the Court of Auditors is important. The first is the impunity with which the Court acts with the massive cases of corruption that affect the two major political parties, of which it has not detected a single one. The second, the diligence and rigour with which it has acted against the Catalan pro-independence movement, from whose leaders it has not hesitated to demand seven-figure dollar fines.

Chapter 5

Partitocracy

The Actors of Repression

5.1 The Control of Justice

The reform of justice promised at the beginning of Spain's democracy by the Socialist Party was soon degraded, in the words of Perfecto Andrés, to a mere "struggle for *power* in the judiciary" (Andrés 2003: 156). What was sought by both the conservative nationalist right and the Spanish progressive left was a law tailored to facilitate control of the judiciary. The key was to exercise watchfulness through the appointment of members of the General Council of the Judiciary. Perfecto Andrés Ibañez explains it in these words: "The judicial question boiled down to a political problem, democratization in exchange for people (now ours), and the heteronomy – of necessity implicit – in the partitocratic co-optation of those in charge of the governance of the judiciary" (Andrés 2003: 157). Luís María Díez-Picazo, a conservative judge and, as such, affected by these measures, called it a "political reprisal."[1]

We shall now set out these *counter-norms*, or mechanisms of political control, in the judicial sphere, given that the judiciary is precisely the most important power of all and the most distant, at the same time, from the system of democratic elections. It is also the most decisive power when it comes to manoeuvring in favour of a lawfare strategy. The aim is to show how, beyond democratically elected governments, by virtue of logical competition between political parties and government programmes, there is a governmental dimension that does not conform to democratic parameters. It conforms to partisan logic and acts as a shadow *sotogoverno*. This *sotogoverno* is not subject to political or jurisdictional controls, nor to public scrutiny. And its actions are not subject to inspection by any court. Debates are held in luxurious offices, in private salons, in restaurants and presidential boxes in football stadiums. They operate in the depths of public administration, deciding and acting, guided by interests and *raisons d'état* that, by their very nature as *metarights*, cannot be part of the political debate.

5.2 Unwritten Tools of Control

We come now to the *counter-normative* mechanisms that allow both the selection and the election of these Spanish judicial elites and the ways they behave. This phenomenon could be called the patrimonialisation of justice or, to put it another way, the appropriation of the administration of justice by the political class. This is today – and has always been – the main malaise of Spanish justice. Hence, the chief pathology of toga power needs to be investigated: its use as yet another tool for politics. This is a serious problem, but the use of justice to eliminate the political enemy is even more serious.

5.2.1 The System of Quotas

The partisan subdivision of the General Council of the Judiciary has solidified a political culture that has been projected onto the system of appointments that have to do with the high echelons of judicial power and the judiciary, including the Constitutional Court. However, in the Supreme Court, as a former judge of the institution, Perfecto Andrés, acknowledges, "decision-making has been practically absolute, reinforced by the open renunciation of self-limitation in the exercise of one's own power" (Andrés. 2003: 159). Neither the General Council of the Judiciary, nor the Supreme Court, nor the Constitutional Court, nor, even worse, the Court of Auditors, have been areas beyond partisan trafficking in appointments according to ideological affinities. The Bandrés amendment caused the installation of a non-aggression, or respect, pact, that introduces the arithmetical variable in the Spanish Congress and Senate into the system of election of those judges who are to act in Spain's top judiciary. This is known as the quota system, in other words the co-opting of judges close to the ideology of political parties based on their arithmetical weight in the two Houses of Parliament.

The politicization of justice, given the tacit implementation of the quota system as a counterweight to the system established in the letter of the Constitution, is precisely this: the introduction of a pact of silence based on election results and the composition of the Congress. This means, in the words of Alejandro Nieto, modifying *de facto* what they *de jure* cannot, or do not want to, do. The risk of enjoying a truly independent, immovable, responsible High Court subject only to the rule of law would amount to an exercise in control of the executive branch in all its degrees and manifestations, and that was not wanted. Although this is the aim of the separation of powers and the system of controls, weights and counterweights shoring up the division of powers, the system of political quotas is a *countermeasure* intended to dilute this constitutional principle.

5.2.2 The Blocking System

The action of blocking the appointments of a particular judicial body responds to the will of the legislator that all judicial bodies are answerable to political power and are thus caught up within the struggle between political parties. This is how it is, as we have seen, in the General Council of the Judiciary (on which the governing vertices of the top Spanish courts, such as the Supreme Court or the National Court then depend), the Constitutional Court and, to a lesser extent, in the Court of Auditors. Blocking the appointment of judges becomes a political technique at the epicentre of which there is no disagreement with the professional curriculum of the barred judge: animosity to particular names is expressed only insofar as they are identified with a political party. That ought not be a problem. The problem arises when a judge, once elected to be part of a particular judicial body, defends the interests and ideological postulates of the party that appointed him. This bond of loyalty, so deeply ingrained in the regime's judiciary, is what the parties reject but at the same time practise.

The history of the blocking of judges in Spain is long and not peaceful. As Ignacio Sánchez Cuenca explains in a study on the delays in the appointment of Constitutional Court judges and their ideological bias, the ideological leaning of the Spanish government has a clear effect on the Constitutional Court.[2] The same can be said of the General Council of the Judiciary. And this is the keystone of the veto system to prevent the normal functioning of the institution, unless it is aligned with the political party that exercises the veto in question. Although the political practice for imposing ideological bias has been present in Spanish democracy since the years of the rolling-out of the Constitution, it was not until 2004, with the arrival of Socialist José Luis Rodriguez Zapatero's government, that this practice became a veritable political battle. The unwillingness to accept the election results of March 2004, conditioned by the Islamist attack on Madrid's Atocha station, led the Popular Party to organize a series of obstructionist manoeuvres to prevent the Constitutional Court from having a majority of progressive judges. In 2007, the Popular Party's refusal to renew the four judges of the Constitutional Court to be appointed by the Senate did not come to an end until 2010: 1,120 days of institutional blockade!

But, as Sánchez-Cuenca says, the 2007 blockade – which lasted until

2010 and overlapped that same year with another blockade, which ended up affecting eight judges of the Constitutional Court – was not an isolated episode in the partisan struggle for control of the top judiciary. The first blocking episode dates back to 1998 and involved a 293-day hold-up. In 2001 there was again a hold-up, due to disagreements over the renewal of the General Council of the Judiciary: 194 days of deadlock. That year, 2001, was crucial, since, with the use of the blocking system, the right took control of the Constitutional Court, the General Council of the Judiciary and the Court of Auditors (Sánchez-Cuenca. 2011: 291). From 2004, the Popular Party tried to compensate for its electoral defeat with a belligerent and utterly partisan use of the constitutional bodies it controlled most easily: the Constitutional Court and the General Council of the Judiciary. The attitude of the members of these two bodies helped. In the case of the General Council of the Judiciary, the active work of opposition to the Socialist Party government cried out, and in the case of the Constitutional Court, its willingness to curb the legislative initiatives of the Socialists.

It is worth noting – following Sánchez-Cuenca – that the sabotage strategy of the Popular Party can be understood as the institutional dimension of the strategy of tension (Sánchez-Cuenca. 2011: 291). In times of electoral weakness of the right-wing, it has intensified its policy of opposition and tension by transferring political initiative and the exercise of government control and scrutiny to the judiciary, especially the General Council of the Judiciary and the Constitutional Court. It is hardly surprising that it was the Spanish conservative right-wing that was to initiate, as we shall see, the strategy of judicial war against the Catalan independence movement.

5.2.3 The Sponsorship System

Once the General Council of the Judiciary has been chosen and the quota or blocking phases have been overcome, it decides on the appointments of the Supreme Court (judges and presidents of Chambers), appoints the President of the High Court of Justice of each autonomous community, and names the judges of the Civil and Criminal Chambers of these Superior Courts. Another of its functions is to appoint the President of the National Court and the presidents of the chambers that make it up. In short, the General Council of the Judiciary is a body with a great deal of power within the judiciary, insofar as it is assigned a broad capacity to decide what the professional career of many judges will be, especially those who, out of ambition or thirst for power, want to get on in the judicial hierarchy. In this sense, it has powers to reward, but also to punish. In a deplorable speech, the President of the General Council of the Judiciary, Carlos Lesmes, defined this power – that of rewarding and punishing – stating that "judges are controlled with a stick and a carrot."[3]

The fact of the matter is that this power, granted to the General Council of the Judiciary, plus the selection of its members in the exclusive hands of political parties, makes the appointments to this body clearly partisan.[4] In fact, if judges want to progress up the judicial ladder, their merits or abilities will be less important than their political contacts. Connections with the top judiciary and, consequently, with top-level politics become the greatest qualification for climbing up to bodies such as the General Council of the Judiciary itself or the Supreme Court. This system of recruiting judicial elites is known as *sponsorship*, or, to put it another way, forging a career in the wake of a politician or a judge with good connections in politics: someone, in short, able to take care of the judicial future of the sponsored judge.

This system – just like the quota system – makes the independence of sponsored judges impossible and raises doubts that their jurisdictional decisions are subject only to the rule of law. The political or judicial godfather, as in the popular imagination, demands loyalty and a return for favours rendered. It is hardly surprising that sponsorship – or as Joaquin Bosch puts it, vassalage – provokes an understandable distrust of the top judicial institution.[5] Bosch speaks of the Supreme Court, but he could say the same about other courts where strategic appointments take place in terms of the political control of the top courts. And, within the Supreme Court, the Chamber most sensitive to political appointments is the Second, or Criminal, Chamber. This is the Chamber in charge of prosecuting on issues as sensitive to public opinion as the trials of those who enjoy political privileges, cases of large-scale corruption, or deciding on matters of great political interest, such as the conflict between Spain and Catalonia. In this sense, getting sponsorships right can be the narrow line that tips the balance in a corruption case or the request for a petition to proceed against someone who has a political privilege, or the admission or non-admission of a lawsuit against a political leader.

5.3 The Politicized Judge

As Alejandro Nieto has explained, Spanish justice has known several types of judges: the *cacique*, who was appointed by the ruling local strongman and who was required to be loyal in the exercise of his function; the *apolitical* judge, who was insensitive to political preferences, which meant that he or she was an unreal judge, but who for many years became the ideal of those who advocated a fair and impartial administration of justice. Finally, the *technical civil servant* judge, who was devised by the Franco regime after a purge of judges during the Civil War, keeping a slot for ex-combatants and for those whose parents had fallen for God and for Spain.[6] In the nineties, the *celebrity* judge came upon the scene, without being a feature exclusive to Spain.[7] On the contrary, the *celebrity* judge has been a global phenomenon that still continues to fill the court pages and, above all, politics.[8]

What we have now is a politicized model of justice, which does not necessarily have to be a bad model, as long as this politicization is put to the service of democracy, political pluralism, and social progress. The problem is not the politicization of judges, as such. They, like everyone else, have political ideals, principles and values, which they express or can express in their sentences, as long as those sentences are legally motivated. The problem has been, as we have seen in the previous section, the partisan politicization of judges provoked by the struggle to colonize spaces of power by the two main parties. The aim was to enjoy the political advantages of having the judiciary under control. However, the top judiciary was no stranger to the carrot technique: it immediately put itself at the service of party politics and soon managed to coexist with the system of rewards inherent in a partisan struggle. A new model of judge was born, which was actually a copy of the old Francoist judiciary: the politicized judge.

In Alejandro Nieto's definition, the politicized judge – who more specifically could be called a partisan judge – is one who "in the exercise of his office lends himself to be an instrument of the interests of political parties" (Nieto.2004: 93). Excluded from this category are those who, despite having a clear political mentality and defining themselves as right-wing, left-wing, liberal or progressive, are able to dispense with their ideology when exercising their profession. Or, at the very least, they put it at the service of democracy and law. The important thing is not to be at the service of the political parties. Because, when the sentences reflect the political interests of the parties that have sponsored the judge handing them down, the necessary judicial independence – and no less necessary submission to the law – remains as a hypocritical aspiration that creates disaffection against the grass-roots judiciary, the one that is closest to the citizens. As Owen Fiss has written, judicial independence requires dual legal and factual components:[9] disconnection from the parties in a case (one cannot be under the influence of anyone), as well as individual autonomy (no one can have power over the judge).

Below we shall offer examples of the different strategies adopted in the process of placing judges in high courts. We are talking, of course, about judges with clear links to political parties that override the basic principles that should guide the judge. These are former MPs, Senators or people with ties of leadership or representation with parties, and who have even belonged to or held organic or elected positions representing the two great dynastic parties. It is not a complete list; it is simply intended to demonstrate the existence of the politicized judge and the politicization of justice that we will see in the last section of this chapter. These names also explain the ease of implementing, in Spain, a strategy of judicialization of politics and a greater involvement of the high judicial elites in a misunderstood judicial activism. And, finally, these names are what make up a real State within the State that we shall see in the second part of this book.

5.3.1 The Colonization of Spaces of Power (the Popular Party)

The list of judges with clear links to the People's Party is a result of the strategy of placing like-minded judges in leading court posts to influence – or try to influence – judicial processes in which the political party has interests. The aim of the Popular Party has always been, in accordance with the mostly conservative nature of the Spanish judiciary, to promote appointments that would allow direct control of the procedure (and all that derives from it: precautionary measures, tempo of the procedure and control of the judicial inquiry) and of the sentence. When analysing the judges related to the Popular Party, we need to start with the presidencies: key posts for the management of the jurisdictional body. As will be explained below, the presidencies of the most important judicial institutions from 2012 to 2017 – the years of the Catalan sovereignty Process – have been in the hands of people of recognized significance within the Popular Party. Once we have analysed the presidencies, we shall do the same with appointments to strategic judicial positions in the top Spanish courts.

The most egregious case of all was that of Francisco Pérez de los Cobos, who was the presiding judge of the Constitutional Court during the years of the Process. De los Cobos not only failed to hide his status as a Popular Party member during the parliamentary procedure of his appointment – as did the Popular Party itself – but, once this situation was revealed, he defended it, despite the controversy that this fact gave rise to.[10] Despite a request for him to be turned down being presented on the grounds of such a blatant bias, it was not granted. Moreover, Pérez de los Cobos had been a well-known adviser to the Popular Party on labour reform, a fact which did not prevent him from taking part in the votes on the unconstitutionality appeals filed against the reform in question.

The prestige of the Constitutional Court was being questioned,[11] especially bearing in mind the pending resolution of cases of strong political significance (the Catalan case, to say no more) and the fact that, in July 2012, the Popular Party had proposed – and the proposal had been accepted – the appointment of Andrés Ollero as a judge. Ollero had been a member of the Popular Party for seventeen years and a party spokesman for Justice. At that time – and with these appointments – a majority arithmetically in favour of the ideological theses of the Popular Party prevailed in the plenary of the Constitutional Court. Ollero had also been turned down on several occasions for his affinity with the Popular Party, but the objections had inexplicably been dismissed.

The Popular Party played its hand again, but this time it affected the presidency of the General Council of the Judiciary and the Supreme Court. The person chosen was Carlos Lesmes. His move from the judiciary to politics took place in 1996, the year José María Aznar became Prime Minister. Lesmes was first appointed Director General of the Office of Conscientious Objection, and then Director General of Relations with the Administration of Justice. The latter appointment gave him a deep knowledge of the bowels of the judicial organization, of the means at its disposal, and of the officials in its service. Lesmes' close ties with the FAES, a conservative think tank linked to the Popular Party, have always been acknowledged and never denied.

The affinity of the President of the Second Chamber of the Supreme Court, Manuel Marchena,[12] with the Popular Party, is also well known. We only need to recall the episode that preceded the trial against the leaders of the Catalan independence movement, in what came to be known as the Cosidó affair. That case proved the extent to which the will to control Spain's top judiciary has always been an issue of State. – It went like this. An agreement to renew the General Council of the Judiciary between the Popular Party and the Socialist Party was to put Manuel Marchena, a judge close to the PP, at the head of the General Council of the Judiciary. The presidency of the General Council of the Judiciary also entailed the presidency of the Supreme Court, a not inconsiderable fact. But a WhatsApp message sent by Ignacio Cosidó – previously Director General of the National Police corps and at the time the Popular Party's spokesman in the Senate – stated that, with the appointment of judge Marchena, the Second Chamber of the Supreme Court would be controlled via the back door. This blew up the deal, as well, of course, as enabling the defendants' counsels to argue that the judge should not act in the case. This argument was not successful.

The case of Judge Concepción Espejel came to light in 2014, when she was closely linked to Dolores de Cospedal, at that time the President of the

Castilla-La Mancha autonomous region. Espejel was the member of the General Council of the Judiciary assigned to that territory when Dolores de Cospedal awarded her the Cross of Sant Raimon de Penyafort. Prior to that, however, the link between Espejel and the Popular Party had already borne fruit. In 2013, she had been appointed President of the Second Section of the Criminal Chamber of the National High Court by virtue of the *ad hoc* change in the system for appointing presidencies to ensure that she presided over the Court that was to hear the Gürtel case and the case of the undeclared funds (the 'B cash box') of the Popular Party.[13] Because of her ideological and personal affinity with members of the Popular Party, the judge could herself have declined the appointment; instead, she was turned down. The conclusion was that the appointment of Espejel was due to the clear will of the Popular Party to have a like-minded judge deal with the main cases of corruption that were harassing it.

But not everything ended there. By the agreement of the General Council of the Judiciary, of May 25, 2017, Concepción Espejel was appointed President of the Criminal Chamber of the National High Court: that is, she was placed as the hierarchical superior of the judges who ultimately had to prosecute the corruption cases affecting the Popular Party and who had removed her by turning her down From this vantage point, Espejel was offered full powers to design the composition of the Courts in charge of judging the most outstanding cases in matters of corruption in the history of the Spanish State.

The case of Enrique López has similarities to those of Espejel and of another judge close to the Popular Party, whose career we shall not dwell too long upon: Juan Pablo González González. The case of Enrique López was that of an investigating judge who, despite his inexperience in prosecuting and handing down judgments, was appointed by the Senate – at the proposal of the Popular Party – to be a member of the General Council of the Judiciary. Later, in 2005, he was appointed judge of the Criminal Chamber of the National High Court, and in 2007 he was appointed to the Constitutional Court, despite his palpable inexperience. Due to this inexperience – and the ideological affinity of the candidate – he was vetoed by the Socialist Party, and this led to an escalation of blockades of Constitutional Court judges that would last three years.

With the arrival of the Popular Party in government, in 2013 Aznar's party got its own way and appointed Enrique López to the Constitutional Court. But he did not last long in office, due to a bout of alcoholism that forced him to resign in 2014. After numerous pressures from the PP's FAES think tank, López ended up topping off his career in the service of the party when he was appointed Minister of Justice, Interior and Victims of

Terrorism for the Madrid region, which had been in the hands of the Popular Party since 2019.

The case of Vicente Magro Servet is different from that of Enrique López. Magro Servet is a judge with a long career and proven legal and technical capacity. But he was Senator for Alicante in the ranks of the Popular Party, good enough evidence of the political commitment to the party. The fact is that Magro Servet was promoted to judge of the Second Chamber of the Supreme Court so that he could rule on appeals against the multiple cases of corruption and illegal funding of the Popular Party.

Fernando Román's case began when he was appointed in 2011 by the then Minister of Justice, Alberto Ruiz Gallardón, as Secretary of State for Justice. He held the position until 2014. He then returned to his post as a specialist judge in the Administrative Chamber of the National High Court, until he was promoted to the Third Chamber of the Supreme Court, as agreed by the Plenary of the General Council of the Judiciary on January 25, 2018. This was a case of judicial revolving doors, which was even described as such by the Civic Platform for Judicial Independence and the Judges for Democracy organization, and it was a case in which other judges who were running for office presented three or four times as many credentials as Fernando Román. But Román's access to the Third Chamber was vital for the Popular Party, as it was the Chamber that had to hear appeals against the agreements adopted by the General Council of the Judiciary itself, more specifically, agreements that decided the appointments of judges to posts at Spain's judicial summit.

5.3.2 *Judicial Revolving Doors (the Socialist Party)*

The list of judges linked to the Socialist Party is not as scandalous as that of the Popular Party, for two main reasons. The first is that the Spanish high judiciary, which lends itself to the game of party politics, is mostly conservative and ideologically right-wing and, as a result, non-progressive. The second is that the Socialist Party's strategy as regards the judiciary has not been the same as that of the Popular Party. The Socialists have deployed the tactic – more subtle, incidentally – of recruiting prominent judges in the judicial career to incorporate them in positions of great political importance in the executive branch. That is why the Socialist Party has been criticized for its obstinacy in promoting the "judicial revolving door."[14] To be sure, the very regulations governing the careers of judges and prosecutors have facilitated this political practice, one that does nothing to depoliticize justice: i.e. Art. 7 of the Electoral Law and Art. 356 of the Organic Law of the Judicial Power.

The start of this practice dates back to the 1990s. It coincides with the appearance of the figure of the celebrity judges, judges who risked their lives investigating cases of great complexity and media presence. In times of political crisis and government weakness, celebrity judges were perceived by the public as the only people with the ability to deal with the most complex cases, linked mainly to financial sharks, drug trafficking and the fight against terrorism. These were the years of Baltasar Garzón (who investigated the indictments of the GAL, ETA and, in 1998, issued the arrest warrant for dictator Augusto Pinochet); of Javier Gómez de Liaño (well known for the investigation of the Sogecable case); and of Carlos Bueren (investigator of the Lasa and Zabala cases). Years later, other important names would emerge. Some would end up linked to Socialist Party governments, such as Fernando Grande Marlaska, and others without any known political affiliation, such as Javier Gómez Bermúdez, who was presiding judge of the Chamber of the National High Court that tried the 11-M terrorist case, and investigating judge Pablo Ruz.

What the Socialist Party has sought, with its strategy of co-opting outstanding names from the Spanish judiciary, has been to associate its image with the image of judges who represented, at that time, the fight against the social scourges that socialism wanted to eradicate: the fight against corruption, illegal party financing, terrorism and tax fraud. It is for this reason that, in the nineties, the Socialist Party included in its electoral lists prestigious names amongst the judiciary, such as Baltasar Garzón, Ventura Pérez Mariño, Margarita Robles and Juan Alberto Belloch. They were the star appointments in the last government of Felipe González. José Luís Rodríguez Zapatero also signed on judges, such as José Antonio Alonso, who was Minister of the Interior and Justice, and José de la Mata, who after his political experience joined the National Court, covering the post of Judge Pablo Ruz and continuing with the investigation of important cases, such as the Gürtel case.

In the course of Pedro Sánchez's term of office, at a time when the fight against corruption is taking over the media agenda and the judicialization of politics permeates the media, there has been a return to Felipe González's commitment. Well-known judges, such as Margarita Robles, who did not leave in the end, and Fernando Grande Marlaska, who had always been in the Socialist orbit, joined the Socialist government. Both Robles and Marlaska coincided in the General Council of the Judiciary as members designated by the Socialist Party. Posts of responsibility were also reserved for family justice and gender-based violence in Pedro Sánchez's new executive. These are the cases of Maria Galobart, a prestigious family judge and wife of the judge who was a member of Parliament in the González years, Ventura Pérez Mariño; and Pilar Llop, a judge specializing in gender violence, appointed as Speaker of the Senate.

With these appointments of prestigious judges, the Socialist Party does indeed secure its share of power, through judicial prestige, in the world of justice. It does not ensure control of the course of court proceedings, but it does make it easier for it to open the office doors of the top court officials. However, the judges who choose to take part in this dynamic of celebrity signings have no qualms about returning to their courts, the most relevant example being that of Baltasar Garzón. Garzón went from his seat in Congress and from the post of Secretary of State, to draft indictments against politicians who until a few days beforehand were sitting either on the opposite bench or occupying offices adjacent to his.

5.4 The Politicization of Justice

The clearest consequence of the existence of the political (or partisan) judge, subject to the instructions or interests of the party that appointed him, coupled with the judicialization of politics and misinterpreted or misunderstood judicial activism, is the emergence of the phenomenon that can do the most harm to a democratic society: the politicization of justice. The definition of this phenomenon is the use of the judiciary as an institutional tool for partisan purposes, under the guise of respect for the law. This includes all the elements that are required of lawfare: legal prosecution of the opponent, cloaked in claimed legality, and a prior or subsequent media lynching of political dissent. This perversion, as Gustavo Zagrebelsky, former President of the Italian Constitutional Court, writes, means "the strongest, most infamous and delegitimizing accusation that can be made of a constitutional court, [...] that of acting or having acted politically; this is a much more serious accusation than that of having made a mistake in a ruling."[15] So there can be no politicization of justice without the acquiescence of the judges themselves.[16]

The politicization of justice – as well as political judges in their partisan ways – is another shortcoming of the party system, a transgression of party democracy. The use of the judiciary to achieve unattainable political goals within particular institutions, in the words of Daniel Innerarity,[17] in order to manage complexity, wrestle with uncertainty, ensure sustainability, and structure accountability, is to distort the political system. Democracy is basically a system built upon the value of discrepancy, the negotiation of dissent and consensus, and the recognition of plurality. It is not for the judiciary to ensure compliance with these variables: it has to comply with just as valuable other variables, but not these. A ruling cannot resolve what should have been debated, amended, transacted and agreed upon by institutions made up of democratically elected people to fulfil this function.

To transfer the function of a power or institution that acts in accordance with a logic and is regulated by a series of processes by virtue of that logic, to another institution that has not been conceived or prepared for this role is to distort the political system. In the case of Spain, as we have seen, this dynamic started at the beginning of the democratic system, based on a calculated deviation from the principle of equality forged by the bipartisanship between the Socialist Party and the Popular Party. The Spanish High Court has handed over its independence and its presupposed submission to the law to a system of political loyalties. The three major associations of the judiciary – the Professional Association of the Judiciary, the Francisco de Vitoria Association of Judges and Magistrates, and the Association of Judges for Democracy – which are aligned with the Popular Party and the Socialist Party respectively – have done little to help in this context. They have moved the struggle of political parties to the realm of judicial associations.

Part Two

Lawfare, or the Criminalization of the Catalan Independence Movement

Chapter 6

Lawfare

The Strategy of Legal Repression

There is a certain consensus that lawfare is the result of the continuation of politics by non-political means. Lawfare requires the connivance of the judiciary with the political promoters of the manoeuvre in the courts and the judicial procedure. At the end of the day, it also requires the violation of the law in the name of the law itself. The aim of the whole operation is to obtain 'political cleansing'. This is how forcefully Silvina Romano expresses herself (Romano. 2019: 29). This "cleansing" of the political adversary is carried out on the basis of several variables:

- Creation or modification of rules to make a criminal offence of claims or conduct that were previously reserved for the political sphere.[1]
- A careful selection of cases taken to the penal courts, as well as the selection of the courts eligible to try the cases.
- If need be, exorbitant demands of prison sentences and civil liabilities, as well as conviction to severe penalties.
- Flagrant disregard for basic rights during all judicial procedures.
- Construction of judicial intelligence evidence to justify precautionary measures for the duration of the proceedings.
- Fabrication of a criminal story in the media that makes a disproportionate condemnation acceptable by public opinion.

And, at the root of this action, there is a clear desire to discourage the exercise of politics (Romano 2019: 29). Law, therefore, becomes a "war weapon" or a punitive instrument that comes into its own by persecuting, retaliating against and eliminating the political enemy through the exercise of violence that is revealed to be symbolic. But violence it is at the end of the day.

Lawfare, however, is an unequal war. Those who promote this strategy are those who control the main instruments of power: the judiciary, the media and the monopoly of those who legislate and interpret the law. And enjoying control of the law, both in its formulation and its interpretation – not to mention its application – means enjoying absolute control of the political, economic and social scene. It can condition or, directly, eliminate freedom. Freedom in all its dimensions: expression, movement, ideology. It can eliminate a person's assets by imposing disproportionate penalties or massive seizures. It can stigmatize, suspending, eliminating or prohibiting the exercise of work or professional activities, and condemning them socially.

That is why a war of this nature is not merely a criminal proceeding. It is much more than that. It requires a synergy between the judicial process, the political will to fuse the powers of the State in the pursuit of a common goal, and the necessary media condemnation to situate the subject against whom the process is directed as part of a dangerous collective. An enemy to be eliminated. A *hostis*.

The pro-sovereignty *Procés* in Catalonia began in June 2010 with the publication of Constitutional Court Judgment 31/2010, known as the "ruling of the Statute," which reached its peak with the Referendum on self-determination held on October 1, 2017, and the unilateral declaration of independence proclaimed in Parliament on October 27, 2017. That was the trigger that activated the defence of the *raison d'état*. The treatment of the pro-sovereignty movement (political parties, civil associations, leaders, organisations and the media) has been the object of a brutal war that began as a police operation and ended up as a judicial one. So-called "Operation Catalonia" was the precursor to a macro-trial that is now being staged in various courts throughout Spain. The whole process was deliberately strategic, as we shall see.

What began as a conflict of a territorial nature, which could be debated and resolved by the two Parliaments – the Catalan Parliament and the Spanish Parliament – became a process of monitoring the constitutionality of the resolutions and decisions taken by the institutions of the Catalan government. But there came a time when the Spanish government decided to raise the stakes. It was no longer enough to annul, or declare the actions null and void, in order to remove them from their binding nature; it was necessary to criminalise this territorial conflict and bring in the criminal jurisdiction through an amendment to the LOTC.[2] The Spanish Public Prosecutor's Office and the courts played the game. And what was a territorially-based political conflict was transformed into a criminal macro-trial with a clear objective: to smash a whole social movement through the imprisonment, disqualification and seizure of the assets of its main political and social leaders. In terms of its objectives, this is the driving force behind the Spanish *lawfare* strategy.

6.1 The Triple Dimension of the Legal War

On the basis of these elements, which we have outlined above, we can determine the characteristic traits that are essential for assessing whether a particular form of political action responds to a desire to activate (or not) a strategy of judicial warfare, based on a twisted and self-interested use of the law. To the extent that lawfare is a strategy of legal warfare, it is interesting to highlight the most important elements in order to provide a more elaborated vision of the phenomenon. Orde Félix Kittrie states that, in order to subsume an action within what we consider to be lawfare, it is necessary to pass two tests: (1) the executor must use the law to create effects equal or similar to those traditionally sought by conventional military warfare, and (2) the motivation of the executor must be to weaken or destroy a political adversary.[3] It is fair to say that Spain's judicial battle strategy against sovereignty passes Kittrie's double test.

However, although Kittrie focuses on lawfare in its international dimension, other authors also warn of the use of this judicial battle strategy to confront internal disputes, clearly political in nature, within a State, with the aim of neutralizing a territorialised minority with strong political aspirations.[4] Indeed, it is this application of *lawfare* that we wish to underline in its three dimensions.

6.1.1 The Strategic Dimension

The purpose of lawfare responds to a political will to use law – the legal system in general – as a weapon of war that replaces traditional military means to achieve an operational objective. This objective is to liquidate the previously identified enemy.

Having established a first element – the legal method – it is necessary to develop a second element, which is the means. Insofar as the method is the use of the legal system, it is logical to question the judiciary as the most appropriate means. It could be said that, in this dynamic of legal warfare, the judges' togas have come to replace military uniforms. There is a further similarity that connects the two estates with lawfare: this phenomenon has been called a soft *coup d'état* (or one in the hands of judges and prosecutors), the traditional *coup d'état* being the sole patrimony of the military establishment. Law replaces arms, a fact that tends to be more digestible for citizens in terms of cost-benefit. This strategic will to transfer power from the executive to the judiciary is one of the reasons that justify the judicialization of politics.

Indeed, the judicialization of politics and judicial activism are two phenomena that hide a clear intention to achieve social mobilisation for the defence of rights and freedoms by placing the interpretation of these rights in the hands of judges. In the case of lawfare, the judiciary assumes a greater degree of activism insofar as it will be called upon to become a powerful tool of war to annihilate the political enemy through a twisted use of the law. It will no longer be just a repression of rights; it will be their violation. In terms of strategy, it means that the judiciary takes over the powers of repression and social control that were previously exercised with absolute diligence by the military. This has been the case in Spain, but also in many countries in South America's 'Southern Cone', especially Argentina[5] (Cristina Fernández de Kirchner) and Brazil[6] (the Lula Da Silva and Dilma Rousseff cases).

An example related to the lawfare against Catalan independence serves to illustrate this transfer of functions from a strong power (the army) to a weaker power (the judiciary). During the Transition period, the defence of the unity of the State was entrusted, by constitutional mandate, to the Army via Article 8 of the Constitution. Today, this defence of unity has ended up being taken over by the judiciary. Both bodies are characterised by a strong sense of statehood, a very conservative political ideology and a close relationship with power. The difference lies in the degree of social acceptability. For this reason, when the machinery of the State was activated, the judiciary proved to be the most reliable means of fighting against Catalan independence and, at the same time, it has not been questioned by a large part of Spanish society. It has even been tolerated by a significant part of Catalan society.

6.1.2 The Judicial Dimension

In recent years, the judiciary has become a powerful position from which to articulate and deploy strategies of destabilisation and political persecution almost without limits. The fact that it is the only power whose creation does not depend on popular sovereignty, but on complex mechanisms of political designation, exchange of favours or subject to loyalties, makes it practically immune to popular scrutiny. This *de facto* immunity, which is often transformed into impunity of action, allows it to operate at the whim of a supposed institutionality that makes use of experts and a jargon full of technicalities and that expresses itself through resolutions that are difficult for the average citizen to understand. This is presented as sophisticated, rigorous, cultured, expert language, far removed from the vulgarity of politics.

Lawfare operates 'from above'. That is to say, by means of judicial apparati that rise above the executive and legislative powers, broadening the room for manoeuvre of the high judiciary to the detriment of the Government or Parliament (Domingo 2009: 50). This transfer of power, by means of the monopoly on the interpretation of the law, from the execution of precautionary measures and the handing down of judgments, provokes the phenomenon that Hirschl called *juristocracy*.[7] The characteristics of the judiciary are distorted, and it takes on the role of a power at the service of a governmental strategy with clear political aims. Juristocracy is a way of curtailing democracy, cutting off the representative and deliberative channel, and leaving in the hands of an executing elite a political operation developed according to military criteria.

This judicial dimension involves one more element, which is at the basis of lawfare and which deserves a separate section: the political use of the law. Judges are no longer independent and are no longer subject to the law or to justice, but are transformed into a power that is subject to a political strategy that has elements typical of the deployment of a wartime operation.

6.1.3 The Media Dimension

Although its objectives are identical to military ones – destruction of the enemy – its forms are more subtle and are tolerated by public opinion. There is a term that sums it up perfectly: soft power. Legal warfare is less violent than traditional warfare, more aesthetic and less costly. It is also more intelligent and more understandable to the general public. Hence, a third necessary strategic element in the deployment of lawfare is the media and social networks. Walter Lippmann, a skilled journalist, was one of the first to write, in 1922, about the importance of the environment, stereotypes and public confidence in the media, with carefully selected and simply formulated messages. Hitler and Goebbels also grasped the importance of the fact that, in huge lies, the public always saw a percentage of truth. Trump is the latest example.

The manipulation of public opinion is another of the pillars on which to build a judicial war strategy. Any criminal case aimed at damaging the public image of a political opponent, in order to limit his freedom or silence his discourse, requires the help of warlike journalism. Negatively influencing public opinion in order to anticipate the consequences of an unjust conviction and damage the right to a defence requires a narrative. This narrative is often deployed by powerful think tanks which, duly financed by conservative governments, are capable of manufacturing expert opinions on issues that are uncomfortable for those in power. They construct self-serving narratives about national politics, about what might threaten the national interest – an indeterminate legal concept that they interpret according to their own needs and convenience – and about what ought to be removed from politics.

The media dimension, therefore, consists of developing and deploying a story to the media and social networks with the aim of creating a climate of hostility against the political target to be eliminated. The ultimate aim of this storytelling is to transform the presumption of innocence into a presumption of guilt, in such a way as to make a judicial conviction inevitable, allowing popular support for it and, at the same time, making it impossible for citizens to have a more critical verdict on the political action deployed. It is a question, as Christian Salmon says, of constructing a fiction and sharing it,[8] making it viral on the social media, confronting narratives, imposing *frames,* in such a way that the media, be they TV, radio or the social media, become the new scenario for *lawfare* operations.

6.2 The Political Use of the Law

Gustavo Zagrebelsky writes that Gustav Radbruch, who initially sympathised with the Nazi concept of law, published an article in 1946 – "Statutory Lawlessness and Supra-Statutory Law" – in which he investigated the reasons for the betrayal of law by German legal science linked to the Third Reich. The reason Radbruch found was the inability to distinguish law from the Law (Zagrebelsky. 2014:19). According to him, the jurists had been recruited by the Nazis using the same methods they had used with the soldiers: loyalty to a slogan. Whereas for the latter "an order is an order," for the former "the law is the law." Thus, as also happened during the Franco regime and during the Transition – the expression "from law to law" dates from that period – an uncritical obedience to the law was galvanized. The law, regardless of whether it was just or not, was the law, and it had to be complied with and enforced. *Dura lex, sed lex*. This is one of the legacies of the Franco regime that is still with us today.

The use of the law that the lawfare strategy proposes is not very far removed from this premise, nor is it a novelty. The basic premise was put forward by the French jurist Jean Bodin when he dealt with sovereignty in the classic *Six Books of the Republic*. Bodin distinguished between law and jurisdiction. Whilst law entailed equity, or the fulfilment of the ideal of justice, jurisdiction was nothing more than the mandate through which the sovereign exercised his/her power.[9] The law was just another expression of the use of force, and the state that acted in accordance with the law was a legitimate state. Nazism, Fascism and Francoism called themselves States of Law because they chose legalised violence as a political weapon. They sought to give legitimacy to their actions in the pursuit of the assassination of the enemy, the imprisonment of the dissident or the definition of someone as different, by means of a legal framework constructed by themselves – customized laws – with the aim of gaining total control of the requirements of legislative production: social consensus, public opinion and technical expertise (Zagrebelsky. 2014: 72).

By this, we mean that the use or distortion of the law, including the construction of rules *à la carte*, detaching them from the value of the law, is yet another of the characteristics of lawfare that connects it with an authoritarian system in its conception of politics. The treatment of the Catalan case is a clear example. The law can be a very powerful tool of war if the person in charge of interpreting and applying it does so for the benefit of one side and to the clear detriment of the other. This is the key to a lawfare strategy: the connivance between the executive power and the legislative power (in its dual role as a parliamentary majority that supports the government and, at the same time, is responsible for legislating) and the judiciary. In addition, of course, to the discursive blessing of the Spanish monarchy.

To be sure, a very legalistic conception of politics has taken root in Spanish political culture. It is as if politics revolved around a continuous interpretation of legal norms, in the context of which is a Constitution that, at present, is a machine that does not admit any other reading than the restrictive ones allowed by the Constitutional Court. This is why a conception of politics that consists of subsuming the incarnation of the facts within a normative framework and extending their legal qualification has taken hold. Hence, only what is legally correct is politically viable, according to the restrictive and narrow interpretation of the constitutional frameworks established by the Spanish high courts. Ignacio Sánchez Cuenca has called this narrow conception of politics *legalistic democracy*. Or, in other words, an interpretation of politics in legal terms: only that which is legally viable is politically possible.

This is how political demands have been interpreted through the various initiatives promoted by the Catalan Parliament and the Catalan government with the aim of holding a referendum or poll to exercise the right to decide Catalonia's future. They have always come up against the vision of the jurist (and not of the politician): as blocked, exclusionary and stuck to the norm. The answers given by the Prime Minister of the Spanish government, always based on the answer "No," entail a new way of facing up to the Catalan problem:[10] negationism. Xacobe Bastida writes that negationists are politicians who apply the jurist's method when they are questioned about any political question that is reasonably complex, such as exercising the right to decide or the right to self-determination. They then move on to the legal treatment of the question and affirm, says Bastida, that they are contrary to this right because article 2 of the Spanish Constitution prevents them from being in favour of it.[11] That is, they identify the juridical treatment of an issue and make it coincide with their ideological opinion.

The problem gets worse when the law is used as a weapon, when the interpretation of the law ceases to seek the ideal of justice and moves towards vengeance. It is then that the law becomes an instrument of social and political control and facilitates the transition from a democracy – which we have often described as legalistic – to a violent authoritarian state.

6.3 Punitive Populism

Gregorio Cámara Villar wrote that, when politics falls to pieces, it is from the justice system that salvation is sought.[12] Specifically, it is from the judge, inasmuch as he is assumed to be the holder of a function of authority from which its former holders (politicians) have deserted. It is in this new scenario – writes Cámara Villar – that "judicialization ends up imposing its penal version on every relationship, be it political, administrative or social" (Cámara 2000: 46). This is none other than the strategy of the judicialization of politics, which is the basis of all lawfare strategies. And this – and nothing else – has been the aim of the Spanish government since the Catalan pro-sovereignty Process was forced to move towards unilateralism: to transform the Spanish State into a "State of judicial justice" or a "rogue State," a state in which judicial decisions enjoy greater legitimacy than political decisions and are much more effective because they have the force of law behind them. Lawfare, therefore, makes it possible to corner politics and transform the activities of a leader, a national minority or a social movement into activities that can be judged according to the certainty of the law.

But not of any law. Constitutional control of political activity through the Constitutional Court is no longer sufficient. With the manoeuvre of lawfare, the idea is to establish whether or not political activity is susceptible to being classified as a crime. Administrative law disappears, constitutional law is swept aside, and criminal law is forcibly broken. All of this has led to a process of delegitimization of political activity and reinforcement of the function of social control by the examining magistrates. The latter are called upon to intervene fully in political activity by issuing provisional measures that are often disproportionate, or directly contrary to the law.

In the Catalan case, the desire to criminalise the pro-sovereignty movement in the context of a constitutional conflict first called for the installation in the collective imagination of the society where the strategy of lawfare is applied, a language that has been defined in the Spanish State as one of tension. In other words, activating all the courts and media outlets that actively collaborate with lawfare in order to pass off a specific political claim as criminal conduct. This is when the crime of rebellion takes on its *raison d'être*, which will be repeatedly invoked insofar as it is the one that best fits in the Spanish collective imagination as a detriment to the national interest. Associating the Catalan pro-independence movement with the Basque terrorist group ETA contributed to arousing inflamatory pronouncements on television and radio and in political forums. This verbal inflation was also to be transferred to the social media.

Recent history confirms that an explosive cocktail in which rebellion, ETA, the *coup d'état* spirit and a desire to establish a Republic – the word Republic in Spanish right-wing and centre-right spheres is simply unacceptable – is the most effective device for calling for the elimination of the political enemy.[13] And when all this happens, then what has come to be known as Symbolic Criminal Law comes to the fore. Or *punitive populism*. And symbolic criminal law or punitive populism is nothing more than the application of the Criminal Code as a response to a supposed demand for security, with the consequent increase in punishments, the ultimate aim of which is to calm the fears of public opinion.[14]

Chapter 7

Dual State

Repression in its Exceptional Dimension

At the theoretical basis of Nazi legal doctrine there are illustrious names that are not unknown to us. Criminal law, philosophy of law, political law (constitutional, in its current version) or theory of State are areas of the social sciences where quotations from Karl Larenz, Alfred Rosenberg, Edmund Mezger and Carl Schmitt himself are abundant. If we talk about the Nazi judiciary, we cannot fail to mention the name of Roland Freisler, a famous president of the People's Court, who was feared and hated inasmuch as he personified the abuse of power. Although authors such as Pérez Luño have described the Nazi legal regime as being "a perversion of the legal system,"[1] it is no less true that, within it, we come across many analogies that might be – and are – occurring today with the way the Spanish State is legally and judicially treating the Catalan independence movement.

Of course, the situations are not comparable, but it does not cease to be worrying that in the 21st century one should need to resort to legal analogies that take us back to one of humankind's most dire periods. And it is in the area of these similarities that we stumble across names of jurists and political scientists, perhaps less well-known but no less important than those already mentioned, who explained Nazism's perversion of the law. They told how a large part of the German judiciary gave up the power to think, and acted under the dictatorship and arbitrariness of the Nazi elites. They tried to explain, based on the theoretical analysis of the legal doctrines of the School of Kiel or the rulings issued by the Nazis, the atrocities of a legal and political weapon designed to annihilate the enemy.[2]

Many of these jurists were forced into exile when Hitler came to power. For this reason their works were written in English before being translated into German, and this probably delayed the interest they present today in explaining certain legal and political situations, such as the one we set out in this chapter. This is the case of Hermann Heller, Otto Kirchheimer, Franz Neumann and Ernst Fraenkel, among others. In particular, we need to take a look at the work of this last author.

7.1 Fraenkel's Dual State

When Ernst Fraenkel – a Social Democrat student of Carl Schmitt who went into exile in the United States – drew up a legal-political theory of the dictatorship, he did so to denounce the existence of a Dual State in Nazi Germany.[3] In this dichotomous State two views of law and politics could be distinguished: (1) the *Normative State,* in which the constitutional legal system governed and legal certainty prevailed, and (2) the *Prerogative State* (or Exceptional State), in which arbitrariness reigned. These two States, which in fact coexisted within the same State, were two sides of the same coin. The Normative State was regulated by rules; in the Prerogative State measures were justified. These obeyed political decisions not subject to any control by the courts, and this signalled the complete collusion between the executive and the judiciary. The executive made decisions outside the existing regulatory framework, and the judiciary disregarded its role as guardian of the system, of the rights and obligations that derive from it. There were no legal rules governing the political sphere.

Fraenkel described a reality in which two worlds coexisted: the State and the Party. Legally constituted authorities and traditional civil servants were part of the Normative State. The Prerogative State was controlled by parallel organizations of the Nazi Party.[4] As the historian and expert on Fascism, Robert O. Paxton, explains, this coexistence of the two States in a single State created a fiction. While the former recruited and promoted civil service elites according to the rules of bureaucracy, in the latter the rule to be applied was the whim of the rulers, the reward for party members or the purported destiny of the *Volk* (people).[5] This coexistence of parallel realities gave the regime a strange mixture of legality and arbitrary violence. It is worth noting that Hitler never officially abolished the 1919 Constitution of the Weimar Republic and never dismantled the Normative State in Germany; but nor did he let himself be held back by that regulatory framework.

The Führer's *decision* was the only source of law. Only he could decide when to do without the Constitution or when to abide by it. It was Carl Schmitt's *decisionism* in its purest form. This way of doing things, praised by the President of Spain's Supreme Court in the presentation of the 2020 judicial year, is what we analyse below, since it has taken place in the final phase of the independence process. The application of Article 155 of the Spanish Constitution is in line with the logic of exceptionality and the application of a Dual State; it is the backbone of the charges in the political trial against the leaders of the Catalan independence movement and is the cornerstone of Spanish lawfare.

7.1.1 Duality and Exceptionality

During the independence Process we have seen several actions by the Spanish State – actions that, we insist, become an option of confrontation in the face of a political problem – that allow one to affirm the existence of this Fraenkelian duality even before the supreme expression of the exceptionality: the application of Article 155. One example is "Operation Catalonia," but it has not been the only one. *Decisive* actions – this is the appropriate word, as we shall see below – by spheres of government, beyond parliamentary and judicial control, have divided the State in two. As we have noted, the source of these measures is a government decision from which they take effect. Let us return to Schmitt and his theory of political decision-making in confronting the enemy. It is at this point that the old debate between Carl Schmitt's decision-making and Hans Kelsen's normativism is reborn, at least in academic terms.[6]

Although we shall analyse it later, let us stop for a moment to look at "Operation Catalonia." That operation was no exception in the independence Process. It was the first practical demonstration of the Dual State. The analysis of what has happened in Catalan politics since the Process became unilateral has to be seen from this perspective, insofar as the actions of the main institutions of the Spanish State, in collusion with a Deep State that has been applying them since then – criminalization of the independence movement and application of Article 155 of the Spanish Constitution – followed criteria, based on convenience and opportunity, to achieve the goal sought. The goal was to pursue and repress political dissent, to slash basic rights and freedoms: in short, to liquidate the independence movement. As Josep Maria Vilajosana writes, this form of action is framed within the defence of the supreme value of national sovereignty, and this defence uses the tools offered by the rule of law, but also the deployment of measures that involve a situation of exceptionality.[7]

The way the referendum of October 1 was treated anticipates institutional violence in the same way that the imprisonment of Jordi Sánchez and Jordi Cuixart – and, later, the political leaders of the Process, including the Speaker of the Catalan Parliament – is the first act in this judicial repression, one that confirms the setting up of a political trial against the independence movement. Can anyone seriously hold that the dirty police war called "Operation Catalonia," the police violence of October 1, the locking-up of the main political pro-independence leaders, and the pressure on the main companies based in Catalonia to change their registered offices to other autonomous regions, amount to an application of the Spanish legal system? Obviously not. This Deep State has acted motivated by the sole purpose of defending the unity of the State. To make this possible, the main lines of action that separate the three powers of the State have had to be blurred. Moreover, a network of political connivance has been set up between the executive and the top levels of the judiciary and the Constitutional Court, and the monarchy as well.

This collaboration in the defence of unity above any other consideration has also entailed costs. The main one is the systematic violation of constitutional rights, which has affected both political representatives and citizens. The victims have not necessarily been politicians or citizens who, individually or collectively, have supported the pro-independence movement; it has also affected citizens and politicians who, according to their line of thought, have been able to question the unity of the State. Freedom of expression and assembly, the right to vote and to be elected, the right to freedom, the right to physical integrity, the right to an impartial judge and to the court established by law, the principle of criminal legality and the right to a criminal trial with all the guarantees: all these rights are recognized in the Constitution and in the European Convention on Human Rights (ECHR), and they are rights that have been violated by virtue of the defence of the unity of the State.

7.1.2 Law and Arbitrariness

As we have already noted, the quality of a political system – its effectiveness in the deployment of its constitutional framework, among other issues – depends on the operation of the mechanisms provided for the control of the exercise of power. These mechanisms, by definition, must be legal and political and must be present in the Constitution. They cannot be limited to legal-political literature; they must have real effectiveness. Uncontrolled power tends to turn a regime into an arbitrary one or, at worst, into a totalitarian dictatorship based on models of total injustice, especially – but not only – when it comes to dealing with minorities. By this we mean that in Spain, in accordance with the legalistic rhetoric inherited from the Franco regime – a constant invocation of the *lawful State* and the *rule of law* – a discourse has been developed which is focused on guarantees and controls. This discourse which, over time, has ended up gaining the support of academics, has been part of political and social agreements and has been adopted by legal operators.

But, as we have seen, as the constitutional framework was being constructed, a system of hidden and tacit countermeasures was being forged in parallel: a kind of Dual State in order to block the functioning of the official system, which, even if it respected the letter, transgressed the spirit.[8] As Alejandro Nieto says, there are two dialogues: (1) the official discourse (politicians, academics and the media praise the constitutional system); and (2) social discourse (the effective application of the defence of guarantees and fundamental rights fails, but no one criticizes it). This is the only way the double discourse of the hegemonic parties in Spain can be understood: when you are in opposition, you criticize the system; but when you are in power, you use it. The fact is that this system of countermeasures is a Parallel State, which is useful in serving the interests of the ruling party or, at best, the two hegemonic parties – the Popular Party and the Socialist Party – in order to defend key points related to political issues which, through tacit agreements, have been removed from public debate. This is what we call *raison d'état*.

It is perfectly clear that this duality – or system of hidden or tacit countermeasures – is a reality which is present in Catalonia. The area of political discretionality has been displacing or gaining ground within the space reserved for the regulatory framework. It should be made clear that this duality is not a political phenomenon that begins and ends with the independence process, but with the independence process this duality has reached its high point in the post-1978 Spanish constitutional era. What has happened with Catalonia is that the dual system (or tacit countermeasures) has been so marked that the interests of the Popular Party government – or the parliamentary majority formed by the Popular Party, the Socialist Party and also Ciudadanos – have been blatantly transferred to the judiciary, merging the three powers into one.[9] And the monarchy also took part, as was evident in the King's speech broadcast on October 3, 2017.

Such a merger is common when two States are fused in a single State. As Robert O. Paxton explains, the Nazi Prerogative State colonized the Normative State and contaminated its functioning until, once the war began, the Prerogative State gained almost total domination (Paxton 2019: 383). When the Dual State is put into operation, the Prerogative State tends to colonize, to impose itself, to absorb the Normative or Constitutional State.

The essence of the Catalan independence Process has been to question the *demos* in the framework of the Spanish State: which is the sovereign entity capable of making a decision on that concept which jurists, such as Mercè Barceló,[10] have called the natural and fundamental *metalaw*, the unity of the State? Given the importance of the challenge, the duality – or the deployment of countermeasures – has not only taken place in the judicial sphere. Other strategic areas have also been subjected to counterbalances. One of the areas in which the Dual State has penetrated

Catalonia most forcefully is the economy. The Economics Ministry has been a bulwark in the application of Schmittian decisionism since the independence Process advanced along the path of unilateralism. The finances of the Generalitat were affected long before the application of Article 155 of the Spanish Constitution. The State did everything it could to persuade companies to move their headquarters away from Catalonia, in an unprecedented political decision in a European democracy. The only justification was the appeal to fear and the dread of losing competitiveness with an independent Catalonia.[11]

7.2 Specifying the Deep State

The duality we have theorized about implies the existence of a Deep State – up to now we have described it as a Prerogative State – that operates within the State. Deep State is a concept that has returned to the media after years of silence. It could be said that the Deep State is the updated version of Fraenkel's Prerogative State. It has returned in the midst of conspiracy theories that have tried, at best, to explain Donald Trump's accession to the White House.[12] These elites – or political operators – defend interests that are not aligned with democratic variables or the general interest, but comply with incentives that are not entirely clear, but that protect and defend outside what can be decided by legitimately elected governments. From now on, we shall call it Deep State: a State within the State.

North American society, however, is no stranger to internal wars provoked by a mysterious State power operating in the shadows or outside the interests of the government apparatus. The assassination of the Kennedy brothers or the corruption of Richard Nixon, in what became known as the Watergate affair, have been explained in terms of theories at the epicentre of which there was a quango operating outside the State or being confused with the State. No one knew who they were, although their existence was known to all. The emergence in American public life of figures such as Roger Stone and Steve Bannon once again put on the public agenda the existence of a shadow State capable of exercising a counter-power to prevent or to tolerate the deployment of public policies driven by the Trump administration. In Spain, the coup attempted by Civil Guard Colonel Tejero on February 23, 1981 is one of the still unsolved mysteries, but in the explanation of which a theory of the Deep State takes root.

C. W. Mills wrote about the Deep State phenomenon many years ago. His is the classic *The Elite of Power*, published in 1956.[13] Mills reasoned that the powers of the common man – his work, his family life – were controlled by forces that could never be understood. But Mills went even further when he argued, in relation to the United States in the 1950s, that the country was ruled by a diffused reality or, rather, by an interconnected network of family elites who had attended the same schools, who belonged to the same clubs and secret societies, the same boards of directors, and which even arranged marriages amongst themselves. These elites were the ones who truly made decisions about the direction that American politics should take. But this sociological explanation did not make an impact beyond the academic world.

Robert Dahl also tried to explain, but at the local level, specifically in the city of New Haven (Connecticut), in the no less classic *Who Governs?*,[14] how the decision-making process was really articulated. The question Dahl asked was, Who decides? A democratically elected City Council based on a democratically based deliberative process, or an elite mobilized to impose its preferences? This was a field of academic research that began to interest economists, sociologists, and political scientists around the world.

Lately researchers from prestigious universities have begun to investigate who is pulling the strings, who is behind the most important State institutions, and how these elites reach the leading posts in the shadows.[15] In recent years, specialized journals, such as *Administration & Society* and *Administrative Theory & Praxis,* have published articles that try to explain phenomena such as governance from the bowels of the State by elites who have not been democratically elected and are not accountable to anyone.

Journalists have also tried to explain the configuration of a space of power that is blurred, active, transversal, but limited to a few social strata with a great capacity for decision-making and influence. Investigative journalism, or more or less essay literature, has tried to offer an explanation for this hidden State that operates outside democratic procedures, which is dark rather than transparent, and which responds to the designs of elites' preferences, far removed from the public interest. A case in point is a classic piece of modern journalism, *All the President's Men*, by Carl Bernstein and Bob Woodward, granted that one of its most important characters (Mike Feld, a former FBI agent) insisted on being identified by the nickname *Deep Throat*.

7.2.1 The Spanish Deep State

The Deep State in the Spanish framework could be defined as the senior officials who act in accordance with the political, economic and military elites who – regardless of the party or parties exercising political power, in accordance with results achieved through free and democratic elections –

exercise its decision-making power. They are a State outside the State. As defined by Mike Logfren, one of the elements that best define the characteristics of the Deep State is its hybrid nature: a living organism, which acts and makes decisions, and which becomes the crossroads between different professional bodies (financial, industrial, senior officials), which respond to a variety of political interests.

In Spanish popular culture, this State within the State has been called *poderes fácticos:* i.e. 'The Powers that Be', a term that has been used a good deal when writing about the Transition. Other expressions of this period, such as sabre-rattling, identify something present, even threatening, that operates from the depths with great coercive power to impose its will without – or in connivance with – the institutions. It is this same popular culture that explains how, during the Franco regime, these Powers that Be – in the plural – were the Church, the Army and the big banks. But, as the sociologist Amando de Miguel explains, in his book *Sociología del Franquismo*, the high officials of the Francoist public administration also represented a body with a great capacity for political influence. This group is of particular interest, as the top echelons of public administration, including judges, come out of it later, acting as guardians of postulates that, due to their meta-rights nature, cannot be subjected to public debate.

In his analysis of Franco's public administration, De Miguel divided the stages of Franco's government into three: it was concerned with war, autarky and economic development, it was technocratic, and it was of the civil service. It was in the analysis of the stage corresponding to technocracy – but above all, that of the civil service – that De Miguel explained the importance that Political and Administrative Law academics had attained in terms of ideological discourse.[16] He gave examples of names who had been part of the official elites of the Francoist state: Javier Conde, Luís Sánchez Agesta, Torcuato Fernández Miranda, Laureano López-Rodó, Villar Palasí, Manuel Fraga, Rodrigo Fernández Carvajal, etc. In fact, he associated the political rise of the Professor of Administrative Law, Laureano López Rodó, with his ambitious plan for administrative reform, built around the *Escuela de Funcionarios de Alcalà*, which sought to become a kind of *École Nationale d'Administration*, the prestigious training centre for senior French officials (De Miguel 1975: 111).

The fact of the matter is that the will of the Franco regime was to turn the authoritarian State into a State of officials that would serve the ideological postulates of the regime. It worked perfectly. Moreover, officials – largely administrative specialists – did not limit themselves to executing orders; they went much further in their functions, acquiring significant levels of political power to the point of being confused with government bodies. A culture making the State their own was created. The State was the bureaucrats, in the same way that high-ranking officials are today. This fact, which may not seem very relevant now, was crucial when the Spanish government had to deal with the Catalan independence Process. It is the only way to explain why it responded to demands promoted by the institutions of the Generalitat from a normative point of view, a legacy of the functioning of the Franco administration and of the political conception – also linked to the process of legitimizing the Francoist repressive State – that only what is legal is legitimate, or that only what is supported by a legal norm is democratic. The rest is illegal and, as it is illegal, illegitimate. Or worse: it is likely to be prosecuted under the Criminal Code.

7.2.2 The Judicial Deep State

The journalist and sociologist Andrés Villena states that one tends to think that this network of interests – as he defines the State within the State – forms "an architecture of social power alternative to the main journalistic narrative and even to the textbooks of conventional political science" (Villena 2019: 16). But who belongs to this State within the State? What, in Spain, are these networks of power that Andrés Villena points to? He himself answers the question: "we refer to the main political parties in the system, especially those that have formed recent governments, but also large companies, Spanish or not, integrated in the IBEX 35 Stock Exchange or with bases abroad, and of course top finance." And he concludes: "We also include [...] the elite bureaucratic power, be it judicial, diplomatic, legal or fiscal, inserted in State institutions" (Villena 2019: 16). Consequently, the judiciary, like the Public Prosecutor's Office or the State Attorney's Office, is, according to Villena, one of the components of this Deep State which makes decisions outside government or in agreement with government.

This is where the General Council of the Judiciary becomes important, as a body that both directly and indirectly proceeds to the appointment of the presidencies and members of the chambers of the top Spanish high courts, including the Supreme Court and the National Court. And it is in this context, too, that the pact is imposed between the two major parties to distribute, through the system of sponsorships and quotas, the most important judicial appointments, including the judges of the Constitutional Court and the members of the Court of Auditors. It is at this point that names become important, or, more specifically, the capacity and level of obedience of these names is decisive in order, in their jurisdictional function or taking advantage of their power as judges, to carry out the political guidelines sent by the main parties. All this is part of a system for recruiting judges whom the top Spanish courts co-opt – not all of them, but many.

These names are the last bastion of the system, those who make it possible to achieve a minimum of legal certainty and a maximum of political impunity. The top judiciary is, in practice, the true administrative elite that achieves most power, holds it longest and is not accountable to anyone. It is precisely these elements – the direct appointment by the two major parties, and the capacity for servitude in their political agenda, the permanence over time and their impunity – that characterize them as a State within the State. A true Deep State.

And when are they called upon to act? When is this State in reserve mobilized? When does the Fraenkelian duality begin to unfold as the Deep State?

In our view, it does so when society, politics or the economy attain a certain degree of autonomy that develops into social or legal changes that the Deep State cannot control or does not dare to tolerate, or when these social changes are of such magnitude that they threaten to tear down the main walls on which the *raison d'état* stands. That is when the Deep State decides to act. It does so by means of seemingly legal mechanisms, such as those outlined in the first part of this book. These seemingly legal instruments are not questioned by the public. The State uses the aura of social prestige that usually accompanies the top judiciary. These legal mechanisms in the hands of judges – which we have described as *counter-rules,* or the political use of legal rules, or *à la carte* interpretations of poorly regulated regulatory spaces – allow for the effective deployment of lawfare.

Moreover, these three systems of manipulation of the law allow the exercise of control over constitutionally designed and strategically crucial institutions to exercise, precisely, the control of political power. This is what Alejandro Nieto calls the manipulation of control by the controlled (Nieto 2003: 385). Or, to put it another way, it allows them to deploy a legal battle strategy with the least possible adversity and the maximum consensus among the population.

7.3 The Specification of Exceptionality

Another aspect of the lawfare against the Catalan independence movement that reinforces the exceptionality and duality of the strategy followed by the Spanish State is the way in which criminal law and procedural law are applied. This is so especially in the case of criminal law of exception in its most up-dated version since the 9/11 attacks on the Twin Towers. The last resort in law was the legal-political tool chosen to proceed with the elimination of the enemy by the application of disproportionate penalties and the limitation of his rights and freedoms. The most explicit legal manifestation of this will to eliminate the enemy is Organic Law 4/2015, of March 30, on the protection of public security, better known as the "Gag Law." The aim of the norm was to create a climate of fear in the population – a chilling effect, in the words of the ECHR – to discourage the exercise of fundamental rights linked to protest. Criticism of the government – or State institutions, including its unity – was seen as an act that increased insecurity. From there, the law allowed law enforcement to activate the punitive mechanisms of the discretionary state.

7.3.1 Criminal Law of the Enemy

The Spanish State – and this has been recognized by illustrious criminal law specialists, such as Muñoz Conde[17] – has never renounced the application of the criminal law of exception. Spain was not the only totalitarian State to use the criminal law of the enemy to fight off dissent. The totalitarian regimes of Hitler, Mussolini, Stalin, and the dictatorships of the American South Cone in the 1970s and 1980s (Argentina, Chile, Paraguay and Brazil), applied a harsh criminal law of exception in order to annihilate the political enemy. The case before us, which burst into the Spanish political reality well inside the 21st century, is defined by Muñoz Conde in terms of three premises:[18]

1. To criminalize social conduct that poses no real danger to protected legal assets: this leads to an early application of criminal law to the extent that conduct is criminalized by creating crimes of mere abstract danger, emphasizing new, diffuse supra-individual legal assets, such as public security or public order.
2. To raise the criminal scale of certain offences, to introduce security measures after serving the sentence, to apply life imprisonment and the death penalty for crimes that under normal circumstances would not justify their application.
3. To abolish the right to "due process," which may mean admitting hearsay evidence, or evidence such as wiretapping without a prior court order, or aggressive interrogation techniques, or to extend the duration of police arrest without judicial control or, finally, to establish the creation of special courts.

If we move to the Spanish case and look into the antecedents of the Catalan conflict, we can observe how Muñoz Conde himself sees in the penalization of the call for a Basque referendum imposed by the Aznar government an anticipation of the intervention of Criminal Law moving towards the application of the enemy's criminal law (Muñoz Conde 2005: 41). What the Aznar government did, then, with an outright majority in Parliament, was to criminalize people who, using a democratic mechanism such as a referendum, wanted to challenge part of the citizenry in relation to a political conflict with territorial roots. The threat that Aznar wanted to fight against was not the fact itself (the calling of the referendum) but rather the existence of certain people (the visible head then was the *Lehendakari* – Basque President – Ibarretxe) who deviated from the supreme value that full obedience to the unity of the Spanish nation entailed. This was a phenomenon which not only affected Spain: it is known as *the expansion of criminal law*.

It is totally evident that, in the criminalization of the Catalan independence movement, there is a displacement of the criminal law of the facts to a criminal law of the author. What is important is no longer whether the fact committed fits into a juridical-criminal category; what is transcendental is who has committed the fact, in other words, the author.[19] Or to put it another way: the personal circumstances (thoughts, ideology, will) that have led someone to act in a certain way. Let us return to Edmund Mezger: the criminal law of the facts is the one that applies to citizens. The criminal law of the author is the one that is applied to the enemy. There has been no lack of criminologists who have seen in this citizen-enemy dichotomy, which is at the basis of the theories of Günther Jakobs, a reformulation of the Schmittian friend–enemy doctrine. Let us look at some examples.

For Francisco Muñoz Conde,[20] cited above, this ideological coincidence is that the differentiation of one criminal law for a citizen and another for the enemy – external or internal – is the famous distinction between "*Freund und Feind.*" The position of Guillermo Portilla Contreras is similar. He wrote that "the ideas of Jakobs on the criminal and procedural law of the enemy are closely linked to the concept of the politics of C. Schmitt."[21] Kai Ambos, of the University of Göttingen, is of the opinion that the speeches of Schmitt and Jakobs coincide.[22] They coincide, above all, in the will to create a discourse aimed at justifying the repression of the State so as to exclude entire groups of the population. Schmitt is the predecessor of the criminal law of the enemy, which, later, Gunther Jakobs was to develop. Eugenio Zaffaroni also sees links between the doctrine of Schmitt and Jakobs' theoretical formulation.[23] One of these points of connection is the

Absolute State. In the Schmittian doctrine, the power of the sovereign in the Absolute State has no limits, so that it can assert who is the enemy in order to eliminate it.

The arrest and imprisonment of the two leaders of the main pro-sovereignty Catalan NGOs – Jordi Sánchez, of the Assemblea Nacional Catalana (ANC), and Jordi Cuixart, of Òmnium Cultural – for having climbed onto the roof of a Civil Guard vehicle to call for calm on one of the many peaceful demonstrations experienced during the independence *Procés*, is an example of the application of legal arbitrariness to a situation where fundamental rights were being exercised (freedom of expression, demonstration and assembly). Such was the case, as well, of the pre-trial detention, for up to two years, ordered by Judge Carmen Lamela against Sandro Rosell, former President of Barcelona Football Club, who was later acquitted. Finally, the pre-trial detention, decreed by the same National Court judge, against the members of the Government of the Generalitat and the Speaker of the Catalan Parliament, amounted to the effective deployment of criminal law of the enemy to the Catalan lawsuit. These are examples, but they are not the only ones.

7.3.2 Procedural Law of the Enemy

Procedural Law of the author is part of a broader phenomenon: judicial populism. This consists of taking measures of a jurisdictional nature based on its media impact or on the expectations of one part of society against another, outside the legal system, or at the service of a distorted interpretation of the procedural legal framework. These procedural measures, once decided, are leaked to the press for the appropriate manipulation of this information. Naturally, the defence of those affected is aware of these measures, not through the proper procedural conduits, but through the media that make them public. This theoretical submission to the law that we saw as binding on judges is replaced by the needs, in terms of the political agenda, of the parties or the government. A synergy can be observed between the State and the State within the State.

The defencelessness of the defendant, the violation of fundamental procedural rights and the feeling of impunity of justice become factors that transform the ordinary process into a political process, as we shall see. In this conception of procedural law of the author, the structure of the Spanish criminal process in its initial phase helps the investigation of criminal acts. The Criminal Procedure Act of 1882 (LECrim) is still in force, after being the subject of numerous reforms, with its inquisitorial conception in regard to the investigation phase.[24] It is investigating judges who, from a more theoretical than effective surveillance function, are in charge of the phase of looking into the criminal facts and collecting evidence. At the same time, their function is to issue precautionary measures, with the corresponding danger of using and abusing powerful social control tools, such as pre-trial imprisonment.

But the degeneration of legal logic in the resolutions decreeing pre-trial detention, especially those related to the pro-independence political leaders examined during the investigation, reached its maximum expression in what is called "intelligence reports licence." The main purpose of the "intelligence reports" is to replace the lack of evidence. Their second function is to draw a criminal profile of an investigated political target, creating a story based on decontextualized, distorted or directly invented facts, which are not criminal in nature or which are distorted in order to end up giving them a criminal character. These "intelligence reports" are prepared by police units to provide them with instructions, with the danger, as has happened in the criminal proceedings against the Catalan pro-independence leaders, of it becoming sufficient evidence to order arrests or imprisonment.

These fraudulent procedures, such as the construction and use of scraps of clues as material made specifically to eliminate the political enemy, were then used as evidence in the trial. Once again, the criminal proceedings against Catalan independence meet the acid test. A chronicle by journalist Ernesto Ekaizer is illustrative: "Daniel Baena, a Civil Guard lieutenant-colonel who, under the name of Tacitus, had been considered to be the user of the Twitter account @maquiavelo1984, a vehicle of messages against independence – a circumstance that he denied – had been responsible for the Civil Guard reports in the investigation of the case for the trial, for Judges Antonio Ramírez Sunyer, head of the Court of Investigation No. 13 of Barcelona, for Carmen Lamela, in charge of the Central Court of Investigation No. 3 of the National Court and, finally, for Judge Pablo Llarena in the Second Chamber of the Supreme Court."[25]

There are more examples of this *à la carte* investigation, probably the most egregious of all being the issuing, and subsequent withdrawal, on grounds of political expediency, of a European Arrest Warrant by investigating judge Pablo Llarena, when the extradition had been granted by the High Court of the German *Land* of Schleswig-Holstein for embezzlement, but not for the crimes of rebellion or sedition. This misuse of a jurisdictional tool, such as the European Arrest Warrant, implies the judicial activism of a Prerogative State. A judge who acts according to criteria of political expediency, and not to criteria of legality, is a judge in the service of a Dual State or of a Deep State that blows up the constitutional principles of judicial independence and equality before the law.

All the elements we have seen tend to unfold a legal battle of the kind that Charles Dunlap called 'Unrestricted Warfare,' and what we have referred to as the lawfare strategy. The culmination of this strategy is to subject the enemy to a sham trial: in other words, a political trial.

Chapter 8

The Judicial State

The Implementation of Repression

We call a Judicial State one in which the activity of the government, legislative chambers, parties and political leaders depends on court rulings. In a Judicial State, the rulings of judges and magistrates fill the vacuum left by politics, or rather the renunciation of politics. Javier Pérez Royo has called it "subcontracting," in the understanding that the most transcendental elements that define the political life of a country – such as the success or failure of a motion of censure (or impeachment), the resignation or continuity of a politician involved in a criminal case, or the expansion or regression in the exercise of the most elementary civil and political rights – depend upon an interlocutory or a judicial sentence. Throughout this book we have referred to it as "juristocracy." And the culture of subcontracting, or juristocracy, is the basis of lawfare. The disqualification of an opponent, the validation of an electoral result or the simple fact of legislating, will depend on a judicial ruling issued by a court deformed in its essential functions. Victory in court will mark the success or failure of politics, in such a way that the scope of political action will be subject to the verdict of the courts.

We insist on one fundamental point. For a court, a judge or a prosecutor to enter the political arena, there must be a legal rule or authorization that allows them to do so. Indeed, in all logic, a political will that empowers them to do so. And, in the end, the judge has to play his part. The Catalan independence Process has been proof that these elements – legal authorization, political will and judicial acquiescence – have been fully in place. And they have occurred to such an extent that the Spanish State has gone from being a legalistic democracy (where political debate is reduced to a question of legality) to a Judicial State (where debate is replaced by interlocutory decisions and sentences). In other words, Spanish democracy has been reduced to a fictitious debate to see who was the most patriotic in defending the Constitution and the laws. This could be, in a nutshell, the summary of the pro-sovereignty Process explained in judicial terms.

8.1 The Judicial State. Or the Judicialization of Political Spaces

The judicialization of a country's political life implies an extension of the political power of judges. This is the main consequence of a lawfare strategy. It is tantamount to affirming that, with the judicialization of areas reserved to political action, the judiciary penetrates into spheres that are meant for the exercise of legislative and executive functions and becomes better adjusted to using mechanisms of social control. When the government empowers judges, what it is doing is redefining the relations between the powers or upsetting the balance between them. This tends to happen when the executive and legislative powers of a State – and the Spanish State, in this sense, is a good example – enter into a crisis of legitimacy, for which reason they opt to offer a legitimising discourse of strengthening the rule of law.[1] This is a constant feature of the 20th century, and of the 21st century, in Spain.

Once this consideration has been made, the following warning must be added: in contexts where justice is politicised, where democracy and the rule of law are weak, the judicialization of politics will hardly be able to solve problems of crisis between State institutions (Domingo. 2009: 37). Therefore, another element that characterises the strategy of the judicialization of politics is that it is closely related to the political and judicial culture of the country in which it is to be implemented. This culture has to do with a dichotomy that is at the root of many territorial conflicts. Either democracy is valued as a system on the basis of which disputes are resolved, or, conversely, as is the case in Spain, the rule of law is reinforced as a mechanism for resolving conflicts. To put it another way: to ponder what space democracy and the judiciary occupy – in the institutional design and in the collective imagination – as mechanisms for resolving social disputes. Once again, the constitutional crisis of a territorial nature between Catalonia and the Spanish State is proof that it is difficult for the courts to resolve territorial crises of a clearly political nature.

It is clear that the judicialization of politics is now a global issue, affecting many democracies. The analysis of law and political science can no longer be carried out in isolation from new concepts, such as judicial activism or the politicization of justice. There has been a mutation in judicial culture around the world. Each political system has to be able to implement these concepts according to the reconfiguration of its democratic values and its own judicial system. The tradition of a judge who applies rules on the basis of perfect logic to resolve basically private conflicts stems from civil law. It was the culture of a judge typical of the constitutional movements of continental Europe, in which judges exercised mechanical and apolitical functions. It was the vision of the priest-judge. Or of the "mouth of the law" judge. This tradition has disappeared. Or it has become obsolete.

As rightly exposed by Gustavo Zagrebelsky, the former President of the Italian Constitutional Court, the emergence of new social problems that call for the intervention of the judiciary forces a judge to leave his office and get involved in the resolution of problems that until then he had seen as alien to him. The judge is challenged and leaves the bench to go down to the political arena, from where he is called upon to resolve – based on an interpretation of the legal framework according to the social, political and economic context – controversies of a public nature. It is therefore recognised that the judge also has an ideology. Moreover, it is appreciated that the judge makes politics; but the judge's political ideology must be placed at the service of the law and of the society in which the application of the law takes place. Never at the service of partisan interests. Another phenomenon, known as the expansion of the judiciary, is now underway.[2]

Tate and Vallinder, who are the originators of the expression "expansion of judicial power," refer to the expansion of the radius of action of judges and courts to the detriment of the capacity of institutional politics to act. There is, therefore, a transfer of powers from the executive and the legislature to the judiciary in such a way that judicial decision-making is expanding into political areas where it has never before been present. But not only that: the methods of judicial decision-making are also transferred to public institutions beyond the judicial sphere itself. It is evident that this reduction in the decision-making space of political-representative institutions entails risks for democracy. Or, to put it another way: in systems where democracy is weak or not well established, the expansion of the judicialization of politics can mean that apparently unimportant aspects – such as language, argumentation, or the way of relating to society – become conditioned by the rhetoric of law.

Spain, a country with just over forty years of democracy after nearly forty years of dictatorship, is not at the same level as, for example, the United States. The United States, after two centuries of judicialization of politics – or judicial activity, which is sometimes but not always synonymous – has developed a system of checks and balances that were already provided for in the Constitution of 1787. Each power is limited by another power. This does not happen in Europe. Even less so in the Spanish State, where the powers are diffused into a single power or tend to be colonized, especially from the executive and legislative, to the judiciary. We now move from theory to practice by looking at what has been the unfolding of the lawfare strategy since its beginnings. How lawfare has transformed the Spanish State into a Judicial State, where the impact of police reports, judicial proceedings and the composition of courts is of great political importance. This means that we must focus, albeit briefly, on the police investigations and the communication slogans that are at the forefront of the judicial battle.

8.2 Operation Catalonia

In the nineteen-nineties, during what was known as the "legislature of tension" (Felipe González's last government, between 1993 and 1996), there was an outbreak of political scandals, amongst which State terrorism, led by the Anti-Terrorist Liberation Groups (GAL), was one of the most prominent. These, according to Xavier Casals, "were counter-terrorist squads, active in the French Basque Country between the latter part of 1983 and the summer of 1987, which attacked the left-wing militant group supposedly linked to ETA, causing 27 deaths." For Enrique Gimbernat, Professor of Criminal Law, the GALs were "a gang of murderers, torturers and kidnappers, organised by the Ministry of the Interior (and probably also by the CESID), that took almost thirty lives and made at least two people disappear in quicklime, after torturing them and making them dig their own graves, committing criminal acts that are among the most serious known to the Criminal Code."[3]

The GAL phenomenon, and, by extension, what was known as 'dirty warfare', was accompanied by another form of terrorism, that of the State, practised against the actual or alleged social environment of the terrorist group ETA, always making use of intimidation, torture and assassination. Although the whole GAL network was developed in the early years of the Socialist government led by Felipe González, it was not until the early nineteen-nineties that the 'dirty war' was made public as such. The investigations by Judge Baltasar Garzón and the political tension fuelled by what was known as the 'clamp' (a more rhetorical than programmatic opposition agreement between the PP and the IU), led to a fierce opposition that aimed to overthrow the PSOE government and put an end to Felipe González politically. The GAL case led to the condemnation of the Interior Minister, José Barrionuevo, and the Secretary of State for Security, Rafael Vera, as well as other important figures, such as Enrique Rodríguez Galindo, General of the Civil Guard in the Intxaurrondo barracks.

We have referred to the background of the GAL in order to explain the form of police response that the PP government was to come up with in reply to the Catalan pro-sovereignty Process. Or, to put it another way, the pro-sovereignty Process was not only fought from the judicial sphere; it was also fought from the police sphere. Specifically, the pro-sovereignty movement was a permanent focus of attention for the Ministry of the Interior, led by Jorge Fernández Díaz, with a clear intention to use what has been called dirty warfare, or institutional violence, to combat the independence Process. In order to define what is meant by "Operation Catalonia," we shall base ourselves on the conclusions of the report issued by the Committee of Inquiry into Operation Catalonia (CIOC) on the occasion of the approval of Resolution 529/XI of the Parliament of Catalonia.

The CIOC report considered that "Operation Catalonia is a conspiracy to try to curb political dissidence in Catalonia, and in particular the independence movement, a conspiracy that has been carried out, at least during the years in which Jorge Fernández Díaz (2011–2017) was the Spanish Minister of the Interior." The report goes on to state that "it is specified in a series of political, police and intelligence actions," the aim of which has been to "reduce social support for independence as a political option by discrediting it." For this reason, the Commission's report reaches the conclusion that the operation's nature is "reputational." In other words, it seeks criminalization based on "accusations, suspicions and slander of certain of the visible faces of the movement." The *modus operandi* – still following the CIOC account – was to work by creating police reports "that were constructed on the basis of false information with data obtained fraudulently and with ambiguous or anonymous sources, with the idea of fabricating a story that gives the appearance of an authentic and proven case in order to be able to pass it on later to the press or to be able to prosecute it."

The decision to stigmatise leaders of the pro-sovereignty movement, such as Artur Mas, Oriol Junqueras and Xavier Trias, was a priority objective from the beginning. Moreover, as a result of this desire to defame and undermine the social and political prestige of the leaders of the independence Process in media outlets sympathetic to the Spanish nationalist right, Operation Catalonia has also been known as "Les clavegueres de l'Estat" (the State Sewers). In this sense, another of the conclusions reached by the CIOC is the partisan use of the police under the command of Fernández Díaz: "This partisan use materialised in the creation of units outside the organic structure of the National Police Force." This political-police brigade, led by the Spanish government – according to the conclusions of the CIOC – is made up of "commissioners, detectives, agents, civil servants and senior officials of the Ministry of the Interior, and also members of other institutions, such as the Anti-Fraud Office of Catalonia and the judiciary."

Some key elements define Operation Catalonia as a police-style political device designed to delegitimize the movement from a "reputational" point of view with the aim of gaining social and, in turn, electoral support. One of these elements is the support of media outlets that become engaged in order to amplify the response of the fake news. As the CIOC states, the reports produced by the Economic and Fiscal Crime Unit (UDEF) to build up corruption cases or produce false reports "are leaked in related media (that collaborate with the whole operation), such as *El Mundo,* and are published by journalists who are part of the plot." The other element is the political timing of the moment at which these news items are published. Once again, it is the conclusions of the CIOC that offer the key: "the political calendar was being tampered with, especially taking into account the electoral contests in Catalonia (parliamentary elections, municipal elections, the November 9, Referendum, etc.), with the aim of ultimately affecting the mood of public opinion." The aim of the media smear campaigns was to influence the election results, a fact that no longer entailed a contest against the Catalan pro-sovereignty movement but a threat against the Spanish democratic system itself. In the meantime, the political police of Interior Minister Jorge Fernández Díaz, in collusion with despicable figures from the State's key institutions, such as the now-imprisoned police officer José Manuel Villarejo, was responsible for constructing a whole network of apocryphal reports that served as the basis for introducing the first judicial proceedings, on the basis of which many of the criminal cases against the pro-independence leaders were laid.

8.3 The Macro-Case Against the Pro-Independence Movement

Arguably, special case 20907/2017 is the criminal case with the greatest media impact amongst all those that the pro-independence movement has suffered. The political leaders of the Process have been tried and, moreover, the case was heard at the Supreme Court, with the symbolic dimension that that entails. But it has not been the only cause. The repression against the Catalan independence movement has taken place in many courts throughout Catalonia, Spain and Europe. And the legal proceedings have not only been heard before criminal courts: the contentious-administrative and constitutional courts have also been spheres of conflict where independence has been forced to appear and defend itself, so much so that it is not unreasonable to say that we are facing a macro-case against the Catalan pro-sovereignty movement.

Let us now narrow down our focus and concentrate on the judicial map resulting from the lawfare strategy, analysing the criminal cases and their derivatives, motivated, basically, by the violation and consequent defence of fundamental rights in higher courts. Our aim is to offer a snapshot of the judicial repression exerted against Catalan independence as a manoeuvre to eliminate political dissidence. We start from the special issue of the magazine *Sàpiens*[4] and the articles published in *La Vanguardia* by journalists Jaume Masdeu, Carlota Guindal and Santiago Tarín.[5] We shall distribute the cases by judicial interpellation, starting with the initial magistrates courts and ending with the highest courts in Spain. We shall divide these cases into two categories: ordinary jurisdiction and constitutional jurisdiction.

8.3.1 Cases in the Ordinary Jurisdiction

The first court to be looked at is the 13th Investigation Magistrate's Court in Barcelona. This is where it all began. It transformed a private case – under secret summary proceedings – over an alleged illegal use of personal data into a general case against the celebration of the referendum and against independence, without any legal basis. From the beginning, the competence of this court has been questioned for violation of the rules of distribution and, consequently, violation of fundamental rights.

The suspicions of partiality of the former President of the court, Juan Antonio Ramírez Suñer, were aggravated after he died. In his obituaries, as journalist Ernesto Ekaizer pointed out, the Spanish judicial right praised the fact that, despite the magistrate's illness, he did not cease to investigate the case, inasmuch as it was Spain that was at stake. Needless to say, Ekaizer was referring to *raison d'état*. Ramírez Suñer had given the order to the Civil Guard to enter private homes and the Economy Department on September 20. That operation, known as Anubis, had been under way since the beginning of 2017 under *sub judice* rule protection. It therefore had nothing to do with the events of September and October of that year. It was, therefore, yet another police and judicial operation affecting the independence movement in general. Logically, the Spanish Prime Minister and the Minister of the Interior were involved. It was therefore a question of *raison d'état*.

Over and above the work of Magistrate's Court 13, where around thirty people were investigated for organising the Process, other examining magistrates' courts – in Barcelona, Tarragona, Lleida and Girona – have been carrying out criminal investigations against more than a hundred people supposedly involved in the incidents derived from the publication of the sentence regarding the referendum. Courts around the country have seen mayors and municipal officials summoned to court for their support for the referendum of October 1, 2017. There have also been several investigation courts in which officers of the Mossos d'Esquadra, the Catalan police corps, were investigated for their supposed passivity in the exercise of their duties during the referendum of October 1. There is only one criminal court competent to hear cases involving crimes with sentences of less than five years committed by persons without the status of "*aforats*" (protected by virtue of their office) that has been involved in the process.

The 15th Criminal Court of Barcelona will be in charge of judging Joana Ortega for having worked, it is said, during the period of disqualification for which she was condemned by the TSJC as a result of the 9-N case. Finally, a criminal court has also tried the members of the electoral syndicate of the October 1 referendum: Jordi Matas, Marta Alsina, Marc Marsal, Tània Verge and Josep Pagès, all of them internationally renowned academics. Faced with the acquittal by Criminal Court 11, the Public Prosecutor's Office has lodged an appeal in what is, in the words of Joan Ridao, a display of judicial fanaticism that demonstrates "the desire to continue to judicialise the conflict and to continue feeding a punitive strategy with an execrably vengeful and fanatical zeal." The case, therefore, is by no means over.

The High Court of Justice of Catalonia (TSJC), competent to try persons enjoying parliamentary protection – as it did with Mas, Ortega and Rigau – has been the Court that has tried and sentenced two Presidents of Catalonia: Artur Mas and Joaquim Torra. Both for disobedience. It has also tried and sentenced two Catalan Ministers: Joana Ortega and Irene Rigau, also for disobedience. And it has tried and convicted for disobedience the members of the Speaker's Committee of the Catalan Parliament: Lluís Guinó, Ramona Barrufet, Anna Simó and Lluís Corominas, but with the express exclusion of the Speaker of the Catalan Parliament, Carme Forcadell, who was tried and convicted by the Criminal Chamber of the Supreme Court. It also condemned the Catalan Minister of Foreign Affairs, Bernat Solé, then Mayor of Agramunt, for promoting the celebration of the October 1 referendum. Finally, the TSJC is also investigating two cases against pro-independence leaders – Josep Maria Jové and Lluís Salvadó for the logistical preparation of the 1-O referendum – and Miquel Buch, Minister of the Interior, for the protection abroad of President Puigdemont by the Mossos d'Esquadra .

Let us move on now to State level. The persecutory zeal of the Court of Auditors cannot be explained without relating it to the desire to destroy the assets of the leaders of the Process. There are several financial cases, the aim of which is to claim millions of dollars for the celebrations of the 9-N civic consultation and the 1-O referendum. Also on State level, sedition trials have been held at the National Court against the former Major of the Mossos d'Esquadra, Josep Lluís Trapero, and against police commanders Pere Soler, Cèsar Puig and Teresa Laplana. The Court had no choice but to acquit the top brass of the Mossos. However, the *Audiencia Nacional* (AN) is also carrying out an investigation, with the imposition of precautionary measures of deprivation of liberty, against members of the Comités de Defensa de la República (the CDR) in the wake of what has become known as the Democratic Tsunami. We recall that the AN was the judicial body that issued the first arrests against pro-independence leaders, specifically on October 16, 2017, when Jordi Sánchez (ANC) and Jordi Cuixart (Òmnium) were arrested, followed by the members of the Government of the Generalitat who appeared in order to testify as persons under investigation.

The Supreme Court – and more specifically, the Criminal Chamber – has been particularly active in repression, both in the investigation and the trial of persons under arrest and in the resolution of appeals. In this sense, it is currently in charge of the condemnatory sentence of the TSJC against President Torra. It has also condemned Francesc Homs for the informal referendum held in 2014 and has ratified the sentence of the TSJC that condemned President Mas and Ministers Ortega and Rigau for that same referendum, as well as Joan Josep Nuet for disobedience when he was a member of the Speaker's Committee of the Catalan Parliament. Until recently he was an MP in the Spanish Parliament.

The Supreme Court has also ruled on various procedural incidents for nullity, which it has repeatedly rejected. The Contentious Chamber has also been called upon to rule against aspects related to the independence Process, particularly in the area of appeals against decisions contrary to the interests of independence, or against decisions of the Central Electoral Board, and always in the context of politically important resolutions. This is the case of the appeal filed by Oriol Junqueras when his status as an MEP was withdrawn without legal justification. Or the appeal presented by President Torra when his status as a Member of Parliament was annulled.

8.3.2 Cases in the Constitutional Jurisdiction

The violation of fundamental rights and freedoms has been constant since the beginning of the lawfare strategy. Freedom of expression, in its threefold aspect, has been trampled upon. Citizens' freedom of expression has been persecuted by means of hate crimes, insults and slander. Freedom of expression in the field of communication has been restricted through the persecution of Catalan journalists and media. Freedom of expression in its parliamentary aspect has been seriously violated, ignoring the prerogative of inviolability. Freedom of assembly and demonstration have also been violated. The rights of political participation have been violated in the double condition in which suffrage is presented to us: both active and passive. Parliamentarianism, as we knew it, has disappeared. The interference of the Spanish courts in parliamentary autonomy has meant that parliamentarians have not been able to take part in sessions using their powers as MPs. These judicial interferences have had an impact on the investiture of Presidents of Catalonia and on the formation of governments. They have restricted the freedom of action of the Speaker, which has been subjected to the permanent threat of a lawsuit for disobedience and prevarication.

Whilst all these fundamental rights and public freedoms have been – and still are – at stake, the Constitutional Court has overlooked other things and continued to reject them. The rejection of important appeals against provisional arrest warrants has been constant and repeated, and all political prisoners have been affected. Other appeals have had, as their *raison d'être*, the challenge presented by Josep Rull and Jordi Turull against the refusal of four of the judges of the Supreme Court to disqualify themselves from trying them. Oriol Junqueras, Raül Romeva, and Rull and Turull too, appealed to the Constitutional Court against their suspension from public office. Carme Forcadell and Anna Simó, like Mireia Boya and Anna Gabriel, have brought before the Constitutional Court their objections to the judge predetermined by law and, therefore, the competence of the Supreme Court. Carles Puigdemont, Clara Ponsatí and Lluís Puig have filed a complaint against the decision of the Supreme Court for their trial. In all these cases, the Constitutional Court has turned down the appeals, after holding them up in order to avoid the internationalization of the Process before the final ruling of the Supreme Court.

But the Constitutional Court has not only been involved in Catalan politics by denying the accused persons a pardon. It is the Spanish institution that has triggered the Process from a jurisprudential exercise of the refusal of politics as a pact between legitimate institutions (in this case the Parliament of Catalonia, the Spanish Parliament and the approval of the citizens expressed in a referendum). This is the meaning of the Statute ruling: to place the Constitutional Court at the epicentre of the political debate. Subsequently, the Constitutional Court did not refrain from acting and thus became a leading political actor. With STC 42/2014, the Constitutional Court set itself up as a body for the control of political debate. In other words, political debate – including political debate in the Catalan Parliament, supposedly protected by immunity and inviolability – is conditioned by the Constitution, which becomes the canon of what can be politically debated in a Parliament.

But, however serious that may seem, the Constitutional Court does not stop here. In STC 295/2015 it defines what is legal and what is illegal in a political debate. It then criminalizes debate by considering that it does not respect its will or, ultimately, the Constitution (ATC 123/2017, ATC 126/2017 and ATC 144/2017, among others). But that is not all. The Constitutional Court approves the extensive deployment of exceptionality (SSTC 89/2019 and 90/2019) and validates an absolutely exorbitant application of article 155 CE that violates, once again – and there have been many more instances – several fundamental rights. Indeed, all these resolutions are the result of the judicialization strategy.

8.4 The Courts of the Process. Analysis of the Sociological Profile

We now offer an analysis of the sociological profile of the members of the two courts with the greatest impact on the lawfare strategy deployed by the Spanish State: the Constitutional Court and the Supreme Court. The data we use has been obtained after an exhaustive internet search: mainly, but not only, in the websites of the courts themselves (www.tribunalconstitucional.es and www.poderjudicial.es), interviews and news reports that have given personal and professional profiles of the judges involved. The report on the structure of the judicial career prepared by the General Council of the Judiciary for the year 2019 has also served to compare the judicial elites with the basic judiciary. It has not been easy to obtain data on the year or place of birth, to the point that it has been impossible to find out the place of birth of four judges of the Supreme Court. The same has happened with regard to the universities where they studied. There are eleven judges about whom we do not even know where they trained as lawyers.

This analysis is limited to 2019, because it is the year of greatest judicial intensity – when the oral hearing of the leaders of the Process was held and the sentence condemning them was announced – when the lawfare strategy achieved one of its main political successes: the severe condemnation of the pro-independence leaders, a condemnation that added imprisonment to disqualification from political office. Below, we offer the most relevant data of what would be a shared profile between the two bodies before analysing them separately. This joint analysis is carried out from a gender and generational perspective.

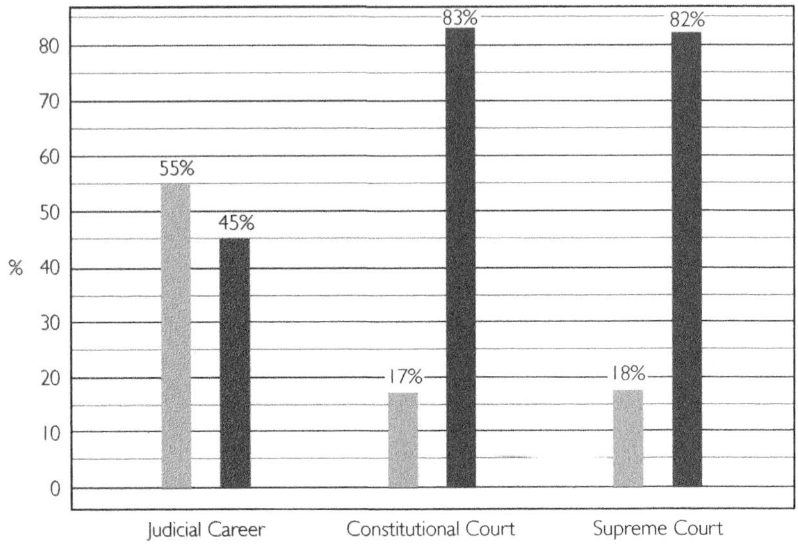

Graph 1 Comparison of the Proportions of Women and Men in the Law Career, in the Constitutional Court and the Supreme Court.

What is most striking, when one observes here the composition of the basic judiciary and compares it with the structure of the Spanish high judiciary, is the difference in terms of gender. The judicial career shows a similar number of male and female judges exercising jurisdictional functions throughout the territory (first instance, pre-trial, criminal, contentious, social and second instance, etc.). When it comes to the judiciary, this parity – or quasi-parity – is altered in favour of men, who become hegemonic. The Spanish constitutional judiciary has the same degree of sensitivity to the gender perspective as the higher courts; in other words, it is practically non-existent. –

Graph 1 shows that in the basic judiciary, 55% of judges are women, whilst 45% are men. The composition of the territorial judiciary is mainly female. However, when these female judges climb up the judicial career ladder and take on tasks of greater responsibility or leadership, they are pushed aside in favour of male judges and magistrates. The latter, despite being fewer at the base, end up imposing themselves in the bodies at the top of the ladder. Women make up a mere 18% of the Supreme Court, while men make up 82%. The data are almost identical in the comparison between the basic judiciary and the composition of the Constitutional Court. The percentage of men in the Constitutional Court is even higher than in the Supreme Court: 83% men and only 17% women.

The gap between the basic justice system and the Spanish high courts is massive, and in 2007, an attempt was made to correct this gap by way of Organic Law 3/2007, a legislative measure to contribute to effective equality between men and women. However, it is a constant feature of the Spanish high courts that they do not feel challenged by certain laws. This situation is relevant to the extent that this distortion ends up being reflected in the judicial decisions of the Supreme Court and the Constitutional Court, which create jurisprudence. The lack of gender sensitivity, and language or the fact that in the face of two possible interpretations of the same instances, the one most beneficial to women ought to prevail, connect directly to the masculine vision of the exercise of the high judiciary. A good way to correct this difference, after more than forty years of democracy, would be to comply with the law and, consequently, to incorporate more women into positions of judicial responsibility.

Once this consideration has been made, it should also be noted that the failure to apply LO 3/2007 is serious, especially since we are talking about an institution, the Constitutional Court, which is responsible for safeguarding fundamental rights and public freedoms. The principle of equality and non-discrimination on the basis of sex is at the core of its composition. Delivering justice from international and constitutional anti-discriminatory legal standards (gender mainstreaming) has to become more than just a legitimate aspiration for a Constitutional Court that wants to be modern and on a par with its European colleagues.

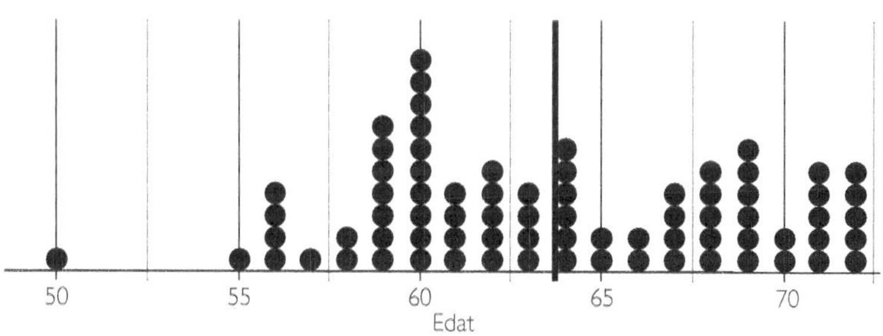

Graph 2 Supreme Court Magistrates' Ages in 2019. The thick vertical line between 60 and 65stands for average age.

Another aspect that attracts attention is the age of the judiciary. In 2019, the average age of the Supreme Court judges was 64 (Graph 2) and the average age of the Constitutional Court judges was 74 (Graph 3). In both cases we are talking about a remarkably high average. And even more so, if

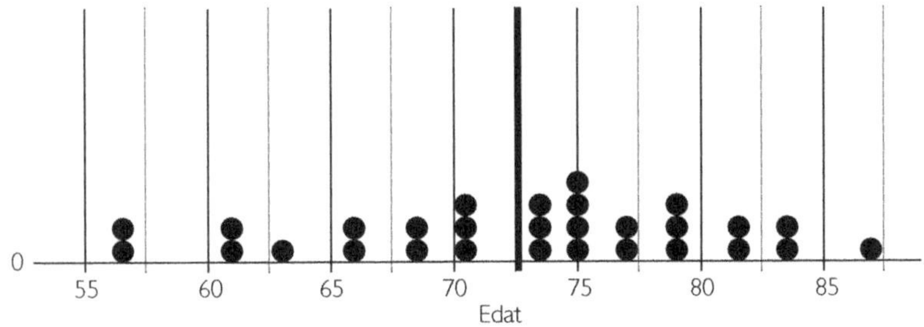

Graph 3 Constitutional Court Magistrates' Ages in 2019. The thick line between 70 and 75 stands for average age.

we bear in mind that people now in their sixties and seventies who opted to study for a university degree usually finished it at the age of twenty-two or twenty-three. The point is that the judges of the Supreme Court and the Constitutional Court studied at university in a pre-constitutional era. And, under the tutelage of professors and intellectuals who had embraced the Franco regime, they had even defended its values and principles and applied its legal framework. This is not to say that, during those years, jurists were trained by a totalitarian or anti-democratic vision of law. However, a vision of law that was not subject to the dissemination, protection and defence of fundamental rights or principles, such as plurinationality and territorial decentralisation, was hegemonic at that time. As we shall see in the following sections and chapters, the Spanish high judiciary has serious shortcomings when it has to deal with international law or when it has to weigh up factual situations in which fundamental rights are affected.

8.4.1 The Supreme Court Profile

The distortion in the composition of the Supreme Court is not only gender-based. When we analyse the data on the place of birth of its judges, we also find variables that allow us to understand why it was necessary to transfer the case against the pro-independence leaders to the Supreme Court. The point was to remove the case from the court that corresponded to it by law and to place it in a much more sympathetic environment as regards the *raison d'état*. Data, such as the place of birth or the place of academic training (law degree), allow us to see the extent of centralisation of the highest court in Spain. Madrid occupies a very prominent position in these two variables (place of birth and place of education).

Madrid, Community	23	29.5
Andalusia	13	16.7
Castile and Leon	9	11.5
Valencia	6	7.7
Aragon	4	5.1
Catalonia	3	3.8
Galicia	3	3.8
Murcia, Region	3	3.8
Extremadura	2	2.6
Basque Country	2	2.6
Asturias, Principality	1	1.3
Canary Islands	1	1.3
Cantabria	1	1.3
Castile-La Mancha	1	1.3
Navarre	1	1.3
Rioja	1	1.3

Chart 1 Total number of magistrates, and percentages, of the Supreme Court with respect to the Autonomous Community they were born in.

The Madrid region is the birthplace of almost 30% of the Supreme Court judges, whereas Catalonia (3.8%), the Basque Country (2.6%) and Galicia (3.8%) – each with its own language and legal institutions – have a marginal presence, if not an irrelevant one. This irrelevance contrasts with Catalonia's importance within the Spanish state in terms of population, economic weight, cultural and political relevance and historical character. This under-representation is aggravated if we compare it with other autonomous communities, such as Andalusia, which, with 16.7%, is the second region with the highest presence of lawyers in the high court. The region of Castile and Leon, with 11.5%, and Valencia with 7.7% are above Catalonia, the Basque Country and Galicia.

The importance of Madrid is reinforced when we add the place of academic training – at one and the same time, a geographical space for learning and for socialising. In other words, Madrid becomes the place where the future magistrate lives and adapts to the socio-cultural elements that are available to him. The magistrate makes these elements his own until he creates his own identity. It is difficult for a conservative profile to be unaffected by a centralist, Castilian and unifying position. And, if Madrid makes up 29.5% in terms of place of birth, it goes up to 33.3% as the place for the university careers of lawyers in Spain. That is to say, Madrid increases its preponderance even more. Andalusia and Castile and Leon

Madrid	26	33.3
Unknown	11	14.1
Andalusia	9	11.5
Castile and Leon	7	9
Aragon	5	6.4
Valencia	5	6.4
Catalonia	4	5.1
Murcia	4	5.1
Galicia	3	3.8
Basque Country	2	2.6
Asturias	1	1.3
Navarre	1	1.3

Chart 2 Total number of magistrates, and percentage, of the Supreme Court with respect to the Autonomous Regions where they were trained.

continue to be the second and third most important regions, with 11.5% and 9% respectively. Far behind are Catalonia with 5.1%, Galicia with 3.8% and the Basque Country with 2.6%. The cultural diversity that comes with university education in specific geographical areas, which could provide a plurinational or more decentralised vision, more respectful or more empathetic to differential factors, is not reflected in the Spanish judiciary. With these data we can affirm that the Supreme Court is a highly centralised judicial body, with a strong presence within it of the capital, Madrid. This centralisation is endorsed both by the place of birth of the judges and – most importantly – by the place where they undertook their university studies.

8.4.2 The Constitutional Court Profile.[6]

When we look at the territorial distribution of the members of the Constitutional Court, the same thing happens as when we looked at the members of the Supreme Court: Madrid once again occupies a central place in the biographies of its judges. And this is clearly reflected in jurisprudence. Especially when it comes to debating and analysing aspects related to the Territorial Constitution. Thus, the Constitutional Court's position and the legal criteria used in STC 31/2010 on the Catalan Statute are no exception. The participation of magistrates belonging to, or appointed by, the historic nations of the Spanish State – Catalonia, the Basque Country and Galicia – has been a theoretical aspiration. Or, to be more precise, not even that.

STC 101/2008 dismantled the dream of autonomous participation in the election of the judges of the Constitutional Court, insofar as it accepted that the autonomous regions could propose candidates for the Constitutional Court. But it also stated that it was in the power of the Senate to decide whether to present its own candidates if the regional candidates were not to its liking. In other words, if it did not like the candidates proposed by the Parliaments of the historical nations of the State, the Senate could propose others. The only thing missing was to come clean and add "to safeguard the centralist position of the Court." This was not the constitutional spirit, which once again the Constitutional Court ignored. When the Spanish Constitution divides the appointment of judges to the Constitutional Court between the two chambers of Parliament, it does so bearing in mind that the Senate is a chamber of territorial representation, not because it seeks to reflect the projection of a particular political majority. Indirect electoral legitimation was already reflected in the election of judges by the Spanish Parliament (Joaquin Urías. 241). Ergo: the logic of the Senate was different and was circumscribed by its desire to convey to the Constitutional Court a greater territorial sensitivity, based on the proposals put forward by the autonomous Parliaments.

Madrid	7	24.1
Castile and Leon	5	17.2
Andalucia	4	13.8
Catalonia	3	10.3
Castile-La Mancha	2	6.9
Aragon	1	3.4
Cantabria	1	3.4
Valencia	1	3.4
Extremadura	1	3.4
Galicia	1	3.4
Murcia	1	3.4
Basque Country	1	3.4
Uruguay	1	3.4

Chart 3 Total number of magistrates, and percentage, of the Constitutional Court with respect to the Autonomous Region they were born in.

When it comes to finding arguments in favour of appointing judges who are sensitive to the plurinational nature of the State, we can go back to the precedents of the Republican Constitution of 1931. Article 122 of that

Constitution stipulated that the Court of Guarantees would have one representative from each of the regions of the State. Comparative experience also goes in this direction: in federal states, the decentralised territorial political entities participate in the appointment of magistrates who are to sit on the constitutional bench. The Spanish state is outside that reality, as the data show.

The centralism of its members is another of the characteristics that is perceived regarding the Spanish constitutional justice system. Madrid tops the list of birthplaces of magistrates, with 24.1%. Far behind again are national regions with their own culture, law and language, such as Catalonia (10.3%), the Basque Country (3.4%) and Galicia (3.4%). In fact, this 3.4% in the Basque Country and Galicia translates into a single judge per community: Adela Asúa in the Basque case and Cándido Conde Pumpido in Galicia. In the Catalan case, there are three: Eugeni Gay, Encarna Roca and Juan Antonio Xiol. In the case of Madrid, the 24.1% translates into seven judges: Ramón Rodríguez Arribas, Pablo Pérez Tremps, Francisco José Hernándo, Luís Ignacio Ortega, Pedro José González Trevijano, Alfredo Montoya and Ricardo Henríquez. But this centralism, in its socialising and formative aspect, is increased even further when we look at the place where the judges undertook their academic training:

Madrid	12	41.4
Andalusia	4	13.8
Catalonia	3	10.3
Castile and Leon	2	6.9
Valencia	2	6.9
Aragon	1	3.4
Asturias	1	3.4
Extremadura	1	3.4
Galicia	1	3.4
Murcia	1	3.4
Basque Country	1	3.4

Chart 4 Total number of magistrates, and percentage, of the Constitutional Court with respect to the Autonomous Community.

Madrid has gone from 24.1% of lawyers born in the capital to 41.4% of lawyers who have been trained and have socialised there. The three historical nations stay put. This variable is of interest in order to relate the level of centralism of the Constitutional Court to the lack of willingness to offer a real development of the Territorial Constitution. There has been no shortage of experts who have seen in the role of the Constitutional Court – and more specifically in the ruling on the Catalan Statute – the beginning of the constitutional crisis that has led to the Catalan pro-sovereignty Process and the start of the judicialization of Spanish politics at its maximum expression.

Chapter 9

The Political Trial

The Implementation of Repression

We shall now look at the construction of an exceptional framework that is just one more of the many screens of a lawfare strategy. We shall see how the Catalan independence movement confronted one of the latest stages of lawfare, probably the most mediated and most relevant of all: the phase of the criminal process. We shall try to analyse the legal-political elements that make up this hybrid warfare strategy, from the beginning (criminal complaint), through the investigative phase (with the consequent adoption of measures) to the hearing, including the outcome in the form of a sentence. The analyses published by legal journalists will help here. Aware as they were that the hearing against the leaders of the independence Process was a historic event – it was an anomaly that, within the framework of the European Union, a constitutional controversy of a democratic nature and territorial scope, could be resolved through the application of the criminal law of the enemy – journalists have made contributions in the form of valuable monographs that will help us narrate the moments of maximum political interest of a procedure that, on paper, was only criminal.[1]

Inasmuch as we describe the trial as political, we shall first see what theoretical elements a political trial requires in order to be considered as such. At the same time, in our analysis we shall be interested to see how procedural tools were used in order to cause damage to the political enemy without resorting to the use of force. To put it another way, we shall see the use of procedural mechanisms to put a spoke in the wheel of the normal development of the exercise of politics through the practice of what has been called a Strategic Lawsuit Against Public Participation (SLAPPS).[2] This is simply a lawsuit that is intended to prevent or discourage citizen participation and to silence voices critical of the political action of a government or the business action of a large corporation.

9.1 The Concept of a Political Trial

In his classic *Political Justice*, Otto Kirchheimer states that the function of the courts in the context of a political trial is to eliminate the enemy according to certain rules laid down in advance.[3] The rules that Kirchheimer refers to are those of a constitutional legal system. And within this system are the rules of the criminal trial, which were neither designed to pursue political dissent nor predetermined to exclude the enemy from the game of politics. But, continuing with Kirchheimer, the need to resort to criminal proceedings as a form of political action arises when, amongst other things: (1) the formal restriction of liberty may be necessary in order for police and security operations to be successful; (2) one opts for a policy of total repression against enemies, restricting their political activity through the use of legal proceedings against them; and (3) a direct repressive effect is sought in order to dramatize the struggle with the opponent and thus regain public support (Kirchheimer 2001: 21).

Although *Political Justice* was written in 1941, it already laid down the underlying elements of a lawfare strategy. In fact, we have already analyzed how the formula referred to by Kirchheimer is not unknown to the political elites of the Spanish right and extreme right. Moreover, this formula, used with different intensity during the Franco regime, has never been explicitly condemned by the Spanish political right. The judiciary, the criminal process and the law have been the bulwarks on which the Spanish State has built repression, especially when political dissent or the need to deepen self-government have come from Catalonia. Criminal procedure has become a deterrent against Catalan political aspirations. And this trial is no exception: it is the confirmation of this strategy.

But are we really talking about a political trial? Kirchheimer's definition, which we share, is similar to that of expert jurists in this type of legal proceedings, such as Jacques M. Vergès or, in Catalonia, Benet Salellas. In 1968, Vergès published a pioneering work in this regard: *De la stratégie judiciaire*.[4] In addition to pointing out the most important political trials in history – Jesus, Socrates, Joan of Arc, Louis XVI, the Dreyfus affair, the Dimitrov case or the Nuremberg trials – he raised a type of political defence, which he called "defence of rupture," to offer a minimum guarantee of success in political trials. This "defence of rupture" involved not recognizing the legitimacy of the court, appealing to rules of international law, and seeking the complicity of public opinion. It was not a rule-based defence; it was constructed on the basis of political arguments, since the procedure was not of a jurisdictional nature, but of a political one.

Benet Salellas, who was a member of the defence counsel in the Trial of the Independence Process (or The October 1 Trial), wrote that in the political judiciary "the legal machinery and its procedural mechanisms are put in motion in order to attain political objectives that transcend the mere satisfaction of the custody of public order. The court is appealed to so it can exercise influence on the distribution of power and thus increase the sphere of political action."[5] Salellas continues by defining the actors who form part of the political process, affirming that "in this logic, it is the constituted power that has the capacity to undertake certain actions, and more often than not it holds the monopoly of the exercise of criminal action through the institution of a more or less dependent prosecutor" (Salellas 2018: 19).

9.2 The Construction of a Political Trial

In order to create a criminal macrocause against the independence movement, there was a need to pivot the whole accusation on a crime of special political transcendence and with severe prison sentences, which is what prosecutor José Manuel Maza did. That crime was *rebellion*. Rebellion had both advantages and disadvantages for the lawfare strategy. Among the advantages was the application of Article 384bis of the LECrim with political ends, the high penalties of prison of the penal type and the media and electoral effect that would entail persecuting Catalan independence rebellion. But it also had weak points that only the deep Judicial State could neutralize: the lack of violence and, consequently, the non-existence of rebellion as such. That was the weak point of the criminal process: that the independence movement was not – and had never been – violent. Rebellion implied a violence with such a capacity as to bend the will of the State. So the deeds being judged could not properly be subsumed under rebellion.

Another weakness was the competence of the court. Given that the preparatory investigation was for rebellion, the courts competent to hear the case were the courts of investigation of Barcelona or, at the very most, the Superior Court of Justice of Catalonia, given the parliamentary privileges of most of the leaders of the Catalan independence Process. These privileges, incidentally, had disappeared, due to the application in Catalonia of Article 155 of the Spanish Constitution and the loss, by the pro-independence leaders, of their status as MPs and members of the Government of the Generalitat. In this case, the competent court was to be a Barcelona court of investigation. In no case, then, were the National Courts or the Supreme Court competent to try the case of rebellion.

As we shall see, the effective deployment of the mechanisms of a Dual State, and the setting in motion of the Deep State for the specification and effectiveness of the lawfare strategy, make the law yet another tool for eliminating the enemy. The interpretation favorable to the interests of the Spanish State – and logically contrary to the independence movement – making the law say what it did not say, or ignoring what it did say, has been so blatant that the trial against the independence movement was, above all and most evidently, a political trial with the aim of eliminating, humiliating and punishing the enemy.[6]

9.2.1 The Construction of a Lawsuit

The legal battle against the Catalan independence movement burst onto the political arena when the Attorney-General's Office announced the filing of a criminal complaint against the entire government of the Catalan Government and the Speaker's Committee of the Catalan Parliament. That is when a criminal macro-trial against the independence movement began to take shape on the Catalan political scene. The Spanish political and media platforms had aleady been working for a long time to build up a discourse aimed at associating independence with a violent movement of a terrorist nature. The title of the press release issued by the Attorney-General's Office to report on the criminal complaint for the crimes of rebellion and sedition, in addition to the crimes of embezzlement and disobedience, continued the story unfolded by the influential Madrid platforms. The title of the press release was: "The Harder They Will Fall." It was from this moment on that the legal battle strategy and the will to fabricate a criminal trial to eliminate the pro-sovereignty movement were made public.

This lawsuit, however, was not the beginning of the criminalization of the pro-independence *Procés*, nor was it the gateway to criminal law. The trial of Catalan President Artur Mas, and of Joana Ortega and Irene Rigau, became a kind of pilot project. As such, it was preceded by a strong controversy that revolved around the need to use – or not use – the path of criminal jurisdiction to resolve issues of a political nature. The entrance of criminal law was not unanimous in the Spanish prosecution. In fact, for ten days there was an unprecedented crisis at the headquarters of the Public Prosecutor's Office, which, weeks later, would lead to the resignation of the State Attorney-General, Eduardo Torres-Dulce.[7] The prosecutors of the High Court of Justice of Catalonia had decided, unanimously, to oppose the filing of a criminal complaint against Artur Mas for the unofficial referendum of November 9, 2014, as they took into consideration the "absence of a concrete, precise and determined order from the Constitutional Court."[8] In other words, they saw no contempt of court.

The pressure, in the form of public statements by Spanish Ministers, such as Interior Minister Jorge Fernández Díaz, and the Presidents of autonomous regions, such as the Galician Alberto Nuñez Feijóo, forced the prosecution to reconsider. But the statement that hurt the prosecution the most, especially in terms of credibility, was that of Popular Party senator Alicia Sanchez-Camacho. On November 11, 2014, Sánchez-Camacho publicly stated that "the lawsuit was solid," that "it would be filed in the next few days," and that it would include the offences of prevarication and bribery. The complaint was neither solid nor would it be filed in a few days, because there was no complaint. But the pressure paid off. It forced the State Attorney-General to convene the Board of Prosecutors of the Supreme Court to expose the facts that had provoked the controversy and try to change the opinion of the prosecutors.

In the end, the lawsuit was filed against President Artur Mas, Vice-President Joana Ortega and Minister of Education Irene Rigau for the crimes of serious contempt of court, prevarication, usurpation of public office and embezzlement. There was no shortage of significant voices in law and politics warning of the political consequences of such an action.[9] The use of criminal law to hold back a legitimate political aspiration supported by a clear social majority was confirmed. On Friday, December 19, 2014, the media opened with the resignation of the State Attorney General, Eduardo Torres-Dulce, due to repeated disagreements with the Spanish Government.[10]

The November 9, 2014, poll criminalization strategy worked. Artur Mas, Joana Ortega, Irene Rigau and Francesc Homs were convicted and barred from holding public office. But the worst thing – and here the will to humiliate, ridicule and destroy, personally and in terms of assets, was confirmed – was that, in spite of acquitting them of the crime of embezzlement, the Court of Auditors opened a case to call for them (as well as other people in the government) to pay €4,988,620.11, plus interest. 'The Harder They Will Fall' confirmed that prosecutor Maza's complaint – with questionable legal rigor as regards the main offences and with requests for pre-trial detention for all defendants – was not an isolated episode to prosecute specific deeds. It was a strategy of judicializing politics that reached the desired scenario: the criminalization of the movement, thanks to charging it with crimes in the Penal Code that carried with them prison sentences of over 25 years.

There was a return to the application of criminal law of the enemy: the typology of tax law of the doctrine of Carl Schmitt. This doctrine was very much in line with the political thought that the Spanish nationalist right, then in the government of the Spanish State, had adopted since the Franco regime and had never abandoned. The prosecution also acted in this way. The Public Prosecutor's Office had adopted criminal law, as advocated by Günter Jakobs. This was the starting point. Aim at the enemy and confront it with legal instruments of a criminal nature. It was one of the first stagings of the lawfare strategy, including a title – 'The Harder They Will Fall'.

Barcelona Court of Investigation No. 13, which for months had been investigating the main political leaders in the independence Process and feeding the case using intelligence reports of dubious credibility, and the National High Court, became the two courts on which lawfare was constructed. The prosecution was the third. The fourth would be the Second Chamber of the Supreme Court. But, to get there, the law needed to be distorted, or, to put it another way, fundamental rights, such as that of the judge predetermined by law – in order to transfer the case to Madrid – or the principle of legality or parliamentary immunity, had to be violated, among others. And, for that to happen, a much more serious crime was needed than disobedience: rebellion. In order to instil credibility regarding rebellion, two elements that characterized this offence during the Franco era had to be recovered: its broad interpretation and countering violence.

9.2.2 The Construction of an Offence

In order to build a solid criminal narrative around the Catalan sovereignty movement, recovering well-known discourses – such as "It's All ETA" – was needed, with the aim of linking independence to a narrative held up or strengthened by the variable of violence.[11] In fact, it is around this variable, as Mercè Barceló wrote, that a *corpus iuris* began to be created to deal with the Catalan case from a legal war strategy (Barceló 2019: 167). We must not forget that what was being prosecuted disproportionately and without legal coverage was an action – calling a referendum – that had actually been decriminalized by the Zapatero government, precisely with the argument (and this was stated in the explanatory memorandum of Organic Law 2/2005, of June 22, amending the Penal Code) that the repealed articles "refer to conduct that does not have sufficient weight to merit criminal reproach, far less so if the punishment attached to it is a prison sentence."

In 2008 the former judge of the Criminal Chamber of the Supreme Court, Adolfo Prego, gave a lecture, organized by the PP's FAES Foundation, entitled "Criminal Law and Defence of the Constitutional Order," in which he defended a reform of the 1995 Penal Code.[12] In Prego's view, this reform of the Penal Code needed to put right the deficits in the classification of the offence of rebellion that it had suffered as a result of the 1995 Penal Code reform. In the face of the threat of a referendum on Catalan self-determination or a unilateral declaration of independence, the State had to protect itself, or rather, it had to protect national sovereignty, which was one and indivisible, and it had to do it criminally. According to Prego, with the current Criminal Code, public authorities who disobeyed could only be fined or disqualified. The reform, on the other hand, made it possible to criminalize them. The Penal Code, therefore, did not offer an adequate response to prevent actions aimed at achieving the independence of a territory.

The situation referred to by Adolfo Prego had occurred in the Committee on Justice and Home Affairs held on June 7, 1995.[13] The draft Organic Law on the Penal Code, specifically the Title on "Crimes Against the Constitution," was debated, the first of which was that of rebellion. After a Parliamentary session in which MPs Leocadio Bueso Zaera (Popular Party), Diego López Garrido (IU), Emilio Olabarría Muñoz (PNB), José Maria Mohedano Fuertes (Socialist Party), Lorenzo Olarte Cullen (CC) and Jordi Casas i Bedós (CiU) all spoke, it was stated that the point of friction between the parliamentary groups was the vagueness with which the crime of rebellion was drafted as regards one of its most important elements: violence. The proposal being discussed specified that "those who publicly rise up for any of the following purposes" would incur rebellion. The fifth assumption read: "Declare the independence of part of the national territory."

The Basque PNV MP, Emilio Olabarría, wanted the meaning of "rising up publicly" to be specified. Did it mean to defend it at a rally? Or in a discussion with an audience? Although MPs Diego López Garrido and José Maria Mohedano Fuertes insisted that the public uprising had to be violent – even armed, they said – to be considered a rebellion, the fact is that the criminal category did not specify the element of violence. The omission of the term 'violent' in the wording of the concept raised doubts. The intervention of the Canary Islands Coalition MP, Lorenzo Olarte Cullén, was to prove decisive. He aligned himself with Emilio Olabarría's position to ask that, if the Code itself differentiated between non-violent conduct and other conduct with weapons, why not define the offence of rebellion as based on its violent nature, which would – said Olarte Cullén – clarify problems of interpretation.

This was when Diego López Garrigo proposed a solution that would explicitly include violence in the wording of the precept. In the first paragraph he argued that, "in order to make everything totally clear, his Parliamentary Group would propose a transactional amendment, in which the following would be said in the first paragraph: 'Those who rise up violently and publicly for any of the following purposes are culprits of the offence of rebellion'." With this, he assumed, the concern of Messrs. Olabarría and Olarte would be completely satisfied.[14] The aim of the legislator was therefore twofold: on the one hand, to specify that the action of rebellion should be characterized by violence and, on the other, to decriminalize a declaration of independence promoted in a parliamentary chamber. Such a case remained outside the scope of criminal law and could only be considered a crime if the declaration was accompanied by violence. Violence, then, became the key element of the offence: in other words, without violence, there was no rebellion.

In fact, this is how the Constitutional Court itself had interpreted it in CC Judgment 199/1987, issued on the occasion of the appeals of unconstitutionality presented by the Parliaments of Catalonia and the Basque Country against certain aspects of Organic Law 9/1984, of December 26, against the action of armed gangs or terrorist elements, further to Article 55.2 of the Spanish Constitution. The Constitutional Court equated rebels as a subject, as its name suggests, associated with the conduct typical of a rebellion, that is, regarding them as armed gangs or terrorist elements. In this context, it stated: "rebellion is the most serious of the criminal actions that can be carried out, or attempted, by an armed gang." Then it went on to define what rebellion should be. It did so in these words: "By definition, rebellion is carried out by a group whose purpose is the illegitimate use of weapons of war or explosives, with the aim of destroying or overthrowing the constitutional order" (4th legal basis).

In other words, in order for someone to be considered rebellious, the Constitutuonal Court required, first and foremost, that person to be part of an armed gang; and they would possess weapons, firearms, bombs, grenades, explosive substances or devices or incendiary means of some kind. Consequently, the breach of the constitutional order by peaceful means was outside the sphere of criminal law, because it belonged to the political sphere.[15] The legislator, in line with the same doctrine of the Constitutional Court, had come to the same conclusion: peaceful and democratic conduct, even if it became a rupturist statement made in a parliamentary chamber, could not be treated using criminal justice.

The Public Prosecutor's Office – in the political statement '*The Harder They Will Fall*' – started with an absolutely subjective interpretation of the crime of rebellion that converged with the predominant interpretation in the times of the Franco regime. Nicolàs Garcia Rivas explains that the Public prosecution – and the High Court as well, later on – set the axis of the legal-criminal devaluation on the intention, and not on the deed. That is just the opposite of what the principle of guilt requires.[16]

But rebellion was not a legal term; it was a political weapon. Or, as Javier Pérez Royo wrote: rebellion was the excuse – the subterfuge, the pretext – for many things: to dodge the principle of the judge predetermined by law and divert the case to the National High Court, first, and to the Supreme Court, later; to justify the adoption of precautionary measures of deprivation of liberty; and to violate the most important political rights for the exercise of public office through the application of Article 384bis of the Criminal Procedure Act.[17] Ultimately, rebellion was intended to dominate the political and media narrative during the years of the trial against the leaders of the Catalan pro-sovereignty movement and to continue to deploy the effects inherent in a legal battle strategy.

9.2.3 The Construction of a Special Judge

One of the first issues that the lawfare strategy highlighted was placing the case in one of the top courts in Madrid, whether it be the National High Court or the Supreme Court. It did not matter that the right to an ordinary judge, predetermined by law, was being violated and, on the contrary, that the court was being irregularly chosen. What was being sought was an "exceptional judge" or a "special judge" capable of a political reading of the criminal process. Or a "centralist judge" with a clear vision and conception of the unity of the State, which was the legal prize that was really at stake.

In addition, taking the case to the Supreme Court meant increasing the difficulties for the defence. For instance, once the case went to the highest court – the Supreme Court – the appeals system was severely curtailed. First of all, because there would be no second instance that could review the sentence, which was certain to be conviction. as the Supreme Court has no hierarchical superior. But, secondly, because, in a case followed in the Criminal Chamber of the Supreme Court, the appeals raised by the defence counsel against the procedural decisions of the investigating magistrate, are resolved collegially by three magistrates belonging to the same chamber. So the impartiality of the rulings is not guaranteed, given the "close professional and personal relationship between judges" (IEA 2020: 46).

As regards the power of the National Court to hear the criminal complaint against the pro-independence leaders, the prosecutor of the National Court, Pedro Rubira, in the hearing held on February 5, 2019, ruled in favor with a singular argument that exposed the lawfare strategy underlying the criminal process: the non-existence of "impartiality" and "serenity" if the case was tried in Catalonia. As the report of the Institute for Self-Government Studies states, "the extraordinary gravity of these words, which pointed to the existence of reasons outside the law to justify the competence of the National High Court, led on the same day, February 5, 2019, to the Governing Chamber of the Superior Court of Justice of Catalonia, constituted as a Standing Committee, issuing a statement in which, amongst other things, it described as unusual and very worrying that a judgment of intent could be used in support of a procedural claim" (IEA 2020: 40).

The distancing of the independence movement from the natural judge became a priority to ensure, from the investigation phase, the application of precautionary measures that had to be read from various perspectives, the most elementary of which was the political one. These provisional measures would be implemented in two ways. First, the application, from the outset, of pre-trial detention, which gave the criminal proceedings a clear repressive, exemplary and media dimension. Second, the application of article 384bis of the Law of Criminal Procedure (LECrim), which made it possible to automatically suspend the functions of public officials charged with rebellion. Consequently, with the transfer of the case to Madrid, the application of deprivation of liberty by virtue of pre-trial imprisonment and the suspension of functions of political office depended on one single circumstance: the admission to proceedings of the criminal complaint and the opening of an investigation phase for the possible commission of the crime of rebellion.

9.2.4 The Construction of an Investigation

For both the investigating judge, Pablo Llarena, and the presiding judge in the trial, Manuel Marchena, the successful completion of the criminal proceedings was a priority. All the decisions, both in the investigation and in the oral hearings, were subordinated to this goal: to prevent the criminal procedure from derailing. We are talking about decisions that affected the exercise of fundamental rights – including the rights of political representation incumbent on elected officials and the citizens who elected them – that were laid aside so as to ensure a guilty verdict. This is the only way to explain a reading of the Constitution subordinated to the Penal Code. The necessary weighting exercise, involving the limitation of fundamental rights, was severely disrupted. The Supreme Court decided to give greater importance to the exercise of the *ius puniendi* of the State, to the detriment of the protection of the rights of political participation of the defendants and those they represented.

In the exercise of this *ius puniendi*, rebellion emerged – as it had been during the Franco regime – as the keystone of the investigation. The vector of violence was not needed. There was no need for an insurrectionary and violent uprising. On the contrary, according to the prosecution – and following the investigating judge – a demonstration (that is, a crowd of people), in open opposition to the legal and constitutional system, created enough intimidating power to deter the forces of this constitutional order from acting as they would have liked to do, or to prevent them from acting. However, this crowd, no matter how peaceful it might be, became a potential insurrectionary movement, or, in other words, a danger that could – despite having been expressing itself peacefully for more than seven years – degenerate into open violence. Yet this violence no longer even required to be physical. It was enough for it to be psychic or intimidating, or even "normative violence," and hence the reference – by the prosecution – to Kelsen's *coup d'état*. If there was a coup, there was rebellion.[18]

Given that the subjective elements of the crime of rebellion were not apparent, it was decided, during the investigation, to support them via intelligence reports prepared expressly by the political police. As for the subjective elements, the prosecution noted that the rebels sought the independence of Catalonia. To support this criminally, they narrated what had been perfectly well known: parliamentary resolutions, government decisions, holding consultations of the public. Even the *Llibre Blanc per a la Transició Nacional* (White Paper for the National Transition), prepared by experts in the academic field, became, according to investigating judge Llarena, evidence to be used against the defendants. To use the distortion of facts of a clear political nature to subsume them into such serious criminal categories as rebellion and sedition amounted to a twisted use of Constitutional and Criminal Law. This way of applying the law would occur in both the investigation phase and the hearings themselves.

But the investigation was not a bed of roses for the investigating judge. The problems came to light when Pablo Llarena issued the European Arrest Warrants (EAWs) with the clear aim of influencing the political agenda. That is when the criminal procedural law of the enemy came into the open, when the weaknesses of the investigation became more palpable, as this made it easier to compare the Spanish penal system with other penal systems inspired by guarantees and non-repression. The rejection of the EAW for the crime of rebellion by the Schleswig-Holstein High Court became an amendment to the whole of an investigation flawed in its procedural guarantees, at the epicenter of which was the tumor of rebellion. For Pérez Royo, the rejection of the EAW was not just a blow to the prestige of the Supreme Court; the most important thing was that it was stated "that the investigation of which Pablo Llarena is the protagonist is tainted at its very roots and that it is a null and void investigation in its own right for the violation of fundamental rights."[19]

The underlying problem, as Pérez Royo explained in his article, is that the crime for which the Catalan sovereignty movement was being investigated did not stand up to a test of "recognizability." The crime had to be "recognizable" in the sense that, in the conduct of those investigated, elements should be seen that could support the media lynching they were being subjected to.[20] It was clear that the investigation could only be held up on political grounds that were outside criminal law. And the main issue, inherent in the lawfare strategy, was the need to remove the political leaders of the Catalan independence Process from the front line.

Judge Pablo Llarena's investigation also had the clear aim of exercising control over the Catalan political agenda. An example of this occurred when he refused the release of Jordi Sánchez so that he could stand in the investiture session, given that he had been proposed by the Catalan Parliament as a candidate for the Presidency of the Generalitat. The doctrine of the Supreme Court that had allowed the release of ETA member Juan Carlos Yoldi, then in pre-trial detention, in order to be able to take part in an investiture debate, was no longer valid; in that debate Juan Antonio Ardanza (PNB) was finally elected. Although Llarena acknowledged, in the interlocutory statement of March 9, 2018 that they were two similar situations,[21] he differentiated between them by claiming that, for him, Jordi Sánchez presented a greater risk of escape. Put another way, for the investigating judge, Sánchez, a university professor and human rights activist, was a much more dangerous criminal than a recognized and self-confessed member of ETA.

In an unprecedented – given the illegality of the interpretation – application of article 384bis of LECrim, Llarena denied Jordi Sánchez the possibility of attending the investiture plenary by applying the referred precept, though without saying so, that is, by using rebellion. Art. 384bis demands the firmness of the indictment, which is why Llarena avoided quoting it in his negative resolution. As Javier Mira explains, the maintenance of the charge of a crime of rebellion played a decisive role during the investigation phase, although it foundered in the sentence: "it helped to artificially magnify the facts and criminalize the entire independence movement."[22]

This desire to influence the Catalan political agenda or to directly influence Spanish politics was seen when Llarena issued an order for the pre-trial detention of MPs of the Parliament of Catalonia who were free and exercising their duties normally. But what is most remarkable is the fact that this measure affected a candidate for the Presidency of the Generalitat in the middle of an investiture debate. "The message that this judicial decision puts out acquires remarkable symbolism: the criminal process is interposed in the middle of a parliamentary procedure of extraordinary importance – the investiture of the President of a region with a strong and sustained vocation of self-government – and it truncates it by making it unfeasible" (IEA 2020: 74). Nor, in this judicial decision, is there the minimum exercise of weighting that is required when dealing with rights of political participation. What there is, undoubtedly, is an obsession with the fulfilment of the success of the criminal procedure.

If at any stage of the Process the lawfare strategy is absolutely clear, it is during the investigation phase. The adoption of security measures that restricted fundamental rights was taken during a procedural phase in which the presumption of innocence had not been destroyed. So the investigating judge operated on the basis of hints, and not of evidence. As Javier Mira says, this way of acting makes one think of an anticipated punishment that could – and did – cause irreparable damage (Mira 2020: 58).

9.2.5 The Construcction of an Indictment

Once the investigation phase was closed, a procedural moment was reached that would help to accentuate the political nature of the criminal process: the statement of the facts and the allocation of punishments. It is at this point that the political narrative and the lawfare strategy intersect to unfold a narrative that involved calling the Catalan independence movement a *coup d'état*. As Oriol March says: "The consideration of a *coup d'état* to refer to the key period of the independence process is essential to understanding the entire narrative that the Prosecutor's Office has built from the indictment – and even before that – to the very last day of the hearing" (March 2019: 146). In this mantra is rooted a maxim, endorsed by the Spanish historical experience: there is no coup without violence. Violence is the coagulating element of the prosecution's narrative, from the slogan 'The Harder They Will Fall' until Javier Zaragoza's final report.

That the indictment of the prosecution is a document that conveys a political narrative is also supported by the fact that it is developed in the same terms in which the political leaders of the Popular Party, and of Citizens and Vox, express themselves when they refer to the Catalan independence movement (March 2019: 146). This desire to unify the narrative is reflected in the punishments sought against the pro-independence leaders. In this issue – and in many others – they also went hand in hand. The Public Prosecutor's Office called for a total of 25 years in jail and 25 years of disqualification for Oriol Junqueras. For the civil leaders, Jordi Sánchez and Jordi Cuixart, and for the Speaker of the Catalan Parliament, Carme Forcadell, 17 years in jail and 17 years of disqualification. And for the imprisoned Ministers, 16 years in jail and 16 years of disqualification. Vox, an ultra-right, anti-Catalan party that defends the postulates of the Franco regime, adopted a warlike narrative, and the Court allowed it to exercise a popular prosecution in which it called for 74 years in prison – since it included the charge of criminal organization – and million-dollar-plus fines. The more cruelty, the more votes, and therefore the better the electoral outcome.

There is more than one hidden message in the sentences demanded: hidden and at the same time present. First of all, there is a clear will to tarnish the independence movement and transform it into a subversive movement with a *putschist* aim. Secondly, there is a desire to chastise, to warn, to caution. And thirdly, there is a clear thirst for revenge. But there is also an aspect, at least as significant, if not more so, in political terms, that goes back to the origin of the conflict between Catalonia and the Spanish State, and that becomes, on its own, the final proof. The indicator that we are facing in a political trial is that "One of the relevant outcomes of both the prosecution's report and, to a lesser extent, that of Vox, is the preeminent role played by the so-called "constitutional order" over and above fundamental rights" (March 2019: 159). That is the key: *constitutional fundamentalism* or *neo-constitutionalism*, i.e. the Constitution as the source of all other democratic rights or principles, including human rights.

But there is still a last reading. The indictment of independence is a fierce defence of the Spanish Constitution; specifically, what had never been discussed and would never have been discussed, had it not been for the independence Process: the unity of the State, in other words, the unique and indivisible sovereignty also of the symbol that represents it, the Monarchy. Hence the speech of King Philip VI on the evening of October 3, a speech that was anything but democratic or conciliatory. This unity is what, in Mercè Barceló's words, is *metalaw.* At the beginning of this book, we defined it as one of the *raisons d'état*.

9.2.6 The Construction of a Trial

The media expression of the political trial was the hearings. And one of the incentives to follow the hearings was one of the great protagonists of the procedure: Judge Manuel Marchena.[23] Journalist Oriol March defines him as "one of those indispensable figures of the Deep State, often with more power and influence than the political representatives – the latter conditioned by the volatility of the polls – and who knows perfectly well the resources he has at hand to maintain the status quo" (March 2019: 162–163). Precisely: Marchena embodies the Deep Judicial State aligned with the *raison d'état* that needs to be above the law, however much the rule of law is invoked. This profile begins to become visible as the trial runs through the hearings. One episode, however, connects Marchena directly with politics and turns him into a political judge – clearly linked to the Spanish nationalist right and more specifically to the Popular Party – who should never have presided over the court that handed down the ruling against the leaders of the Catalan independence Process: the message for the Popular Party sent by Ignacio Cossidó which acknowledged that the appointment of Marchena to preside over the General Council of the Judiciary meant the control of the Second Chamber of the Supreme Court via the back door.

Behind the polite formality hid a judge – as Josep Maria Brunet explains – with hands of steel inside silk gloves.[24] He exercised powerful control over the courtroom and made it clear from the outset that he would not leave a single procedural loophole that could favour the presentation of counter-evidence that would refute the narrative of violence. One thing is what would be written in the sentence; another was what the trial could reveal. It was along this line that the first controversial decision was made, as it achieved a clear political importance: not to compare the narrative of the prosecution witnesses – National Police and Civil Guard officers who were operational on October 1, 2017 during the referendum – with the images of the videos provided during the investigation phase and which had been accepted as documentary evidence. Images of violent police crackdowns on defenceless civilians. Not to counter the narrative of the witnesses – subjective and one-sided – with the evidence of the images – objective and clarifying – amounted to preventing the two realities that confronted each other in that trial from being compared: the truthful one and the imagined one. Peaceful, popular demonstrations and demands by Catalans of many persuasions could not be confronted with the prosecution's narrative of supposed hatred, resentment and violence. Marchena's decision was therefore clearly political.

Another political decision, as it continued to remove the possibility of confronting two narratives, was the refusal to allow a face-to-face confrontation at the trial between Diego Pérez de los Cobos (Colonel of the Civil Guard) and Ferran López (head of the Catalan Mossos d'Esquadra), as requested by defence lawyer Xavier Melero. It is true that, during the hearing, prosecution and defence witnesses offered many contradictory versions. But the contradictions between the two top police officers of the two major corps instructed to exercise functions of direction and control of the police operation during the referendum deserved to be countered by the procedural technique of confrontation. As Joan Queralt said in an interview with the weekly *El Temps*, Marchena was inventing a new procedural law, or reinterpreting the current one, against the right to defence.[25]

The role played by Marchena was one of feigned neutrality that has not withstood the passage of time. Had the trial lasted a month, its jurisdictional function would surely have overshadowed the true political intent of his appointment. But, being a long and tedious trial, a Marchena emerged who treated the parties – or rather, the evidence available to the parties – unequally. For instance, whilst hundreds of National Police and Civil Guards were able to deploy the language needed to sustain, to the end, the narrative of violence – the expressions "hateful looks," "human ramparts," "tumultuous mass," "hostility," "pre-war," "powder keg," "insurrectionary climate" – became a common denominator in the prosecution's witnesses, the defence witnesses were prevented from fully expressing their personal assessments. Such was the case with Marina Garcés' testimony.

The aim was the preservation, in the media arena of televised justice, of the narrative of violence associated with the Process. This was a media asset to be preserved. This alone could ensure the public stigmatization of the independence movement and the acceptance of a sentence of rebellion or sedition, with significant prison sentences for the Catalan leaders. In return, Marchena also helped the Prosecutor's Office. This would maintain, by raising the provisional conclusions to definitive, the charge of rebellion, with the maximum possible penalties. The position of the prosecution, in a cause-and-effect move, also benefited Marchena. He could hand down a seemingly Solomonic sentence, dismissing rebellion but accepting sedition, which also implied very significant prison sentences. The judge, with a sentence of this nature, would preserve his position of feigned neutrality. But the result of the sentences would also be the result of a purely political reasoning.

Marchena would put criminal proceedings – the *ius puniendi* of the State – over and above substantive guarantees of fundamental rights, which meant transforming democracy into a bureaucracy or an *administrativistic democracy*.[26]

The clearest examples, however, will be seen in two decisions that will be discussed later: one, the application of Article 384bis (LECrim) to the MPs and Senators elected in the April 2019 elections; and two, the request to the CJEU for a preliminary ruling on the scope of the institution of immunity that gave rise to what has come to be known as the Junqueras doctrine.

9.3 The Construction of a Political Sentence

The judgment of October 14, 2019, which culminates one of the battles – so far, the most important one of all but not the last one – of the lawfare strategy against the Catalan sovereignty movement has been described in many ways and from various points of view. We shall give some examples. From a legal standpoint, it has been described as pre-constitutional.[27] In a more benevolent analysis, it has been considered to be Solomonic.[28] In a dissenting analysis, the sentence was deemed insufficient and should have involved conviction for rebellion,[29] or ill-advised because it was the result of a pact between separatism and the Socialist Party.[30] There has been talk among journalists about the practice of *thanatoplasty*, which buys the narrative of the prosecution, although it ends up ruling out rebellion (March 2019: 11). For political science, it was the exercise of legal creativity[31] for its willingness to equate the sit-downs of citizens during the October 1 referendum with an "uprising." However, it has always been described as historic. And, in fact, it is. But above any other consideration, the sentence is a political sentence. Moreover, it has culminated a political strategy that has used the mechanisms of criminal and procedural law and the complicity of the Deep Judicial State to eliminate the pro-independence enemy. That was the goal, and it has accomplished it.

A political analysis of the judgment – which is what we offer now – which complements a legal analysis, must necessarily be based on the proven facts, which is what in procedural law is called an assessment of inference. In other words, the court must express, by what logical-deductive means and on the basis of what evidence, it has come to the conclusions of the proven facts which it has finally reached. These proven facts will, of course, be qualified according to legal rules. And this area of deductions, evidence and arguments must be confined to the perimeter of the trial. Outside of the trial, no other factual or probative reality can be assessed. Based on this premise, the sentence, as Joan Queralt says, is built upon a pre-constitutional structure (Queralt 2019). Expressions were used to deem certain facts to be proven, without the evidence being identified at any time. This is pure war fiction, without documentary, expert or testimonial evidence to support it.

The journalist Oriol March wrote that the court bought the narrative of the rebellion defended by the prosecution, fed by the Spanish nationalist right and far right (Vox, but also Popular Party and, above all, Citizens), and amplified by the most influential Madrid platforms and by think tanks with roots within the more radicalized Spanish nationalism like FAES or the Elcano Institute. The Court did indeed adopt it. To verify that it is a political and not a legal account, we refer to the proven facts.

The narrative is built on a climate of violence and hostility, which the Court infuses into the factual narrative, especially from the ninth fact (page 41). It describes the situation on September 20, 2017 – a demonstration in front of the Catalan Economics Ministry in protest against the searches and arrests taking place there – as a situation in which 40,000 protesters (no report or police or experts specifying this figure is quoted) "packed" – we quote – "in an environment in which cries of protest against the presence of the court commission and the entertainment coexisted" (page 43). The source of the evidence is not identified, but the sentence is intended to contrast two realities, one illegal and the other permissible, as if cries of protest were an offence and leisure events a virtue.

One sentence, in this section, narrates an improbable situation. It explains how the Ministry was "surrounded" (page 43). But what happened in front of the Economics Ministry was a demonstration and not a siege. Joan Queralt writes about this aspect of the judgment – and we agree with him on this – that "words are not innocent, 'surround' gives the feeling of siege, which considerably increases the dramatic nature of the facts" (Queralt 2019). But the desire to infuse drama into the narrative doesn't stop there. It is aggravated further when reference is made to the officer of the administration of justice who carried out the search. It is stated that "the court commission was prevented from carrying out its normal functions." This is not true: the search was carried out. Nothing was prevented. And this, as Queralt says, is not a minor aspect of the narrative. Sedition is being constructed, since impeding "is a possible element in sedition: one of the purposes provided for in the criminal law" (Queralt 2019).

The narrative goes on to say that, in order to leave the Ministry, the officer had to be "infiltrated among the spectators" (page 45). 'Infiltrating' is a police or military term that does not correspond to the situation here. These are not the only expressions that aim to place the independence movement within the Schmittian logic of the friend–enemy, or of the *hostis*. Expressions such as "vast crowd" (page 45) or "hostile concentrations" or "with marked hostility" (page 48) correspond to this desire. The narrative goes into the October 1 referendum – proven fact No. 12 – with the supposed multiple injuries to police officers. It even states that they required medical assistance. If so, where is the medical documentary evidence to support this part of the narrative? Once again, the lack of supporting evidence in the conclusions reached gives the narrative a marked political intent.

This whole narrative aims to lead to an "uprising." Because, without an uprising, there is no rebellion, nor sedition either. Uprising is a fundamental and characteristic element of sedition. And, not being able to offer an uprising, the sentence takes as an uprising passive resistance, passive opposition, mass demonstrations or hostile looks. This is the uprising on which a criminal case is being built, which in the end adds up to a total of a hundred years of prison sentences. A hundred years is the result of the anti-democratic, arbitrary and authoritarian application of criminal law.[32] Once again, we take up a phrase written by Joan Queralt: "We are facing a perfect, finished, rounded, immaculate example of the criminal law of the enemy" (Queralt 2019). But we also have the question posed by Valeria Gaillard, in the prologue to the translation of the articles published by Émile Zola when he denounced the Dreyfus affair (the case of the Jewish soldier falsely accused, tried and convicted of espionage): "What happens when *raison d'état?* [...] imposes itself above justice?"[33]

Nothing. Nothing happens in Spain. France pardoned Alfred Dreyfus. Moreover, the French Supreme Court annulled the two courts martial that had unjustly condemned him for high treason, and a law passed by the National Assembly allowed him to rejoin the army with the rank of major. Alfred Dreyfus regained his freedom and, most importantly, his honor.

Chapter 10

The International Jurisdiction

Or the Weakness of Lawfare

It is clear that the lawfare strategy limited to the Spanish judicial sphere has been a resounding success for its promoters. The system of election of the high judiciary in charge of investigating and judging, based on a normative corpus duly interpreted according to the interests at stake, has been used as a steamroller against the Catalan independence movement. Information watchtowers have used the narrative as an effective tool to point out the enemy in a time marked by post-truth.[1] The results confirm the success of the tactics used. Much of the enemy has been condemned and imprisoned, much of the enemy is pending trial, and the rest of the enemy see their political activity conditioned, due to the *angst* that the Spanish judicial state continues to show, to this day.

But when this strategy has had to be confronted with international courts, the defeats of the strategists – or the thinking minds of lawfare – have been devastating. More and more so. In Europe, it has been shown that the macro-cause against Catalan independence has been – and is – a political macro-cause, far removed from the values and principles of European justice and directly connected with the vengeful intentions of Spain's high courts, ones that date, at least, from the times of Franco.

International courts, more guarantor and less authoritarian, more independent and less politicized, have emerged as the great hope of the pro-independence leaders of the Process to win the legal battle. The pro-sovereignty movement has always known that the path to European justice would be complex, long and not without obstacles, and that when the results arrive, they will hardly have an impact on the personal and political situations of the imprisoned and exiled leaders. But the independence movement has always been very clear that judicial defence must be based on the legal arguments inherent in the doctrine of fundamental rights that inspires the European legal and political framework.[2] Gonzalo Boye explains this when he says that the Spanish jurisdiction is where the sowing is done, and the international jurisdiction is where one can reap the harvest.[3]

Below we offer a political analysis of the results that allow us to be optimistic about the international jurisdiction to win the lawfare battle in the distant future.

10.1 The Fiasco of the EAWs

The European Arrest Warrant (EAW) turned out to be Judge Pablo Llarena's nightmare. Each EAW he issued involved placing the Supreme Court's investigation in front of the mirror of courts outside Spain. It was a test of the Spanish penal and constitutional system when compared with other European systems. This comparison had to be made in terms of procedural guarantees of the defendant, the scope of fundamental rights and the democratic quality of criminal justice systems. The first – and clearest – obstacle to the Supreme Court's investigation was the justification of the crime of rebellion and sedition, and the pre-trial detentions already carried out. The facts underlying the investigation could hardly be subsumed within a criminal framework that required a sufficiently violent uprising to bend the will of the State. Such harmful measures were still less justified for defendants who had appeared, of their own free will, before the Spanish courts. It seemed difficult to persuade modern legal systems that the conduct of members of the Government of the Generalitat could be considered a crime of rebellion and sedition when in fact fundamental rights inherent to their political activity were being exercised. And it was even more difficult to justify pre-trial imprisonment.

Llarena's first European legal order soon petered out. He had to withdraw it, due to an issue of form. But he sent it back. The Belgian Prosecutor's Office and the defence lawyers of the exiled Catalan Ministers Toni Comin, Lluís Puig and Meritxell Serret once again warned of formal defects that prevented the success of the extradition without having to go into the nuts and bolts of the issue. It was the precedent of the Bog-Dogi case that led to the rejection of the EAW presented by the Supreme Court. Every EAW must be accompanied by a prior national arrest warrant, a procedural requirement that, in this case, was not met.

One of the shortcomings of the Spanish top courts, which we pointed out when analyzing the judicial elites inherited from the Franco regime, was the knowledge and application of international law. Traditionally, the Spanish top courts – many of whose members were trained in a pre-constitutional era – have refused to apply international regulatory frameworks. They neither knew European law nor saw the need to apply it within a framework of jurisdictional action circumscribed by Spanish sovereignty.

In other words, the Spanish legal system was quite enough. But this reality clashed with the European judicial framework when the processing of a judicial cooperation tool was rejected for formal, and not for substantive, reasons. It is worth noting that Llarena did not accept the fiasco of the first two EAWs as his own fault, because they had been drafted by Judge Carmen Lamela when she was acting as an investigating judge in the National High Court.[4]

10.1.1 The Puigdemont Case

The worst setback for Llarena's investigations took place in Germany. This was the extradition process against Catalan President Puigdemont, before the Schleswig- Holstein High Court. The judgment did not just reject the request made by the Spanish Supreme Court; it built a legal assessment on violence and the use of criminal law. The German court based itself on the premise that criminal law must act in moderation in the face of political disputes inherent in a parliamentary democracy. This was the initial premise. From here, a double criminality check was made. The petition did not pass the test, insofar as the crime of rebellion is not one of the 32 crimes that could involve the automatic extradition of Puigdemont under the June 2002 framework agreement. But Llarena added more crimes, just to make doubly sure. The Court of Schleswig-Holstein chose the crime of embezzlement. But embezzlement did not carry the punishment that the investigation of the Supreme Court wanted. Llarena had failed again.

The Supreme Court did not succeed when the case crossed the borders of Spanish jurisdiction. Or rather, when it tried to twist the law in a clear lawfare strategy that its European colleagues saw through. The investigating magistrate, Pablo Llarena, did not consider giving up the EAW before the Schleswig-Holstein Court; what he did was withdraw it and refuse the extradition of Carles Puigdemont for embezzlement. If he had accepted extradition for embezzlement, he would have given up a trial for rebellion and sedition. Embezzlement did not fulfil the will to humiliate and ridicule, to destroy the political enemy, because it would have meant leaving the enemy alive. And that could not be allowed by the Spanish Deep Judicial State.

As we have said, the ruling of the Schleswig-Holstein Court was an amendment of the whole investigation phase and made it very difficult for Europe to support a future conviction for rebellion. But the decision to renounce extradition was based on criteria of political opportunity, which were not explained in judicial terms. Moreover, it was a reasoning clearly linked to the goal of the lawfare strategy. The success or failure of lawfare meant resolving the dilemma inherent in any dichotomy: rebellion or nothing. And it was nothing.

10.1.2 The Puig Gordi Case

The case of the Minister of Culture, Lluís Puig Gordi, although it reaffirms the failure of the Spanish high justice system when it crosses national borders, is different from that of Carles Puigdemont. The refusal of the Brussels Court to extradite Lluís Puig Gordi to be tried for a crime of embezzlement of public funds was a matter of jurisdiction. The Belgian judiciary considered that the Supreme Court was not competent to try Lluís Puig Gordi. He had been dismissed as Minister on October 27, 2017, pursuant to Article 155 of the Spanish Constitution. Yet he was not a member of the Government of the Generalitat and, therefore, enjoyed no parliamentary privilege when Prosecutor Maza filed the lawsuit. In addition, the events had taken place in Catalonia. The case against Lluís Puig Gordi should have been brought before an investigating court in Barcelona, not before the Supreme Court in Madrid. Europe took the fundamental right to a judge predetermined by law very seriously. And not justice *à la carte* or the special judge – the application of the procedural law of the enemy – which the Belgian judiciary did not swallow.

To be sure, the Lluís Puig Gordi case was not just a formal matter; it was the application of the most basic doctrine of fundamental rights that should guide any procedure, especially when it comes to criminal proceedings. For Lluís Puig Gordi, apart from being an issue of fundamental rights, it was also a matter of collective justice, inasmuch as the doctrine could be applied to other political exiles for whom Spanish justice had issued extradition requests. As Javier Pérez Royo says: "If the decision of the Belgian judge becomes firm, the doctrine established by the Belgian judiciary would affect all those convicted in the trial and would provide an argument of enormous value to the defence counsels before the very Spanish Constitutional Court itself, and especially before the ECHR."[5]

The decision of the court of first instance was the subject of an appeal. The surprise came when the Brussels Court of Appeal upheld the rejection of the EAW, but added one more argument: the risk of violating the presumption of innocence if Lluís Puig Gordi was extradited to Spain. The second instance supported its argument on public statements made by Spanish judges, prosecutors and political authorities against Catalan pro-independence leaders. And it cited such public statements that were not in line with European Union Directive 2016/343 on the presumption of innocence.

10.2 The Junqueras Doctrine

The so-called Junqueras doctrine has been the big black hole in the Spanish Supreme Court's Second Chamber trial and the issue that brought into the open the political profile of Judge Manuel Marchena. Its origin lies in the request of a preliminary ruling before the CJEU. The ruling of the Court of Justice of the EU – Grand Chamber – of December 19, 2019, revealed various aspects of the legalistic democracy that the Spanish State has become. The least important aspect was that swearing the Constitution could be dispensed with as a requirement for access to the office of MP or Senator. The most important was the violation, by both the Supreme Court and the Constitutional Court, of fundamental political rights and freedoms. It wasn't the first time it had happened, nor would it be the last. This exceptionality was becoming the norm. And this is precisely what the ruling of the Grand Chamber of the ECJ showcased.

A brief analysis, from a political point of view but also from a legal one, involves a first element. Since July 13, 2019 – and in accordance with the tenor of the CJEU resolution – Oriol Junqueras, but also Carles Puigdemont and Toni Comin, could have moved completely freely both inside and outside Spain. And also across Europe. As a result, they could have attended the sessions of the European Parliament, including the constituent one. For all intents and purposes, they were MEPs. This was not the case by the express will of the Spanish Supreme Court. Nor did the body to which the Spanish Constitution entrusts its fundamental rights do anything about it: the Constitutional Court. Some by action, and others by omission, flagrantly violated the right to personal liberty, the right to active suffrage of politicians and the right to passive suffrage of voters who on May 26 had elected Junqueras, Puigdemont and Comín to represent them in the European Parliament.

In the face of this violation of fundamental rights with clear political intent, can it be argued that Supreme Court and Constitutional Court judges have turned out to be impartial? The answer is no. When the Supreme Court saw the need to raise the question before the CJEU as to the extent of the immunity of the MEP who was being tried, it was well aware that, until it obtained a ruling, the process had to be suspended.[6] The jurisprudence of the CJEU was clear in this regard. Since June 15, 1995, it has been claiming – uninterruptedly – that the national trial in which a preliminary ruling has been requested should be suspended pending the decision of the CJEU. But the Supreme Court did not suspend the trial.

Why not? Why didn't it suspend the criminal proceedings? Manuel Marchena knew – or could sense – the result contrary to his interests or the interests of the *raison d'état*, and he decided to ignore the Community regulations. And he handed down a sentence fearing a Community ruling that would force the Court to release Oriol Junqueras and not resume his trial until the parliamentary waiver had been obtained. Too much time and too much hindrance for those like Marchena who put the effectiveness of the *ius puniendi* above the protection of fundamental rights. There was also another issue that cannot be ignored. On October 16, 2019, Jordi Sánchez and Jordi Cuixart's two-year pre-trial imprisonment was to run out. The Jordis' pre-trial detention had been criticized by the UN Working Group on Arbitrary Detention. And this time limitation made Marchena expedite a final resolution of the criminal case.[7]

The issue, however, was still serious. Once again, the Supreme Court made a political decision. And it did so by using the artifice of considering the elements contained in the preliminary ruling to be a part independent of the judgment. It was a way of saying – without actually saying so – that the result of the ruling of the CJEU would be irrelevant, or considered irrelevant, by the judgment that the Supreme Court was to issue. It is still unusual for a court decision to be taken out of a desire to create jurisprudence and not to have practical effects, as Jordi Nieva wrote.[8] To understand an action of the Supreme Court that can only be explained in terms of political opportunity – and not for legal reasons – and in defence of the interests of the *raison d'état*, we need to return to the moment when Oriol Junqueras was elected MEP. That is, at the moment when he could exercise the right to active suffrage but could not materialize it. And he could not materialize it when, just a few days before, he had been able to do so, albeit with limited effects, when he was elected a member of the Spanish Parliament. What had changed?

The first issue that had changed was of a formal nature. Oriol Junqueras had not been able to fulfil the requirement of swearing loyalty to the Spanish Constitution before the Central Electoral Board (a requirement that the CJEU would leave, in its judgment of December 19, 2019, without effect). But he had not been able to do so, not because he did not want to, or did not ask to, but because the Supreme Court denied him permission to do so. The second issue, as Antoni Bayona explains, is more fundamental. What the Supreme Court has sought to hide is the protection of "the criminal case as against the effects of parliamentary immunity which is linked to the status of MEP."[9] If the Supreme Court had complied with EU law, it would have had to deal with the parliamentary waiver request, as Junqueras' immunity would have remained in effect until there was a final ruling. The waiver request would have, of necessity, entailed what was to be avoided: debating in Europe whether the case against the Catalan leaders was a political trial or a criminal trial with a clearly vengeful background. The debate would have been a torpedo below the lawfare waterline. The Supreme Court's action eliminated this debate. But it certified, by way of the facts, that the motivations of the case followed in the Second Chamber were political and nothing but political.

There was no shortage of writers who, from important media forums, argued that the ruling of the Grand Chamber was against the Spanish Constitution and that complying with it would be equivalent to violating the Constitution. One of them was Tomás de la Cuadra Salcedo.[10] He does not recognize that there is intelligent legal life beyond the Spanish legal system. But there have also been voices, such as the aforementioned Jordi Nieva or Antoni Bayona, as well as Javier Pérez Royo[11] and Joan Queralt,[12] who have argued in the opposite direction, namely that, with this resolution of the CJEU, the sentence of the Supreme Court, with regard to Oriol Junqueras, adds more legal arguments to those already available to conclude that its judgment is null and void.

Conclusion

Returning to Politics

In 2010, the Constitutional Court issued a judgment limiting the state of the Autonomous Regions. That was the starting point of the Catalan independence Process. Nine years later, in 2019, the Supreme Court handed down a ruling that liquidated the rule of law. That was the end of the Process, at least of the Process as we had known it until then.

With the 14 October 2019 judgment of the Criminal Chamber, the Supreme Court formulated unprecedented restrictions on the exercise of individual and collective fundamental rights and delimited, even more than Constitutional Court judgment 31/2010, the development of self-government. The relevance of this judgment – which is not the last that, from the criminal jurisdiction, will be dictated in the framework of the lawfare deployed to eliminate a part of the independence movement and to deter the other part from wanting a sovereign State – is that it will condition the practical development of Spanish democracy in the coming years.

From a fundamental rights point of view, this resolution, which puts an end to the first of the episodes of a long lawfare, is a resolution that proves the existence of a *raison d'état* that needs to be defended, whatever the cost. The violation of fundamental rights – including their criminalization – such as the right of assembly, freedom of expression and the right to political participation, has been a necessity in order to protect a *metaright*, such as the single and indivisible nation, from political debate. The right to the judge predetermined by law, parliamentary inviolability or the principle of legality: all of these are nuclear elements of the rule of law, and have been trampled on, despised and wiped out to shield a *raison d'état*, which does not want to be subjected to political debate. No one can claim a debate on this, because a debate on the principle of unity of the State, or on the monarchy that represents this unity, is an illegal debate. The Constitution does not allow it or, at least, the Constitution according to the interpretation of its highest interpreter, the Constitutional Court.

Based on these premises, the judgment of the Second Chamber of the Supreme Court set the threshold of criminal significance of mere passive resistance or peaceful protest of those who, symbolically or not, want to put this *raison d'état* at the epicentre of political debate. But it set that threshold based on pre-democratic criteria. The Supreme Court ruled – and the October 14, 2019 judgment is a clear example of this – that both the effective exercise of passive resistance and peaceful protest can be subsumed within the criminal nature of sedition. With this decision, the principle of proportionality – as happened with the principle of legality – was blown apart. They were not the only limitations. Parliamentarianism has also seen its capacity for political debate censored – it must be confined to the Constitution – and the prerogative of inviolability is no longer worth the paper it is written on. And it has not been the legislator who has set limits: it has been the high courts – the Constitutional and Supreme Courts – that have pushed the State back to pre-constitutional times. The government of the judges has imposed its conservative, authoritarian, centralist and pre-democratic logic.

In this scenario, where is the place for politics?

A paradigm shift is needed to engage politics. It will not be easy. It will not be immediate. The culture of litigation, which is the antithesis of politics, is too ingrained in Spanish political culture. Politics is dialogue, negotiation, transaction, yielding and conceding; it is a way of seeking collective gain. Obsessive litigation is fueled by the duality of Them and Us, where only one of the two wins. And, when it comes to *raisons d'état* – and the possibility of controlling the judiciary and the ability to interpret or tailor laws – there is more interest in litigation than in politics. It is hardly surprising that the rhetoric of the enemy is part of the daily life of the statements of Spanish political leaders, especially those of the right and far right. The successes of the judicialization of politics are so evident, at least in terms of repression of the enemy and in the defence of the unity of national sovereignty, that the Deep State will hardly dispense with the power conferred on it by the tacit Constitution, which is unwritten but is in effect applied.

There seems to be no place for politics.

Perhaps there is no interest in politics. That could be the reality. A Constitution was approved in order to return politics to its rightful place, but it soon became apparent that politics entailed making concessions that the Spanish elites were unwilling to allow. Hence the drawing up of a tacit rule of not reforming the existing Constitution. And now, at a time when politics has turned out to be a sum of hard-to-manage complexities, simplifying everything to the deployment of a lawfare strategy is a low-cost way out. Daniel Innerarity wrote that "the main threat to democracy is not violence, corruption or inefficiency, but simplicity."[1] This is the core problem.

I do not deny that the picture is bleak. But nor shall I deny that a return to politics is needed, by facilitating spaces, reconstructing discourses, rewriting narratives, softening forms, restoring confidence, weaving complicity around what brings us closer. Let us start with issues that unite, such as the defence of fundamental rights, but without forgetting those that require mechanisms of direct democracy, such as a referendum or a poll for the citizens of Catalonia. There is only one thing that stands out above all others: abandoning repression. The Spanish State can only engage in politics if, once and for all, it forgets the authoritarian impulses that, in the field of national politics, are called tension, but, when they are aimed at national minorities, are nothing but repression. And repression has made the Spanish State a small State, where there is no room for democracy or pluralism, nor, as has been said, for politics. Only laws have a space, though not the Law.

So a return has to be made to politics.

Notes

1 Conceptual Framework

1 LAKOFF, George. *Don't Think of an Elephant! Know Your Values and Frame the Debate: The Essential Guide for Progressives*. White River Junction, VT (USA): Chelsea Green Publishing Company. 2004.

2 WERNER, Wouter G. "The Curious Career of Lawfare. Historical and Semiotic Origins of Lawfare". *Case Western Reserve Journal of International Law*. Vol. 43, Issues 1 and 2. 2010. p. 63.

3 FREEDMAN, Lawrence. *Strategy: A History*. Oxford: Oxford University Press. 2013. p. xi.

4 VON CLAUSEWITZ, Carl. *De la guerra*. Barcelona: La Esfera de los Libros. 2014.

5 For a theoretical analysis of lawfare, see ROMANO, Silvina. *Lawfare. Guerra judicial y neoliberalismo en América Latina*. Sevilla: Política y hegemonía. 2019.

6 DUNLAP, Charles J. *Law and Military Interventions: Preserving Humanitarian Values in 21st Conflicts*. Cambridge, Carr Center for Human Rights, John F. Kennedy School of Government. Harvard University, Working Paper. 2001.

7 COMAROFF, John L. "Colonialism, Culture, and the Law. A Foreword". *Law & Social Inquiry*. Vol 26. Núm. 2, 2001. pp. 305–314.

8 PRONER, Carol. "El *lawfare* como herramienta de los neofascismos". In Guaman, Adoración; Aragoneses, Alfons i Martín, Sebastián (eds.). *Neofascismo. La bestia neoliberal*. Madrid: Siglo XXI. 2019. pp. 219–228.

9 PRONER, Carol. "Guerres híbrides al Brasil i la guerra jurídica per derrocar la democràcia". *Revista Eines*. Núm. 36, desembre de 2019. p. 36.

10 MONTAIGNE, Michel Seigneur de. *Les essais* (ed. Marie de Gournay, 1595).

11 In this context, see the article by SÁNCHEZ-CUENCA, Ignacio. "Querulància". *La Vanguardia*, February 8, 2020.

12 ECO, Umberto. *Inventing the Enemy. And Other Occasional Writings*. Boston, New York: Houghton Mifflin Harcourt. 2012. p. 2.

13 BACHERO, Juan Luís. *La neutralización del adversario político. La deportación en la España del S. XIX*. Madrid: Centro de Estudios Constitucionales. 2020.

14 Carlos Lesmes referred to the very first sentence, that defines sovereignty, in the book by Carl SCHMITT, published in an English translation (by George Schwabb) as *Political Theology: Four Chapters on the Concept of Sovereignty*, Chicago: University of Chicago Press. 1985. – For Judge – Lesmes' speech, see: "Discurso del presidente del Tribunal Supremo y del Consejo General del Poder Judicial en el solemne acto de apertura de tribunales 2020". 7 September 2020.

https://www.poderjudicial.es/stfls/SALA%20DE%20PRENSA/NOTAS%20DE%20PRENSA/20200907%20Discurso%20presidente%20TS%20y%20General Council of the Judiciary%20apertura%20A%C3%B1o%20Judicial%202020.pdf

15 To appreciate Carl Schmitt's prestige in the political elites and legal brains of Spanish nationalism, see the work of SARALEGUI, Miguel. *Carl Schmitt. Spanish Thinker*. Madrid: Trotta. 2016. On the current significance of Carl Schmitt in a broader political and social context see MOUFFE, Chantal (ed.) *The Challenge of Carl Schmitt*. London – New York: Verso, 1999.

16 LÓPEZ GARCÍA, José Antonio. "La presencia de Carl Schmitt en España". *Revista de Estudios Políticos (Nueva Época)*. No. 91. January-March 1996. p. 140.

17 SCHMITT, Carl. *The Concept of the Political: Expanded Edition*. Chicago: University of Chicago Press. 2007.

18 Nationalsozialistische Deutsche Arbeiter Partei (German National Socialist Workers' Party), also known as the Nazi Party. But his connection with the Führer went further. In his capacity as a renowned jurist, Carl Schmitt entered the German Academy of Law, chaired by Hans Frank, he was director of the Group of University Professors of the National Socialist League of German Jurists and editor of the leading law journal then: the *Deutsche Juristen-Zeitung*. In his capacity as Kronjurist, too, he justified the most reprehensible actions and laws of the Nazi regime.

19 ZARKA, Yves-Charles. *Un détail nazi dans la pensée de Carl Schmitt. La justification des lois de Nuremberg du 15 septembre 1935*. Collection Intervention philosophique, éditions Presses Univ. de France. 2005. These laws were the Reich Flag Law, the Civil Rights Law and the German Blood and Honour Protection Act.

20 LEGAZ, Luís. *Introducción a la Teoría del Estado Nacionalsindicalista*. Barcelona: Bosch. 1940. p. 170.

21 MEIER, Heinrich. *Carl Schmitt, Leo Strauss y El concepto de lo político. Sobre un diálogo entre ausentes*. Buenos Aires: Katz. 2008. Popular Party. pp. 36–37.

22 BARBERO, Marino. *Política y Derecho penal en España*. Madrid: Tucar Ediciones. 1977.

23 NUÑEZ SEIXAS, Xosé M. *Suspiros de España. El nacionalismo español. 1808–2017*. Barcelona: Critica. 2018. pp. 45–46.

24 This is the perfectly documented thesis by MARFANY, Joan-Lluís. *Nacionalisme espanyol i catalanitat (1789–1859). Cap a una revisió de la Renaixença*. Barcelona: Edicions 62. 2017.

25 BENET, Josep. *L'intent franquista de genocidi cultural contra Catalunya*. Barcelona: Publicacions Abadia de Montserrat. 1999.

26 ESTEFANÍA, Joaquin. "Teoría de la crispación". *El País*. April 19, 2007.

27 FERRER I GIRONÈS. Francesc. *Catalanofòbia. El pensament anticatalà a través de la història*. Barcelona: Edicions 62. 2000. p. 54.

28 MORENO CABRERA, Juan Carlos. *Determinació nacional. Catalunya davant l'ofensiva espanyolista (2009–2018)*. Argentona: Voliana Edicions. 2019. p. 24.

29 COMPANY, Enric. "El mal momento catalán y español". *El País*. November 23, 2017.

30 The leader of the Popular Party in Catalonia, Xavier Garcia Albiol, used the expression *"A por ellos"* as a rallying call with which to launch the campaign for the elections to the Parliament of Catalonia called on December 21, 2017 in application of Article 155 of the Spanish Constitution.

31 Rafael González Fernández writes: *"Tanto la simbología nacionalista como la introducción de los temores y los miedos respecto a la amenaza de "los otros" constituyen dos ingredientes primordiales para hacer eclosionar –mediante la correspondiente incitación y demagogia política– la violencia colectiva y el fratricidio (...)"*. ("Both nationalist symbolism and the introduction of fears and apprehensions about the threat of "the others" are two key ingredients for the emergence – through the corresponding political incitement and demagoguery – of collective violence and fratricide."). GONZÁLEZ, Rafael. "Historia y psicología social: perspectivas complementarias para un análisis de la violencia colectiva". In González Fernández, Rafael (ed.) *Violencia colectiva. Estrategias políticas del odio*. Madrid: Catarata. 2018. p. 202.

2 Francoism

1 RODRIGO, Javier. "Violencia i fascistización en la España sublevada". A Morente, Francisco (Ed.) *España en la crisis europea de entreguerras. República, fascismo y Guerra Civil*. Madrid: Catarata. 2011. p 81.

2 MARTÍN, Sebastián. "Los juristas en la génesis del franquismo ¿Un contraste posible?" A Birocchi, Italo i Loschiavo, Luca. *Il giuristi e il fascino del regime (1918–1925)*. Roma: RomaTrE Press. 2015. p 395.

3 SESMA, Nicolás. "Sociología del Instituto de Estudios Políticos. El "grupo de élite" intelectual al servicio del partido único y el estado franquista (1939–1969)". A Ruiz Carnicer, Miguel A (Ed.). *Falange. Las culturas políticas del fascismo en la España de Franco (1936–1975)*. Zaragoza: Institución Fernándo el Católico". 2013. p. 253.

4 ZAFFARONI, Eugenio R. *El Derecho Penal Nazi. La dogmàtica penal alemana entre 1933 y 1945*. Buenos Aires: Ediar. 2017.

5 In this sense, see FERNÁNDEZ-CREHUET, Federico. "Revista General de Legislación y Jurisprudencia (1941–1955) ¡Una revista para Castán, por favor! A Fernández-Crehuet, Federico (coord.) *Franquismo y revistas jurídicas. Una aproximación desde la Filosofía del Derecho*. Granada: Comares. 2008.

6 Del Rosal wrote these words in his work DEL ROSAL, Juan. *Acerca del pensamiento penal español y otros problemas penales*. Madrid: Editorial Aldecoa. 1942. Pàg. 269. As FERRÉ explains, the work of Del Rosal is full of references to Nazi constitutionalists and criminal law experts, such as Schmitt and Karl Larenz.

7 AROSTEGUI, Julio. "Opresión y pseudo-juridicidad, de nuevo sobre la natu-

raleza del franquismo". *Bulletin d'Histoire Contemporaine d'Espagne*. Núm. 24, December 1996. pp. 31–46.

8 BERDUGO, Ignacio. "Derecho represivo en España bajo la dictadura franquista (1939–1975)". *Revista de la Facultad de Derecho de la Universidad de Madrid*. Núm. 3. 1981. pp. 97–128.

9 An example of what we mean is what came to be known as the "Salamanca Papers" case. This practice responds to the documentation looted from the Generalitat de Catalunya and other Catalan organizations, entities and individuals by Franco's forces from the moment they set foot in Catalonia between 1938 and January 1939. This documentation was subsequently deposited in the San Ambrosio School in Salamanca, a police depot later converted into the National Historical Archive of Salamanca in the democratic era. The Spanish state has been reluctant to return to its rightful owners the plundered heritage, despite the fact that, from 2005, there began a timid return of some documents under a law passed that year. The truth is that the return of documents is still not complete today, many having been burnt as heating fuel. See: CRUANYES, Josep. *The Papers of Salamanca: the Plunder of the Documentary Heritage of Catalonia (1930–1939)*. Barcelona: Edicions 62. 2003.

10 RAGUER, Hilari. *Escrits dispersos d'història*. Barcelona: Institut d'Estudis Catalans. 2018. pp. 161–165.

11 VILAR Pierre. *La Guerra Civil española*. Barcelona: Crítica. 2017. pp. 22–32.

12 PORTILLA, Guillermo. *La consagración del derecho penal de autor durante el franquismo. El Tribunal Especial para la Represión de la Masonería y el Comunismo*. Granada: Editorial Comares. 2010. p. 5.

13 In this sense, see ÁLVARO DUEÑAS, Manuel. "Los militares en la represión política de la postguerra: la jurisdicción especial de responsabilidades políticas hasta la reforma de 1942". *Revista de Estudios Políticos (Nueva Época)*. No. 69. Julio-septiembre 1990. p. 149. Also the article by ALVARO DUEÑAS, Manuel. "El decoro de nuestro aire de família". Perfil político e ideológico de los presidentes del Tribunal Nacional de Responsabilidades Políticas". *Revista de Estudios Políticos (Nueva Época)*. No. 105. Julio–septiembre 1999. pp. 147–173.

14 TOCORA, Fernando. *La renuncia a la autonomía judicial. La pérdida de juicio en los jueces*. Barcelona: Bosch Editor. 2019. Pàg. 90.

15 AGUILAR, Paloma. "Jueces, represión y justícia transicional en España, Chile y Argentina". Revista Internacional de Sociologia (RIS). Vol. 71, núm. 2. Mayo-agosto 2013.

16 See DEL ÁGUILA, Juan José. *El TOP, la represión de la libertad (1963–1977)*. Barcelona: Editorial Planeta. 2001. p. 16.

17 On the function and relevance in repression of dissidence practiced by the Social Political Brigade at the end of Francoism, see the book by CASANELLAS, Pau. *Morir matando. El franquismo ante la práctica armada*. 1968–1977. Madrid. Catarata. 2014.

18 On the repressive function of the army, see GIL VICO, Pablo. *La noche de los generales. Militares y represión en el régimen de Franco*. Barcelona: Ediciones B. 2005.

19 JIMÉNEZ VILLAREJO, Carlos & DOÑATE MARTÍN, Antonio. *Jueces, pero parciales. La pervivencia del franquismo en el poder judicial*. Barcelona: Ediciones de pasado & presente. 2012. p. 51.

20 BOSCH, Pere. *El primer procés contra Catalunya. Repressió i resistència després del 6 d'octubre*. Vic: Eumo Editorial. 2019.

21 That is to say, the judges became the echelon that whitewashed the regime.

22 ÁLVARO DUEÑAS, Manuel. *"Por ministerio de la ley y la voluntad del Caudillo." La Jurisdicción Especial de Responsabilidades Políticas (1939–1945)*. Madrid: Centro de Estudios Políticos y Constitucionales. 2006. p. 47.

23 Professor and judge Juan José del Águila also highlights the paper of the special jurisdictions as instruments of coercion and repression of political dissidence: "The special jurisdictions – of which Public Order was one – during the Franco regime had the role and function of being institutional legal instruments, created from and by the political power, so that, with coercive, procedural and penal techniques, together with other mechanisms, they should serve to impose themselves on their political and social adversaries through institutionalized violence by way of repression" (Del Águila. 2001: 16).

24 Vegeu BASTIDA, Francisco J. *Jueces y franquismo. El pensamiento político del Tribunal Supremo en la Dictadura*. Barcelona: Ariel Derecho. 1986.

25 LANERO, Mónica. *Una milicia de la justicia. La política judicial del franquismo (1936–1945)*. Madrid: Centro de Estudios Constitucionales. 1996. p 273.

3 The Transition

1 A first contribution to the demystification of the official account of the Transition was the doctoral thesis, published years later in Spanish, by ANDRÉ-BAZZANA, Bénédicte. *Mitos y mentiras de la transición*. Barcelona: El Viejo Topo. 2006. See also GALLEGO, Ferrán. *El mito de la transición. La crisis del franquismo y los orígenes de la democracia. 1973–1977*, Barcelona: Editorial Crítica. 2008; GONZÁLEZ, Damián (Coord.) and ORTIZ, Manuel. *El Franquismo y la transición en España. Desmitificación y reconstrucción de la memoria de una época*, Madrid: Libros de la Catarata. 2008.

2 CLAVERO, Bartolomé. *Constitución a la deriva. Imprudencia de la justicia y otros desafíos*. Barcelona: Pasado & presente. 2019. p. 17. See also, by the same author: *España 1978. La amnesia constituyente*. Madrid: Marcial Pons. 2014.

3 BABY, Sophie. *El mito de la transición pacífica. Violencia y política en España (1975–1982)*. Madrid: Akal. 2018. p. 32.

4 The Constitutional Court itself, based on Judgment 259/2015, of 2 December 2015, bans debating, in parliament, issues related to the independence process that are not, solely and exclusively, for the reform of the Spanish Constitution.

And not only does it forbid it, but it warns the Speaker of Parliament that he/she may incur a crime of contempt of court if a parliamentary debate is allowed on aspects relating to the independence process.

5 ROVIRA, Marta. *La Transició franquista. Un exercici d'apropiació de la història.* Barcelona: Pòrtic. 2014.

6 COLOMER, Josep Maria. *La transición a la democracia. El modelo español.* Barcelona: Anagrama. 1998.

7 The political scientist Adam Przeworski has emphasized the fact that in Spain there were a series of events that guaranteed the continuity of the previous regime, so one cannot speak of a rupture. Przeworski says that in Spain "democracy was established [...] without a break in the armed forces, without a purge even of the political police, without a very obvious degree of politicization and with two major parties that emerged almost overnight." PRZEWORSKI, Adam. "Algunos problemas en el estudio de la transición hacia la democracia." In O'Donnell, Guillermo; Schmitter, Philippe; Whitehead, Laurence. *Transiciones desde un gobierno autoritario. Perspectivas comparadas.* Vol. 3. Buenos Aires: Editorial Paidós. 1995. p. 101.

8 ESCUDERO, Rafael. "Sin memòria ni reconocimiento. Una Consitución de espaldas a su pasado". In Escudero, Rafael; Martín, Sebastián. *Fraude o esperanza: 40 años de la Constitución.* Madrid: Akal. 2018. pp. 18–19.

9 We refer to the book by SÁNCHEZ-CUENCA, Ignacio. *Atado y mal atado. El suicidio institucional del franquismo y el surgimiento de la democracia.* Madrid: Alianza Editorial. 2014.

10 The Spanish electoral system laid down, pursuant to the Law for Political Reform of January 1977 (the last of the Fundamental Laws of the Kingdom adopted by the Francoist Parliament) and the Royal Decree Law of 15 April 1977, calling elections in that same year, granting the right of a sufficient majority to be able to command the Transition process, to fix the composition of the top representative body of popular sovereignty through which the Constitution would be drafted and adopted; and, moreover, to control the initial membership of the governing body of judges in democracy.

11 DEL ÀGUILA, Rafael. *La senda del mal. Política y razón de Estado.* Madrid: Taurus. 2000. p. 11.

12 One of the first journalistic approaches to the concept of the *de facto* power that operated during the Transition was that of CAVERO, José. *Poderes fácticos en la democracia.* Barcelona: Espasa Calpe. 1990. Cavero identified three main groups: the Church, the Banks, and the Army.

13 PÉREZ-FRANCESCH, Joan Lluís. "Raó d'estat i repressió". *El Matí digital.* 3 January 2020.

14 Ruben Uceda's graphic novel can be highly recommended, due to the virtue of combining text with cartoons, which transforms it into a highly pedagogical book on the renunciations of the Transition. See – UCEDA, Ruben. *Atado y bien atado. La Transición golpe a golpe (1969–1981).* Madrid: Akal. 2018.

15 Pérez Royo reports that Spain is the only state in Western Europe that has not

reformed its constitutional text, as France has done since the Third Republic or Germany since the Constitution of Weimar and, above all, with the Bonn Basic Law, or Italy, Austria and Portugal. See PÉREZ-ROYO, Javier. *La reforma constitucional inviable*. Madrid: Catarata. pp. 30–31.

16 Javier Tajadura explained this, quoting professor Pedro de Vega, in "El problema de la reforma". *El País*, 9 December 2017.

17 In this context, see SOUSA SANTOS, Boaventura. *Sociología jurídica crítica. Para un nuevo sentido común en el derecho*. Madrid: Editorial Trotta. 2009. pp. 105–107.

18 Aguilar quotes Mónica Lanero's idea of "cohesion around secrecy" as a strategy for weaving a network of complicities between the various groups and actors involved in the repression of dissent. A sort of "pact of silence" with which, should the occasion arise, to protect each other from crimes and brutality exercised in the past. Aguilar also refers to students of Franco's violence who speak of a "blood pact". See, then, CASANOVA, Julián (coord.). Morir, matar y sobrevivir: La violencia en la dictadura de Franco. Barcelona: Crítica. 2002.

19 JIMÉNEZ VILLAREJO, Carles; DOÑATE MARTÍN, Antonio. *Jueces pero parciales. La pervivencia del franquismo en el poder judicial*. Barcelona: Editorial Pasado y Presente. 2012.

20 "The provisions of the decree abolishing the TOP did not, however, prevent its former judges and prosecutors from continuing to practise in other jurisdictions, or even from being assigned to the highest courts in the country, such as the Presiding Chairs of Provincial Courts and the Chambers of the Supreme Court" (Del Águila, Juan José. 2001: 293).

21 See TOHARIA, José Juan. *El juez español. Un análisis sociológico*. Madrid: Tecnos. 1975. p. 65. An article published fully fifteen years later offers a different view of Spanish justice, basically due to the incorporation of women and the entry into the jurisdictional function of judges under the age of 35. See – TOHARIA, José Juan. "El juez español. Quince años después". *Revista del Centro de Estudios Constitucionales*. No. 3. May-August 1989. pp. 345–364.

22 SÁEZ, Ramón. "Los jueces y el aprendizaje de la impunidad, a propósito de los crímenes del franquismo". *Mientras tanto*, No. 114. 2010. p. 42.

23 This lack of sensitivity on the part of Spain's judiciary as regards applying international law on the subject of Human Rights – in contrast to other judicial systems, such as Argentina's, which also undertook the transition from a dictatorship to a democracy – is perfectly explained in the book by CHINCHÓN, Javier. *El tratamiento judicial de los crímenes de la Guerra Civil y el franquismo en España. Una visión de conjunto desde el Derecho Internacional*. Bilbao: Ediciones Universidad de Deusto. 2012.

4 Democracy

1 Essays and academic chronicles usually quote the work of the late transition period politician, Jordi Solé Tura, to narrate the genesis of Article 8 of the Spanish Constitution and the decisive participation they had on the part of bodies or sectors that had no role in the drafting of the Constitution, that is to say the Army, which was key in the final wording of the precept. In this sense, see SOLÉ TURA, Jordi. *Nacionalidades y nacionalismos en España*. Madrid: Alianza Editorial. 1985.

2 The Organic Law for the Harmonization of the Autonomic Process.

3 CAPELLA, Juan-Ramon. "La Constitución tácita". In CAPELLA, Juan-Ramon. *Las sombras del sistema constitucional español*. Madrid: Editorial Trotta. 2003. pp. 17–41.

4 NIETO, Alejandro. "Mecanismos jurídicos de control del poder". Juan-Ramon. *Las sombras del sistema constitucional español*. Madrid: Editorial Trotta. 2003. pp. 383–400.

5 The book was published in Spanish by Tecnos in 2010. In this sense, see, LAMBERT, Edouard. *El gobierno de los jueces y la lucha contra la legislación social en los Estados Unidos*. Madrid: Tecnos. 2010. It was translated and adapted by Felix de la Fuente and has an interesting introductory study by Luís Pomed.

6 LIFANTE, Isabel. "El guardián de la Constitución". AAVV. *Fraude o esperanza. 40 años de Constitución.* Madrid: Akal. 2018. p. 228.

7 AJA, Eliseo. "La elección de magistrados del Constitutional Court". *El País.* June 17, 1998.

8 BANDRÉS, Juan Maria. "Yo tuve la culpa". *El País*. October 31, 1990.

9 NIETO, Alejandro. *El malestar de los jueces y el modelo judicial*. Madrid: Trotta. 2010.

10 ANDRÉS, Perfecto. "Sobre asociacionismo e independencia judicial". *Jueces para la Democracia*. Number 25. pp. 88–94.

11 DE LA OLIVA, Andrés. "El invento de la Audiencia Nacional". *Actualidad Económica*. No. 1036. 1977. p. 10.

12 Note that the National High Court was the first judicial body to admit the complaint filed by the Attorney General of the State, Manuel Maza, for the crime of rebellion when its most immediate jurisprudential antecedents – interlocutory 34/2008 AN – explained that "the crime of rebellion has never been the responsibility of this National Court."

5 Partitocracy

1 DÍEZ-PICAZO, Luís Maria. *Régimen constitucional del Poder Judicial*. Madrid: Civitas. 1991. p. 140.

2 SÁNCHEZ-CUENCA, Ignacio. "Los retrasos y los sesgos de la composición del Tribunal Constitucional". *Informe sobre la Democracia en España 2011*. Madrid: Fundación Alternativas. 2011. pp. 283–293.

3 For a fairly accurate chronicle on the person of the President of the Supreme Court and the General Council of the Judiciary, Carlos Lesmes, see journalist Pablo Ordaz's "El fracaso más amargo de Lesmes". *El País*. November 11, 2018. And for a definition of the stick and carrot technique, see NIETO, Alejandro. *El desgobierno judicial*. Madrid: Trotta. 2004. pp. 136–140.

4 This has happened lately – while these pages are being written – when it was found that an interim General Council of the Judiciary had appointed a total of 46 posts, the vast majority of which are related to Carlos Lesmes and the Popular Party (Lesmes himself was a senior official of the government of Aznar). See the headline of the newspaper *Público* of December 4, 2019: "The interim General Council of the Judiciary appoints 46 posts, most related to Lesmes and the PP, and conditions Justice for the next 20 years."

5 BOSCH, Joaquin and ESCOLAR, Ignacio. *El secuestro de la justicia. Virtudes y problemas del sistema judicial*. Barcelona: Roca Editorial. 2018.

6 MARTÍN PALLÍN, José Antonio. *¿Para qué servimos los jueces?* Madrid: Catarata. 2010. p. 128.

7 For an analysis of the figure of the star judge that burst into Europe, especially after the birth, in 1992, of the Mani Pulite group, led by prosecutor Antonio Di Pietro and the emergence of a group of anti-mafia judges. led by the charismatic Giovanni Falcone and Paolo Borsellino, both murdered, see the work of TIJERAS, Ramon. *La revolución de los jueces. De Falcone a Barbero: una cruzada contra la corrupción política, el crimen internacional y la razón de Estado*. Barcelona: Temas de Hoy. 1994.

8 For a more up-to-date view of the figure of the star judge see ÁLVAREZ, Javier and RODRÍGUEZ, Luís Fernándo. *La última trinchera. Un retrato inédito de los jueces que protagonizan la actualidad de nuestro país*. Barcelona: Península. 2016.

9 FISS, Owen. *Los mandatos de la justicia. Ensayos sobre Derecho y derechos humanos*. Madrid: Marcial Pons. 2013. pp. 37–39.

10 "*El presidente del Tribunal Constitucional defiende su militancia en el Partido Popular*» (The president of the Constitutional Court defends his militancy in the Popular Party). *El País*, July 19, 2013. This fact was widely criticised, and we highlight the comment made by José Antonio Zarzalejos in the pages of La Vanguardia: "A man who, out of ineptitude or folly – his or of those who put his name forward – forgot or hid his membership of the conservative party in his nomination hearing before the Chambers, made a more relevant omission than the fact of paying a quota for political affiliation" ZARZALEJOS, José Antonio. "Un Tribunal caducat". *La Vanguardia*, July 23, 2013.

11 As Daniel E. Herrendorf rightly says, in relation to the appointment of judges as a key element for the legitimacy of their functions, "the origin of a civil servant can give us the key to what his conduct will be. It is not impossible for loyalty systems to impose on the appointees a certain obedience with respect to the appointer". HERRENDORF, Daniel E. *El poder de los jueces. Como piensan los jueces que piensan*. Buenos Aires: Abeledo-Perrot. 1998. p. 53.

12 For a journalistic portrait of Manuel Marchena see Carlota Guindal's article:

"El jutge més poderós" (The most powerful judge). *La Vanguardia*, 21 November 2018. For a more literary treatment, see REMIREZ, Carmen. *Marchena. El poder de la justícia*. Barcelona: La esfera de los libros. 2020.

13 Both the Association of European Democratic Lawyers (ADADE) and the Socialist Party, who were acting as private prosecutors, filed motions for Espejel's recusal for her ideological and personal proximity to the Popular Party; they were successful, as stated through court order 83/2015, dated November 13, of the Plenary Session of the Criminal Chamber of the National High Court, which saw a connection between the links of friendship and affinity of the judge with the appointments of which we had taken advantage.

14 See, in this regard, the newspaper article signed by GAREA, Fernándo. "*La puerta giratoria de la Justicia*". *El País*. May 22, 2016.

15 ZAGREBELSKY, Gustavo. *Principios y votos. El Tribunal Constitucional y la política*. Madrid: Trotta. 2008. p. 37.

16 On this issue, see the newspaper article by PÉREZ OLIVA, Milagros. "*El Gobierno a través de los Jueces*". *El País*. January 5, 2020.

17 INNERARITY, Daniel. *Política para perplejos*. Barcelona: Galaxia Gutenberg. 2018. p. 145.

6 Lawfare

1 A clear example of criminalisation of political conduct was the PP's reform of Article 506 (2), which criminalised the holding of an illegal referendum. The new offence, which was part of Lehendakari Ibarretxe's desire to hold a referendum in the Basque Country, carried a prison sentence of 3 to 5 years and suspension from office of 6 to 10 years. The headline of the news item in the newspaper *El País*, dated 29 November 2003, is quite explicit and forceful: "The Government reforms the Penal Code to imprison Ibarretxe if he calls the referendum."

2 The very Constitutional Court (CC) declared the reform of the LOTC constitutional by way of Judgments 185/2016 and 2015/2016, but with three dissenting votes that undermined the unanimity that until then had presided over all the CC's rulings on the Independence Process.

3 KITTRIE, Orde F. *Lawfare: Law as a Weapon of War*. Nova York: Oxford University Press. 2016. p. 8.

4 RAMIRES SANTORO, Antonio E i FRIAS TAVARES, Natalia L. "El uso del sistema penal como *lawfare* político". *Revista Jurídica de la Universidad de Palermo*. Year 17. Number 1. November 2019. p. 10.

5 BIELSA, Rafael i PERETTI, Pedro. *Lawfare. Guerra judicial mediática. Desde el primer centenario hasta Cristina Fernández de Kirchner*. Buenos Aires: Airel Argentina. 2019.

6 RAMIRES SANTORO, Antonio E and FRIAS TAVARES, Natalia L. *Lawfare Brasileiro*. Belo Horizonte: Editora D'Plácido. 2019. In this book, Ramires

Santoro and Frias Tavares argue that operations "Lava Jato" and "Impeachment" are inscribed in a coordinated strategy of *lawfare*.

7 HIRSCHL, Ran. *Towards Juristocracy. The Origins and Consequences of the New Constitutionalism*. England: Harvard University Press. 2007.

8 SALMON, Christian. *Del storytelling a la era del enfrentamiento*. Barcelona: Península. 2019.

9 BODIN, Jean. *Los seis libros de la República*. Madrid: Tecnos. 2006.

10 To the expression "I neither want nor can authorise a referendum in Catalonia," used by PP Prime Minister Mariano Rajoy in December 2013, must be added a further "I neither want, nor do I believe it, nor will there be a referendum," expressed at a meeting of the Cercle d'Economia held in Sitges in May 2017.

11 BASTIDA, Xacobe. "El derecho de autodeterminación como derecho moral: Una apología de la libertad y del deber político". A Cagiao, Jorge and Ferraiuolo, Gennaro (coords.) *El encaje constitucional del derecho a decidir. Un enfoque polémico*. Madrid. Catarata. 2016. p. 231.

12 CÁMARA VILLAR. Gregorio. "Justicia política en la España democrática (Una reflexión a propósito de los llamados jueces estrella y la judicialización de la política". *Revista de Derecho Político*. Núm. 47, 2000. pp. 27–52.

13 Just after the 27-S "plebiscite" elections, the professor of Criminal Law, Luís Rodríguez Ramos, in an article published in the newspaper *El Mundo*, exposed the uncrossable lines of the Catalan conflict in order to criminalise it. In this sense he wrote the following in reference to rebellion and sedition: "the conduct common to rebellion and sedition is the 'uprising', with or without violence, in pursuit of the declaration of independence of Catalonia, whether or not it is achieved, by means of a resolution agreed in Parliament, which goes beyond the mere expression of a desire in breach of the Constitution and other legal provisions."

It is noteworthy that violence, the core element of the criminal offence in question, is not necessary to classify the conduct as a crime of rebellion. See RODRÍGUEZ RAMOS, Luís. "Criminalizar el conflicto catalán?" *El Mundo*, October 5, 2015.

14 POZUELO, Laura. *La política criminal mediática. Génesis, desarrollo y costes*. Madrid: Marcial Pons. 2013. Apart from "Symbolic Penal Law" we must include another phenomenon: the loss of interest and confidence in politics, alongside of which, by activating the penal solution, politicians see their legitimacy reinforced.

7 Dual State

1 PÉREZ LUÑO, Antonio E. "El Estado totalitario contra el derecho subjetivo. La teoría jurídica de Karl Larenz". *Sistema Revista de Ciencias Sociales*. No. 212. September 2009. pp. 3–13.

2 In this context it is well worth referring to the book by MÜLLER, Ingo. *Los*

juristas del horror. La "justicia" de Hitler: el pasado que Alemania no puede dejar atrás. Bogotá: Librería Jurídica Álvaro Nora. 2009.

3 We refer to the classic work, originally published in 1941, by FRAENKEL, Ernst. *The Dual State: A Contribution to the Theory of Dictatorship*. Clark, NJ: The Lawbook Exchange, Ltd. 2006. Fraenkel originally published this work in German in the 1930s. But it wasn't until the following decade that it was published, in English. After World War II, the book was finally published in its original language.

4 This duality, or this «larval» State that, from 1938 onwards, was replaced by the Nazi Party, is explained in ARENDT, Hannah. *The Origins of Totalitarianism*. New York: Schocken. 1951.

5 PAXTON, Robert O. *The Anatomy of Fascism*. New York. 2004.

6 The following works are illustrative of the debate between the views of Carl Schmitt and Hans Kelsen on constitutional justice: *Der Hüter der Verfassung*. Weimar, 1931; Lars Vinx (editor and translator), *The Guardian of the Constitution: Hans Kelsen and Carl Schmitt on the Limits of Constitutional Law*. Lars Vinx (editor and translator). Cambridge: Cambridge University Press, 2015; SCHMITT, Carl and KELSEN, Hans. *La polémica Schmitt / Kelsen sobre la justicia constitucional: El defensor de la Constitución versus ¿Quién debe ser el defensor de la Constitución?* Madrid: Tecnos. 2009.

7 Vilajosana puts it this way: "If one accepts this view of sovereignty and describes the current situation in Spain as one in which sovereignty is at stake, then the question will become not what the rules of the Spanish legal system say, but who will emerge as sovereign and make the *political* decision", VILAJOSANA, Josep M. "L'Estat dual a Espanya. Context i justificació de l'aplicació de l'art. 155 CE". *Revista Catalana de Dret Públic (Número espacial)* 2019. p. 141.

8 Alejandro Nieto, for example, refers to the mechanisms of judicial control that are nullified by a system of countermeasures that blocks its ordinary development: the high degree of politicization of its governing body (General Council of the Judiciary) and the presiding judges of the most important Courts. The countermeasures, in this case, soften control measures so as to achieve political goals, such as the repression of minority movements, invoking the defence of national sovereignty or the unity of the State. (Nieto. 2013: 384).

9 This interference reached such an extreme that the Association of Judges for Democracy published, on February 5, 2018, a communiqué "on political interference in the judiciary and the Constitutional Court" which had to do with the independence process.

10 BARCELÓ, Mercè. "Crisis constitucional del Estado o cuando la "unidad de España", como metaderecho, se impone a los derechos fundamentales de la ciudadanía". In Lasagabaster, Iñaki (coord) *Crisis institucional y democracia (A propósito de Cataluña)*. València: Tirant lo Blanch. 2019.

11 See the report "Així va fer l'Estat la guerra econòmica contra Catalunya". *Ara*, 7 October 2018.

12 LOFGREN, Mike. *The Deep State. The Fall of the Constitution and the Rise of a Shadow Government*. Nova York: Viking Press. 2016.

13 We refer to the classic book on Economics, Sociology and Political Science by MILLS, C. Wright. *The Power Elite*. Oxford: Oxford University Press. 1956. Also Published in México DF: Fondo de Cultura Económica. 2013. Another classic, published in 1969, is *Who Rules America?* Englewood Cliffs, New Jersey: Prentice Hall.

14 Another Political Science classic is the book by DAHL, Robert A. *Who Governs? Democracy and Power in an American City*. New Haven (CT): Yale University. 1961.

15 In the case of Spain, the following work is especially relevant for the subject under study: VILLENA, Andrés. *Las redes de poder en España. Elites e intereses contra la democracia*. Barcelona: Roca Editorial. 2019.

16 DE MIGUEL. Amando. *Sociología del Franquismo*. Barcelona: Editorial Euros. 1975. p. 111.

17 MUÑOZ CONDE, Francisco. *De nuevo sobre el "derecho penal del enemigo"*. Buenos Aires: Editorial Hammurabi. 2005. p. 26.

18 MUÑOZ CONDE, Francisco. "Derecho en la guerra contra el terrorismo; el Derecho de la guerra, el Derecho penal internacional y el Derecho de la guerra dentro del derecho penal interno ("Derecho penal del enemigo")". *Revista Justiça e Sistema Criminal*, Vol. 5, No. 9. 2013. pp. 90–91.

19 The words of the chief prosecutor of the Supreme Court, Javier Zaragoza, reveal the conception of the author's criminal law – and famous –, the paraules of the Prosecutor in Cap, when, in the final report in the trial held in the Supreme Court in the criminal case, he affirmed that "holding a referendum in contravention of the constitutional order is a crime, even if it has been decriminalized."

20 MUÑOZ CONDE, Francisco. "¿Es el Derecho penal internacional un "Derecho penal del enemigo"?". *Revista Penal 21*. 2008. pp. 93–102.

21 PORTILLA, Guillermo. "Bases teóricas del "nuevo" derecho penal schmittiano: el derecho penal y procesal penal del "enemigo". *IUS Revista del Instituto de Ciencias Jurídicas de Puebla*. No. 19. 2007. p. 34.

22 AMBOS, Kai. "Derecho penal del enemigo". Cancio Melià, Manuel and Gómez-Jara, Carlos (coords.). *Derecho penal del enemigo: el discurso penal de la exclusión*. Montevideo-Buenos Aires: B de F Ltda. Vol. I. 2006. pp. 119–162.

23 ZAFFARONI, Eugenio Raúl. El enemigo en el derecho penal. Buenos Aires: Ediar. 2012. p. 159.

24 RODRÍGUEZ RAMOS. Lluís. "¿Progresión o regresión constitucional de la justícia penal española? Irrupción del populismo judicial y del derecho penal de autor". *Teoría y Realidad Constitucional*. No. 43. First semester 2019. pp. 220–223.

25 EKAIZER, Ernesto. *Cataluña Año Zero. El proceso, el juicio y la sentencia*. Barcelona: Espasa. 2019. p. 223.

8 The Judicial State

1 DOMINGO, Pilar. "Ciudadanía, derechos y justicia en América Latina. Ciudadanización-judicialización de la política". *Revista CIDOB d'Afers Internacionals*. Núm. 85–86. May 2009. p. 37.

2 This expression was formulated in the now clàssic work by TATE, Neal C. and VALLINDER. Torbjorn (Eds.). *The Global Expansionof Judicial Power*. Nova York: New York University Press. 1995. p. 13.

3 GIMBERNAT, Enrique. *Ensayos penales*. Madrid: Tecnos. – 1999. p. 112. The link between the GALs and the Ministry of the Interior was proven in the sentence of the Supreme Court of July 28, 1998.

4 AAVV. "Un judici per a la història". *Revista Sàpiens*. Special edition.

5 GUINDAL, Carlota; MASDEU, Jaume i TARÍN, Santiago. "Més de 70 casos sobre la taula". *La Vanguardia*. January 26, 2020.

6 In order to carry out this analysis of the composition of the Constitutional Court during the entire period of the Catalan pro-sovereignty Process, we have used the period from 2006, when the Statute of Autonomy of Catalonia was challenged and the Spanish constitutional crisis began, to the present day. Therefore, the judges analysed range from 2006 to 2019. This means that the number of judges of the Constitutional Court exceeds 12, as it includes the emeritus judges, 29 in all.

9 The Political Trial

1 Other outstanding journalistic chronicles on the trial of the pro-independence leaders of the sovereignty process are: MARCH. Oriol. *Judici 1-0*. Madrid: Catarata. 2019; SÁENZ DE UGARTE, Iñigo. *El Juicio*. Barcelona: Roca Editorial. 2019; ORDAZ, Pablo. *El juicio sin final*. Alcobendas: Círculo de tiza. 2019; BUSQUETS, Lluís and GRABULOSA, Jordi. *El judici. Els líders independentistes a la banqueta*. Maçanet de la Selva: Editorial Gregal. 2019; and MARTÍNEZ, Guillem. *Caja de Brujas. Procesando el proceso al Procés*. Madrid: Lengua de trapo. 2019.

2 CANAN, Penelope and PRING, George W. *SLAPPS. Getting Sued For Speaking Out*. Temple: Temple University Press. 1996.

3 KIRCHHEIMER, Otto (1961b): *Political Justice. The Use of Legal Procedures for Political Ends*. New Jersey: Princeton Univ. Press. p. 7. – When we talk about political judgment we are referring to what Kirchheimer calls classical political judgment: that is, one that involves the government's intent to incriminate the public conduct of its enemy in order to expel him from the political scenario.

4 Jacques M. Vergès' book was translated into Spanish and published in 1970 by the Anagrama publishing house, with the title *Estrategia judicial en los procesos políticos*. It has gone through several new editions since then.

5 SALELLAS, Benet. *Jo acuso. La defensa en judicis polítics*. Lleida: Pagès Editors. 2018. p. 19.

6 In this context, we shall draw upon the January 2020 report carried out by the Institute for Self-Government Studies. See IEA. "La Sentència del Tribunal Suprem sobre el referèndum d'autodeterminació de Catalunya de l'1 d'octubre de 2017" ("The Judgment of the Supreme Court on the referendum on self-determination in Catalonia of October 1, 2017." Generalitat de Catalunya. *Institut d'Estudis de l'Autogovern*. June 1, 2020.

7 In order to grasp the level of tension that was experienced within the Prosecutors' Office, see the report published by *El País* on November 18, 2014, entitled "Diez días que sacudieron a la Fiscalía."

8 See, in this context, the information published by *La Vanguardia* on November 18, 2014, entitled: "Los Fiscales catalanes decidieron por unanimidad no presentar querella por el 9-N". The news piece, signed by journalists Josep Maria Brunet and Santiago Tarín, speaks of a report that the Prosecutors of the High Court of Justice of Catalonia sent to their hierarchical superiors in Madrid. The refusal to file a criminal complaint was based on the absence of a specific, precise and determined order from the Constitutional Court addressed to the President of the Catalan Generalitat and the government ministers in charge of the deployment of the November 9, 2014 poll.

9 Francisco Rubio Llorente wrote: "The political forces that dominate Spanish politics will have thus rendered a double service to the Catalan independence movement: first, by flatly refusing the proposal to hold a legal and purely consultative referendum; and now, by not undertaking the reform of the Constitution. A new and serious manifestation of this rampant paralysis that can end with the implosion of our constitutional democracy and return us to a past from which we thought we had emerged." RUBIO LLORENTE, Francisco. *La Vanguardia*, December 1, 2014.

10 See the headlines: "El fiscal general dimite tras un prolongado acoso del Gobierno", *El País*, December 19, 2014; "El fiscal del Estado dimite por sus continuos choques con el Gobierno", *La Vanguardia,* December 19, 2014.

11 The variable violence introduced during the investigation phase in the criminal process – on which the crime of rebellion was built – is the criminal type that allowed the pre-trial detention of the defendants to be upheld until the conclusion of the trial, and, almost two years later, is what has become journalistically known as the 'Llarena theorem'. See JULIANA, Enric. "El relat de la Catalunya violenta". *La Vanguardia*, April 13, 2018.

12 We refer to Jordi Amat's article: "The State of Judgment". *La Vanguardia*, January 27, 2019. Amat explains that since its creation Judge Prego had been the honorary patron of the far-right Fundación para la Defensa de la Nación Española (DANAES). In addition, as stated by López-Fonseca in the newspaper *Público* on June 21, 2009, "he has intervened in recent years in at least two public events in which he justified the military coup of 1936" and added: "and eight months after the second of these acts, and while he was still a

member of the General Council of the Judiciary, Magistrate Prego signed a manifesto against the Law of Memory which was published after its approval." For a profile of the magistrate Adolfo Prego we draw on the work of Carlos Jiménez Villarejo and Antonio Doñate Martín already mentioned – *Jueces pero parciales. La pervivencia del franquismo en el poder judicial* (i.e. *Judges, But Partial. The Survival of the Franco Regime in the Judiciary*).

13 See *Diario de Sesiones del Congreso de los Diputados*. Comisiones. Año 1995. V Legislatura. Núm. 516. pp. 15801–15812.

14 Diario de Sesiones del Congreso de los Diputados. Comisiones. Año 1995. V Legislatura. No. 516. p. 15810.

15 MARTÍN PALLÍN, José Antonio. "Rebels sense armes". *La Vanguardia*, June 6, 2019.

16 GARCIA RIVAS, Nicolás. *El delito de rebelión militar en el derecho penal.* Universidad de Castilla-La Mancha. 1990. p. 147.

17 PÉREZ ROYO, Javier. "La acusación de rebelión como coartada". *El Diario.es*. 14, 2019.

18 NIEVA, Jordi. "Graus de violència". *El Periódico*. June 20, 2019.

19 PÉREZ ROYO, Javier. "Instrucció nul·la de ple dret". *Ara*, April 7, 2018.

20 PÉREZ ROYO, Javier. "La rebel·lió del Govern: un delicte imaginari". *Ara,* December 13, 2017.

21 See the report signed by CALVET, Josep M. "Per què l'etarra Yoldi sí va poder anar a la investidura i Jordi Sánchez no podrà?" *La Vanguardia*. March 9, 2018.

22 MIRA, Javier (2020). "Reflexiones críticas sobre la aplicación del artículo 384 bis de la LECrim y su (no) reflejo en la STS 459/2019". In Queralt, Joan J. *La sentencia del procés. Una aproximación acadèmica*. Barcelona: Atelier. 2020. pp. 57–58.

23 For a journalistic portrait of Manuel Marchena see the chronicle by GUINDAL, Carlota. "El jutge més poderós". *La Vanguardia,* November 21, 2018. For a portrait of both Marchena and the other judges in charge of judging the pro-independence leaders, see ORDAZ, Pablo. "Marchena: el juez que se convirtió en protagonista". *El País*. October 14, 2019.

24 BRUNET, Josep Maria. "Marchena: un jutge de ferro amb mans de seda". *La Vanguardia*. February 25, 2019.

25 See Xavier Puig's interview with the Professor of Criminal law of the University of Barcelona, Joan Queralt. *El Temps*, April 2, 2019.

26 SÁNCHEZ-CUENCA, Ignacio. "Llei i democràcia". *La Vanguardia*. January 11, 2020.

27 QUERALT, Joan. "Notes de legalitat penal a la sentència del procés". *Blog Revista Catalana de Dret Públic*. December 11, 2019.

28 NIEVA, Jordi. "Justícia salomònica". *El Periódico*. October 14, 2019.

29 GIMBERNAT, Enrique. "La sentencia del "procés"". *El Mundo*. October 28, 2019.

30 DE ESTEBAN, Jorge. "Una sentencia desacertada". *El Mundo*. October 16, 2019.

31 SÁNCHEZ-CUENCA, Ignacio. "Mala consciència". *Ara*, October 17, 2019.
32 GARCIA RIVAS, Nicolás. "Rebelión y sedición en la STS 459/2019: razones para una legítima discrepància". In Queralt, Joan J. (ed.). *La sentencia del procés. Una aproximación acadèmica*. Barcelona: Atelier. 2020. pp. 135–145.
33 We refer to the work by ZOLA, Émile. *Jo acuso! La veritat en marxa*. Barcelona: Angle Editorial. 2019.

10 The International Jurisdiction

1 On the post-truth era, see McINTYRE, Lee. *Post-Truth*. Cambridge MA: MIT. 2018.
2 For a journalistic chronicle of the struggle in international jurisdictions, see CASULLERAS, Josep. *La batalla de l'exili. L'estratègia que ha posat la justícia espanyola contra les cordes*. Barcelona: Ara Llibres. 2018.
3 BOYE, Gonzalo. *Así están las cosas. Como ganamos en Europa*. Barcelona: Roca Editorial. 2020.
4 EKAIZER, Ernesto. "Un juez en su ratonera". *Ara*, 13 July 2018. Carmen Lamela, who sent former Barça President Sandro Rosell into pre-trial detention before he was acquitted after the trial, was rewarded by the General Council of the Judiciary and is now a member of the Second Chamber of the Supreme Court.
5 PÉREZ ROYO, Javier. "Sorpreses judicials". *Ara*, August 13, 2020.
6 PÉREZ ROYO, Javier. "L'ambigüitat del Tribunal Suprem". *Ara*, July 22, 2019.
7 JORDANA, Mirenxu i ZAPATER, Esther (2020). "La cuestión prejudicial ante el Tribunal de Justícia de la Unión Europea a proposito del caso Junqueras: ¿Un asunto de largo recorrido?. In Queralt, Joan J. *La sentencia del procés. Una aproximación acadèmica*. Barcelona: Atelier. p. 204.
8 NIEVA, Jordi. "La sentència del Tribunal de Luxemburg no existeix". *El Periódico*. January 9, 2020.
9 BAYONA, Antoni. "Absències a Estrasburg". *Ara*, July 3, 2019.
10 DE LA CUADRA, Tomás. "Inmunidad o presunción de inocencia". *El País*. January 3, 2020.
11 PÉREZ ROYO, Javier. "Encara no està tot dit". *Ara*, January 13, 2020.
12 QUERALT, Joan. Justícia europea: primera estació. *El Nacional.cat*. December 19, 2019.

Conclusion

1 INNERARITY. Daniel. "Complicar la democracia". *El País*. January 14, 2020.

Index

Page numbers in italics refer to graphs and charts.

Printed and bound by CPI Group (UK) Ltd, Croydon, CR0 4YY
13/09/2026
14961101-0001